798.
240
942
39

SC4

D1327821

# BADMINTON HORSE TRIALS

## THE TRIUMPHS AND THE TEARS

# BADMINTON HORSE TRIALS

## THE TRIUMPHS AND THE TEARS

### DEBBY SLY

*Preface by* HIS GRACE THE DUKE OF BEAUFORT

*Foreword by* HUGH THOMAS

DAVID & CHARLES

# Contents

# Preface

## by *The Duke of Beaufort*

The beautiful Badminton estate and village

Page 1 (*clockwise from top left*): The local Pony Club provides mounted runners who collect results from the fence judges on cross-country day
**John Thelwall** on **The Ulsterman** in 1988
**Kristina Gifford** and **General Jock** at the vet check in 1998
Best bonnets are the order of the day in 1995

Fifty years ago my predecessor – Master – hosted the first Badminton Three-Day Event. He was its greatest enthusiast and yet I am sure at the time that even he did not envisage there being a fiftieth Badminton anniversary to celebrate.

The original aim of the Badminton Horse Trials was to prepare our riders for success at the Olympic Games. This was quickly achieved with team gold and an individual bronze medal for Frank Weldon at the 1956 Stockholm Olympics. How fortunate for us all that Master was happy to see Badminton continue as an annual event.

Over the years Badminton has served its purpose of preparing not only our own riders for international competition, but a host of international competitors as well, raising not only the overall standard but also heightening worldwide interest in the sport of eventing.

Badminton started as a training ground but is now a much coveted competition in its own right – the unofficial individual World Championship.

Anyone reading through Debby Sly's book will, I am sure, enjoy sharing the many moments of triumph and adversity that have formed Badminton's history. I have seen many sides of the event, as spectator, competitor and host and hope that, fifty years on, there will be another major celebration of the world's 'most important horse event'.

*Beaufort*

6

# Foreword

## by *Hugh Thomas, Director*

Although I did not move to the Badminton area until 1990, the Horse Trials has played a major role in my life since childhood. I first came as a spectator with my parents in the late fifties, and all the time I was riding in the Pony Club it was an ambition to ride at Badminton. After several false starts because of lame horses I finally got there in 1973, by which time my trainer Brian Crago had made it clear that I was to aim to win, not just to complete. That was not to be – but to be second in 1976 was a great thrill.

I was then lucky enough to work for the BBC at Badminton for nearly ten years. It was always exciting doing live coverage with all its potential for disaster; I remember in particular an interview with a very concussed rider, and another day when we finished live to camera in a snowstorm about half an hour after the real competition had finished!

All of us who work on the event still get a tremendous buzz when the horses start arriving each year; suddenly all the office work, site preparations and course building are no longer theoretical. The atmosphere builds up steadily through the week, climaxing as the cross-country starts on Saturday. In March I always wonder whether we will get any entries, and at 6am on the Saturday I always wonder if a big crowd will come – so far they have! The most enjoyable part of the week for me is always the Sunday – not surprisingly – when I really can relax a little, concentrate on putting on a good show, and wait for the high drama that invariably develops as the last few horses come in to jump.

Naturally the design of the cross-country course is the most important job, but it takes up a lot less time than organising the loos, litter collection, trade-stand parking and temporary roads! We are lucky, of course, to work in such a lovely village and park; one of the most enjoyable aspects of being the course designer is the time spent quietly walking and driving in the park, trying to conjure up new ideas on what is by now pretty familiar territory.

If I had to name just one aspect of the event that still astonishes me, it would have to be the incredible willingness and enthusiasm of the

countless volunteers without whom we could not possibly run the competition. That has been true since the very beginning in 1949, and I am delighted that it continues. While people come from far and wide, our core is still based on the village, the estate, the hunt... thank goodness they all seem to enjoy it! In a real sense Badminton Horse Trials is an annual reunion of a community – so many old friends from all over the world, so many regular visitors, many of the same riders, and all the volunteers.

I think that Debby Sly has captured in this book a lot of what it is that makes Badminton special. I have enjoyed reading it, and I think that everyone who has helped her has had a lot of fun going back over the last fifty years. Now it is time to look forward, and for us to make sure that well into the next century Badminton remains, as its founders advertised, 'The Most Important Horse Event in Great Britain'.

**Pippa Nolan** and **Metronome** almost hidden in the crowds at the start of the cross-country in 1993

Page 2: The 10th Duke of Beaufort, HM the Queen and Colonel Gordon Cox Cox share a light-hearted moment with Bertie Hill in 1959

Page 3: **Felicity Cribb** on **Carmody Street** jump the beautiful Gondola, part of the Lake complex in 1994

7

**Come rain or come shine...** Badminton has been cancelled only three times in its fifty years. Spectators, well acquainted with the English weather, come prepared for anything from a heatwave to a hailstorm…

TBREAD CHAMPIO

# A world-famous competition

A Badminton landmark: the weathervane in the stableyard

To compete at the Badminton Horse Trials is the ambition of almost every serious event rider: to win it is their ultimate dream. Badminton has become a world-famous competition in its own right, and its success has fuelled the ever-growing enthusiasm for the whole sport; however, it is hard to believe that such a prestigious event is only fifty years old, and that it hasn't been a part of our heritage for much longer. Looking at the event today, with its well earned place in the social and sporting calendar, it is almost impossible to imagine the task that faced those who, in 1948, had the foresight to commit themselves to providing generations of competitors with what has become the ultimate test of horse and rider.

Badminton Horse Trials was born out of the failure of the brave, but poorly prepared British team at the 1948 Olympic Games. Until that time the sport of eventing was unknown in England; it was popular on the Continent, but was confined to riders of the armed forces. Admittedly a British three-day event team did win the bronze medal at the 1936 Berlin Olympics, but they were army officers who would have trained at the cavalry school at Weedon, and even so, their only competition experience would have been the few inter-Forces competitions organised in Europe. Indeed by 1948, for the first Olympics to be held after World War II, the situation was little improved. Our intrepid team of three – Major Peter Borwick, Brigadier Lyndon Bolton and Major Dougie Stewart – rode in front of a home crowd round an impressive purpose-built course at Aldershot, where all the Olympic equestrian events were to be staged, and it must have come as quite a shock to us then, a nation priding itself on its equestrian heritage, to find that we did not exactly cover ourselves in glory. Major Borwick enjoyed a successful round, but Brig Lyndon Bolton suffered two falls, and Major Stewart had to retire when his horse was lame at the start of the cross-country phase.

But the event opened the eyes of many to a sport at which it was felt the British ought to excel; and one particular horseman, the late 10th Duke of Beaufort MFH, was so convinced of its potential success in Britain that he volunteered to run a three-day event on his Badminton estate in Gloucestershire. He first voiced the idea to his friend and neighbour Colonel Trevor Horn. As a council member of the British Horse Society, Trevor Horn was sent to Aldershot to find out more about the three-day event; he walked the course several times and talked to competitors and officials about

Before the crowds arrive at Badminton: chance for a relaxing hack in the crisp early morning sun

what the competition entailed, and so was the best person to introduce the Duke of Beaufort to its challenges. He escorted the Duke round the course whilst an event was in progress, stopping at every fence to watch two or three competitors tackle it, and one can imagine the Duke formulating in his own mind the structure of such an event to be run over his own home estate. His sole aim was to help the British be better prepared for the 1952 Helsinki Olympics.

The British Horse Society agreed to support this bold venture; the Duke of Beaufort, Brigadier Bowden-Smith, Major Peter Borwick, Lt Col the Hon Guy Cubitt and Colonel Trevor Horn, Colonel Babe Moseley and Mr C. Cornell formed the organising committee, with Trevor Horn as Badminton Horse Trials' first director and Babe Moseley as assistant director. Looking back it seems that Trevor Horn handled this daunting responsibility with remarkable calm – it must not be forgotten that most people in Britain did not know what 'eventing' was, and

there had never been a horse trials organised here apart from the Olympic competition. Trevor Horn was granted the use of a beautiful estate, but as far as a three-day event was concerned, it was virgin territory: he had to take this piece of land and mould it into a site suitable for a competition; he also had to devise most of the rules himself as there were no 'official' eventing regulations, only the general rules of the FEI. But in his quiet, unassuming way he produced, from the raw material of the Badminton estate, the first Badminton Horse Trials, as much a success then as it is now.

## Badminton, then and now

Throughout its fifty years' running, the Badminton Three-Day Event has succeeded in retaining its reputation for friendliness and efficiency, although by today's standards the early Badmintons were exceptionally informal and 'homely'. As now, the competition opened with

Hugh Thomas accompanies the late Princess of Wales, with Princes Harry and William at the 1991 presentation, with the present Duke of Beaufort

... and to think that once upon a time dogs were banned from Badminton!

the first horse inspection, although this took place in the stableyard at Badminton; today it is held in front of Badminton House, and attracts a great number of spectators. Since the event's inception, the Badminton estate has stabled every horse that has been entered. The grooms were given accommodation above the stable – although female grooms were housed separately in caravans. In the early days the riders stayed at local hotels. Today, the grooms and overseas riders are housed at Badminton, and British riders have to find their own beds for the night, usually in their horse boxes. Then, the competitors' entry fee was £2 per horse and first prize was £150; today the entry fee is £210 with a first prize of £27,500. For the first Badminton there were twenty-two starters, and the only qualifications required in order to take part were that the riders had to be British and over seventeen years of age, and the horses should not be over ten years of age, the latter proviso to ensure that any horse taking part would still be a good age to compete at the 1952 Olympics if selected. Although at that time ladies were not allowed to ride at the Olympics themselves, a quarter of the first Badminton entry was female.

Today the qualification process in force for those wishing to compete at Badminton is strict, and horse and rider have to have proved themselves capable of taking on the challenge. After a considerable furore in 1997 when there was such a large entry that many horses were balloted out, the qualifications were tightened further, and now only those horses that have been placed in the top 25 per cent at a three-star event, or in the top 50 per cent at a four-star event, in the past two years will be accepted. If there are still places available, then only horses meeting the minimum FEI qualification will be accepted.

## The competition

**The dressage** The first dressage test to be used at Badminton was the BHS Test B, and by today's standards it was very simple. But it has to be remembered that dressage as a sport was virtually unpractised in Britain, to the extent that Colonel Hance – an early *Horse and Hound* correspondent who wrote a series of articles giving

training advice to potential Badminton competitors – felt the need to impress upon people that they should not be put off by this phase! In fact his advice, which still holds true today, was correct: that dressage is nothing more than the training of the horse to be a balanced, supple and obedient ride whatever the job it is being prepared for.

Today's dressage test is still not as complex as those devised for pure dressage competitors, but it must be remembered that the event horse has to be many things: obedient, quiet and graceful in the dressage; strong, fit, bold and athletic for the speed and endurance phase; and supple and careful enough for the showjumping. These other requirements make performing a good dressage test plenty difficult enough for the majority of horses taking part.

The dressage phase used to take up only one day of the competition and was held in front of Badminton House, with farm wagons and straw bales providing the 'grandstands and seating'. However, the high number of entries today necessitates the dressage taking up two days of the event, and in order to provide adequate space and seating for the growing crowd of spectators, the arena is now in the main park, surrounded by purpose-built, covered grandstands. Spectators can now listen to a commentary on the test through the headsets provided.

**The speed and endurance phase** It is speed and endurance day, and in particular the cross-country, Phase D, which Badminton is all about, as is the whole sport of eventing. As far as the dressage and showjumping is concerned, the competitor knows exactly what will be demanded of him at the event itself: he can practise the actual dressage test at home, and can build and ride over showjumping courses which will ask the same questions as those he will encounter in the Badminton arena. But he cannot reproduce the cross-country phase at home; certainly he can take his horse cross-country schooling and hunting, and he can compete at one-day events so as to introduce it to the types of obstacles and questions that he will be faced with – but until he is allowed that first walk round the course at Badminton, he cannot be sure exactly what will be asked of

Inevitably, there is always an unseemly rush to get a good view of the Lake which draws an enormous crowd, all hoping to see some poor rider take a ducking. (The days of ducking the village witch are still with us!) The unlucky riders are **Jo Scott** (opposite and top) and **Caroline Sizer** (above centre)

Above: As is so often the case, the horse gets the last laugh (or in this case a wide grin!)

# A world-famous competition

**Colonel Trevor Horn: the original architect (1949–1953)** By all reports, and not the least judging by the results of his work, Badminton's first director Colonel Trevor Horn must have had all the qualities of a saint and a genius. A keen hunting man, and a great friend and neighbour of 'Master', the Duke of Beaufort, Trevor was delighted to be given the task of running the first Badminton Three-Day Event. However, although he was a brilliant rider and horseman, winning many showjumping classes including the King George V cup at Olympia, his experience of three-day eventing was limited to the two weeks he had spent at the 1948 Olympic Event.

As a council member of the British Horse Society, Colonel Horn was asked to be on the selection committee once it was decided to enter teams for both the Prix de Nations jumping (showjumping) and the three days' event at the 1948 Olympics. Brigadier Bowden-Smith had been *chef d'equipe* of the 1936 Berlin Olympic team, and he was in charge overall, but Trevor Horn was appointed arena manager for the 'Grand Prix de Dressage', and for the three days' event dressage and showjumping. He arrived at Aldershot two weeks beforehand and lived in the barracks with competitors and officials, and being naturally inquisitive he found out as much as he could about the general running of such an event. One of his duties was to escort the Duke and Duchess of Beaufort around the cross-country course, and it was over lunch in the Landrover that the Duke made his now legendary offer of the Badminton estate for Britain's own three days' event.

The British Horse Society needed no persuading to sanction the event, and Trevor Horn was appointed director and told to form a British Horse Society Badminton committee as well as a local committee to organise and run the event.

Despite never having ridden in a three days' event, Colonel Horn put his hunting experience and natural instinct to good use and was quickly able to assess what a horse could jump safely. His first wife had died from TB, but shortly after World War II he had married again and moved to Luckington Court (now famous for being the film set for *Pride and Prejudice*); his second wife remembers only too well how the Badminton Event occupied his mind for the five years that he was director:

'Trevor had nothing very sophisticated to work with,' recalls Mrs Horn; 'The top of the piano in our drawing room acted as his "office" and he would spend hours on the front lawn experimenting with showjump poles to see how his cross-country designs might look. He measured out the speed and endurance course – fourteen miles – on his bicycle, and a neighbour's daughter would do a practice run over most of the fences to give him an idea of how they would ride and what the timing would be like.'

The late dowager Duchess of Beaufort, with Colonel Trevor Horn presenting W. H. Pritchard with a long service award in 1959. Mr Pritchard handed over his job to his son-in-law, Harry Norris

Amongst his responsibilities he had also to arrange accommodation for competitors and officials, to advertise and promote the event, and to organise stabling and accommodation for the horses, grooms and chauffeurs, all of which were housed at Badminton; he had to arrange tentage and catering for competitors, officials and the general public, as well as liaise with the British Horse Society to print the schedules and programmes. Few people are given the chance to create, from nothing, a potentially world-famous event, but that is what Colonel Trevor Horn managed to do. Since he had had to devise the rules himself, there were obviously going to be teething problems as situations arose which no one had allowed for, or had any experience of. His creed was that if he hadn't a rule to cover it, then he made one up on the spot – and he was obviously a natural diplomat, because he seems to have succeeded in doing so without losing any friends along the way.

Colonel Trevor Horn was born in 1889, and he died from emphysema on Boxing Day in 1966.

him. And as the standard of riding has improved over the years, the ingenuity and art of the course designer and builder has been stretched in order to keep providing a sufficient challenge. And that is how a good competitor sees the cross-country phase: it is a challenge thrown down by the course designer, and the rider knows that if he reads it correctly and finds the right answer in terms of riding in a good balance, at a suitable speed and line to the fence, then he will be able to meet that challenge successfully.

The exact nature of the speed and endurance phase has altered over the years in terms of the speeds and distances ridden and the number of obstacles jumped, but the principles remain the same: it is a test of the horse's fitness, courage and agility, and of the rider's skill and horsemanship. The biggest obvious change is in the physical appearance of the cross-country course and the technical nature of the fences. At the very first Badminton Horse Trials the obstacles were described as being rigid and resembling natural objects such as hedges, ditches, farm gates, road crossings and streams. Although the maximum fence dimensions have remained unchanged, the size of the timber used in the fences in those first events was far smaller than that used today; this made the fences less inviting and probably caused many of them to look bigger than they were. Equally, the early courses had very few combination fences, and few were built up to maximum height. The obstacles you met on the course were like those you might expect to meet out hunting. Today's fences are elaborately designed with timber of as large dimensions as possible, and whilst still described as natural, it would be stretching the imagination to say that they might be met out hunting!

Originally the park at Badminton was left very open and the course would meander anywhere it liked; competitors could decide their own line across country in order to be as quick as possible. Today, because so much work goes into preparing the ground, so that the take-off and landing areas at each fence are as secure and 'weather-proof' as possible, the course follows roughly the same track each year, though generally it runs alternately clockwise and anti-clockwise. The vast number of spectators who now attend on cross-country day and wish for a close view of the course has meant that it has become necessary to rope the track off, both for safety reasons and to preserve the track itself. Whilst making for better 'viewing' and easier television coverage, this does mean that for the competitors, some of the fun and challenge has been lost. Many hours used to be spent walking various shortcuts to see if the course designer could be further outwitted by finding a quick route he hadn't anticipated when working out the time allowed! Such deviousness did not always pay off, however; for instance, one competitor thought he had found a shortcut from Phase A out to the steeplechase course. It involved jumping into a field of kale, although that in itself did not present a problem: his undoing lay in the fact that he had failed to notice an electric fence dividing the field, and almost cantered straight into it; his horse stopped dead in its tracks but he didn't, and hit the ground head first on the other side.

**The showjumping phase** Like the dressage, the showjumping was originally held outside Badminton House, but is now situated in the main arena surrounded by grandstands, so that all can watch the final result being played out. In the event's early days competitors jumped a fairly rustic-looking course, more like a working hunter course found in the show-ring; today the showjumps are colourful and elaborately designed, often with a particular theme in mind, and provide much more of a spectacle for both competitors and spectators.

## Badminton's founder and 'Master', the 10th Duke of Beaufort

The Badminton Three-Day Event owes its very existence to the foresight and generosity of the late Henry Hugh Arthur Fitzroy Somerset KG, PC, GCVO, MFH, 10th Duke of Beaufort. Born in 1900, it was soon abundantly clear that his main passion lay in hunting, so much so that on his eleventh birthday he was given a pack of harriers (hounds that hunt hares); from that day on he was referred to with fondness and respect as 'Master'. He was educated at Eton where he

15

# A world-famous competition

whipped in to Gordon Cox-Cox, the young Master of the Eton Beagles, who later in his career as Colonel Cox-Cox was to succeed Colonel Horn as the second director of the Badminton Horse Trials. 'Master' always maintained that Gordon Cox-Cox taught him everything he knew about hunting, but looking back on his life it is obvious that he was very knowledgeable on the subject well before he arrived at Eton. He served in the Royal Horse Guards (The Blues), and at the age of twenty-one, as the then Marquis of Worcester, took on the Mastership of the family foxhounds, managing the pack and its staff for forty-seven seasons!

Henry Hugh Somerset inherited the title 10th Duke of Beaufort in 1924. In 1936 he was appointed Master of the Horse by King George V to serve Elizabeth II, a position in which he was responsible for the Queen's safety on all State and formal occasions when she was mounted on horseback or travelling in a horse-drawn carriage. It was his privilege, as senior to

all on parade, to ride at her side. This same position had been held by the Duke's ancestor Edward, 4th Earl of Worcester, who was appointed in 1588 to serve Elizabeth I.

In 1928 he had been elected President of the British Olympic Association, and it was in this capacity that he visited the 1948 Olympic horse trials at Aldershot. The British team did not do well, and he determined there and then to see Britain succeed in this sport; it is a tribute to this determination that within a year, his family estate was hosting the first Badminton Three-Day Event.

The 10th Duke lived for his hunting and horses, but he always found time for people, too. He served as High Steward of Bristol, Gloucester and Tewkesbury; and as Lord Lieutenant of Bristol and Gloucestershire. He was also President of the MCC. He died in 1984, having enjoyed following his hounds the previous day. He is spoken of today with genuine respect and affection, and is remembered for the inimitable way in which he could inspire friendship and loyalty from all who knew him.

He is succeeded by his cousin David Robert Somerset. The 11th Duke of Beaufort shares his family's love of horses and hunting, and came close to victory himself when riding at the Badminton Horse Trials in 1959. He finished second to Sheila Willcox and High and Mighty. It is fortunate for the eventing world that the current host is as excellent a guardian of the Badminton Three-Day Event as was its founder.

## The Beaufort family and the Badminton estate

The Beaufort family is descended from John of Gaunt, Duke of Lancaster and the fourth son of Edward III. They became prominent at Court during the fifteenth century and have retained strong links with the royal family ever since. Created Earls and then Dukes of Somerset, the legitimate family name disappeared when the 2nd, 3rd and 4th Dukes were all killed during the Wars of the Roses. But Henry Beaufort, 3rd Duke of Somerset, executed after being defeated in the Battle of Hexham in 1464, had an illegitimate son who took his father's title as his surname. Charles Somerset became a favourite of both Henry VII and Henry VIII, and was created 1st Earl of Worcester in 1514. He married the heiress of Raglan and Chepstow, and Raglan Castle became the family home of the Earls of Worcester.

It was the 4th Earl of Worcester who bought the manor of Great Badminton for his youngest son Thomas in 1608; prior to this the house had been in the possession of the Boteler family since 1066. There were no sons produced from Thomas' marriage, and when his daughter died in 1655 the Badminton estate was bequeathed to Edward, Lord Herbert, son of the 5th Earl. Lord Herbert was a fanatical scientist and a devoted supporter of Charles I, and like his father before him, spent enormous sums of money supporting the Royalist cause during the Civil War. King Charles had rewarded the 5th Earl for his loyalty by making him 1st Marquis of Worcester in 1642. His son Edward, Lord Herbert, became the 2nd Marquis of

Worcester in 1646, his father having died in prison shortly after the fall of Raglan Castle, one of the few remaining Royalist strongholds. The castle was taken by Cromwell's Ironsides, but only after a fierce fight which earned it's defenders the respect of their conquerors. When Cromwell took possession of Chepstow a large proportion of the Somerset estate was confiscated by Parliament, but the family was allowed to return to the manor of Great Badminton, with many of their possessions.

In 1655 the Badminton estate was inherited by Henry, the son of Edward, Lord Herbert. Henry was an astute man and set his fortunes fair by becoming a Protestant MP and a friend of Cromwell. He was able to reclaim much of the family's lost fortune, and having decided to make Badminton the main family home, put in place an extensive rebuilding project. In 1660, during the Restoration, he transferred his allegiance to Charles II, who rewarded the family's long-term loyalty to the Crown by creating him 1st Duke of Beaufort in 1682.

The successive Dukes of Beaufort continued to prosper, and Badminton House was further extended and fabulously furnished over the years; the many alterations have transformed it from a Tudor manor to a Palladian-style mansion, although the original great Tudor hall remains. Now called the Old Kitchen, this is used as the grooms' canteen during the three-day event. All the dukes were keen horsemen and huntsmen; it was the 5th Duke who started hunting foxes in preference to deer in 1762, although the 7th Duke was the true founder of the Beaufort Hunt, which continues to thrive today. The 8th Duke was known as the 'Duke of Sport' and showed great interest in hunting, racing, carriage driving and cricket; it was in his house that the game of badminton (that of racquets and shuttlecocks) was invented. The 9th Duke was an exceptionally keen huntsman, and continued to follow hounds by car after an accident in 1919 put an end to his riding career; he was said to be just as capable of finding a fox when riding in a car as when mounted on a horse! From this summary history it would therefore appear that the Dukes of Beaufort have always been sportsmen, countrymen and gentlemen, and remain so today.

Top: A corner of the timeless Badminton estate, bathed in early spring sunshine
Centre: It is easy to forget that the activity in the stables goes on all year-round, this being home to the Beaufort Hunt. Brian Higham's enviable tack room is a cornucopia of sights and smells
Above: Every year there is work to be done on the course, whether maintaining existing fences or building new and more testing obstacles. Here Andrew Witt puts the finishing touches to the Colt Walls, a new fence in 1998

# 1949

## 'The Most Important Horse Event in Great Britain'

John Shedden and the infamous **Golden Willow** were the first to claim the Badminton title

Courage has long been a requirement for those in the world of eventing, and it was manifestly evident amongst both the organisers and the competitors at Badminton's first three-day event. In 1949 eventing did not exist as a sport in Great Britain, and apart from the few who had seen the 1948 Olympic three-day event course at Aldershot, none of the competitors had any idea what to expect. There was no such thing as an 'event horse' – those first competitors were 'having a go' on their hunters, showjumpers and point-to-pointers, and their only cross-country experience was that gained out hunting.

### Olympic testing ground

The task of Colonel Trevor Horn and his assistant Colonel Babe Moseley was to devise an event at Badminton which would be a testing ground for a British Olympic three-day event team. They had a lot to deliver, because not only did this event have to be a challenge fit for potential Olympians, it also had to inspire competitors and spectators to the extent that they would want to see the sport develop in this country – Badminton alone would never be enough to produce a successful Olympic team. Colonel Horn had to draw up the rules for the event, too (an official set of FEI rules did not appear until 1957). The scoring system was the same as that used at the Olympics, namely an official time for the speed and endurance phases with competitors able to earn plus points for beating the time, or incurring penalty points for being slower than the set time.

The publicity posters announced that on 20, 21 and 22 April 1949 'the most important horse event in Great Britain would take place: the Badminton Three Days' Event'. No doubt there were some who thought this a touch presumptive, but in fact as time has shown, a more apt description would have been hard to find. A number of articles appeared in *Horse and Hound* magazine, aimed at helping would-be competitors with their training. Forty-seven combinations entered originally, but as more was heard about what the event would involve, some obviously began to have doubts as to their suitability. Twenty-two remained firm in their resolve, and eventually took part in the horse event which did prove itself to be the most important in the country.

### Dressage day

One thousand people turned out to watch the dressage, judged by Brigadier Bowden Smith, Colonel V.D.S. Williams and Mr Henry Wynmalen, against the magnificent backdrop of Badminton House. The standard varied considerably; most riders had come to enjoy the challenge of the cross-country and were happy simply to 'get through' the dressage phase somehow. As a result few horses could be described as showing an attractive way of going, a fact not helped by the compulsory use of a double bridle and their obvious lack of correct schooling. But there where sufficient glimpses of brilliance to sustain the crowd and encourage the 'Olympic talent spotters'. The best performance was given by Captain Tony Collings riding Remus; thus as the proprietor and main trainer of the Porlock Vale Riding School he could subsequently and quite justifiably tell his pupils to 'do as I say and as I do'. He was thirty-three points clear of second-placed Lt Col Leech and Lucky Chance. The tearaway American Thoroughbred, Golden Willow, ridden by the leading Cotswolds instructor John Shedden, was third.

## Speed and endurance

Then, as now, it was really the cross-country that everyone had come to see. The first section of roads and tracks took competitors to Didmarton where the steeplechase had to be completed. They then hacked back along another section of roads and tracks to the start of the cross-country which was originally just below the stables. There was no ten-minute box, so if anyone wanted a few minutes rest before the cross-country, they had to get round the roads and tracks more quickly to allow for this. The cross-country course ran virtually in a straight line, and although obviously very different from today, it nevertheless took in many features which will be familiar to modern-day enthusiasts. Thus it crossed Luckington Lane, then went through Cape Farm and beyond Centre Walk, came back over the lane, crossed the Vicarage Ditch and finished along Worcester Avenue. There was then a Phase E, or 'run-in', to complete: this was just a long, straight stretch of cantering which gave the horses a chance to wind down.

Colonel Trevor Horn's first cross-country course was designed to be attacked. Whilst the timbers used were nothing like as big and imposing as they are today, the 'questions' asked by each fence were nothing like as complicated. There were two road crossings, a wide open water jump, a formidable drop fence and a big set of parallel bars set in front of a 4ft 6in wide, water-filled ditch, making a spread of 8ft in total. On the whole, the course was designed to replicate the type of obstacles you could expect to meet out hunting. The speed and endurance phases totalled fourteen miles, of which the cross-country course and its twenty-one fences took up three miles. Some concern was expressed when the course was first walked, with the result that five fences were lowered by a few inches and a small brush fence was put in front of the open water jump. However Major Eddie Boylan, who rode at the first Badminton, remembers the course as being tremendous fun to ride: 'During those first few years of the Badminton event the fences were straightforward by today's standards. You needed a horse with more courage than sense, and you could gallop at almost everything and stand off a mile.'

Wet, windy weather made for quite slippery conditions in 1949, and the course caused eight horses to be eliminated. But there were some very impressive performances: Captain Tony Collings and Remus produced a copy-book round, though Remus lacked the speed to allow him to pick up the maximum bonus points. Golden Willow, on the other hand, gave John Shedden a fantastic ride, his huge stride enabling him to power from fence to fence. The late Mrs Vivien Boon (née Machin-Goodall) put up the best performance of the five lady riders entered. Her big, powerful chestnut horse Neptune was well suited to the course – if a little over-enthusiastic when he cleared 22ft at the open water jump! They finished fifth overall. However, this over-bold attitude got him into trouble the following year when he tried to follow Golden Willow's example of jumping the Irish Bank all in one: he caught a hoof in the landing-side ditch and tipped up, giving his rider a crashing fall.

The informal atmosphere at that time meant there were no conventions such as crowd control or a roped-off track, and this gave competitors the freedom genuinely to take their own line from fence to fence – although this also had its dangers. For instance Reg Hindley and Stealaway were enjoying a cracking round when a spectator stepped out in front of them as they took off over a ditch and birch fence. Stealaway twisted in mid-air in an attempt to avoid a collision, but couldn't regain his balance and fell. They were both able to complete the course, however.

19

## Showjumping day

The final day's competition involved a course of twelve showjump-type fences, though these were more like a rustic working-hunter-type course than the imposingly colourful fences we are used to today. But then, as now, they provided a good test as to the horse and rider's all-round ability, and in 1949 only one competitor, Ireland's Ian Dudgeon and Sea Lark, managed a clear round. John Shedden had picked up such a commanding lead after his fast cross-country round that his one showjump down could not deny him victory.

Ian Dudgeon was a worthy runner-up, and third place went to Brigadier Lyndon Bolton and Titus III: Bolton was the only competitor to have had experience of a three-day event, having ridden at the 1948 Olympics, and this showed in the fast cross-country round that he achieved.

## Runaway success for Golden Willow

Badminton's first winner, the American Thoroughbred Golden Willow, proved to be a good indication of the type of horse most likely to succeed in international eventing: a classy blood horse with tremendous scope and presence, enabling him to make all three phases look easy. Golden Willow himself was not so easy in that he was impossibly strong – and according to his rider the late John Shedden, not far off mad, either.

He was foaled in 1943 in America, and was by Cloth of Gold (by Sir Galahad II) out of Pussy Willow. He was owned by Mrs Eleanor Home Kidston who had stabled Pussy Willow with John Shedden prior to the war. The striking light bay Golden Willow came over to England in 1948 and won four hunter trials that autumn. He was a quirky character, described by John Shedden as being both lovable and terrifying – but there was no denying his enjoyment of his new job. Besides, John Shedden was an experienced horseman and knew a trick or two to keep this maverick horse on the straight and narrow. Sheilah Michaels, a close friend who rode for John during the seventies and eighties, remembers him telling her how he used to wear a thimble on one finger with a spike on the end of it: if he pressed the spike into the horse's withers it touched a nerve, and this generally persuaded the horse to walk rather than jog! John himself was always worried about what Golden Willow might do if ever he broke loose, so he always rode with a length of string tied from his belt to the saddle in the hope that if he fell off he might still have a chance of holding on to him! Their inaugural victory earned Mrs Kidston a prize of £150.

In l950 John Shedden became the first rider to compete on two horses at Badminton, finishing second on King Pin and fifth on Golden Willow – although it would seem that some dubious time-keeping possibly robbed Golden Willow of a second victory. Sadly the crowd-pleasing horse was not to get the chance to show his full potential, because to John Shedden's intense disappointment and lasting regret, his owner was persuaded that there were far greater riches to be had in racing. John, however, was convinced that the horse's mind would not cope with the regime of training – and if that wasn't the finish of him, then he considered his lack of brakes would be: he always rode him in a severe 'gag' with a very tight standing martingale. And he was to be proved right, because Golden Willow ran away with his jockey on a training gallop and didn't stop until his tendons broke down after fourteen miles. Eighteen months later he was put back into training, but ran away again with the same result.

After his achievements at Badminton John Shedden moved to Australia where he helped train and develop their combined training and showjumping teams. When he returned to England he rented Greenhill Farm at Chedworth from Lord and Lady Vestey, and here he brought on and sold many horses, and helped a great many competitors with their cross-country riding. His direct approach was much appreciated by those riders who did not expect to be mollycoddled.

Rachel Bayliss, third in l982, was one rider to benefit from his help and advice, crediting him with giving her the confidence and direction that she had previously lacked. But as she explained, he was very blunt and did not 'carry' anyone: 'You had to stand on your own two feet and get on and do what he told you. If you were frightened he had no sympathy at all, because he genuinely believed that there was no place on the cross-country course for fear – you would just end up getting hurt.'

To those prepared to listen, John Shedden was more than helpful, though his direct manner probably meant that much of his great fountain of knowledge was never shared with as many in the horse world as it might have been – but this was their loss, not his, it would seem.

He had a brilliant eye for a horse, often

he had left the army and returned to the family's riding establishment to help out. His father, Lt Col Joe Hume Dudgeon, had trained the British showjumping and three-day event teams for the 1948 Olympics so he was able to give Ian some idea of what to expect – and that first taste of eventing immediately converted Ian to this new sport. He rode a home-bred horse from a reliable family of hunters and showjumpers: Sea Lark was a good showjumper and had been well hunted. Ian was almost unseated over the last cross-country fence, but survived to produce the only clear round in the final day's showjumping.

Ireland's **Ian Dudgeon** took second place at the first Badminton Three-Day Event, and is seen here in 1951, again riding **Sea Lark**. He ruefully admits he spent many years trying to go 'one better', but his first attempt remained his best result

spotting potential that others would overlook. His father had been a great polo player, though this did not afford John an affluent childhood. He started off as a nagsman, learning the hard way by riding anything – but this also meant that he worked with some great horsemen along the way. He always bought his horses cheaply, often because they had been deemed unridable or were in a very poor state, and then successfully retrained them.

## Ian Dudgeon and Sea Lark

For second-placed Captain Ian Dudgeon from Ireland, the trip to Badminton had been the most exciting part of his equestrian career to date. During the war he had been badly shot and had to have a piece of his rib grafted into his leg to repair the damage; then after the war

'It was always a great pleasure going to the Duke of Beaufort's house for Badminton,' recalls Ian. 'Everything was very informal and personal – the Duke would invite us in, and treated us like guests. I was thrilled for my father that his "stable" recorded a good result at the first Badminton – but it meant that I spent all the rest of my time trying to win it in subsequent years! And although we were always there or thereabouts, we never did better than that first attempt. My father and I were inspired to start the Irish Olympic three-day event team, and to have a real go at this sport; I rode at the Olympics in 1952, 1956 and 1960.' Ian was presented with an Armada dish (for five completions) the first year that they were given, in 1964. He then gave up eventing and concentrated once again on showjumping. He now lives on the Isle of Man.

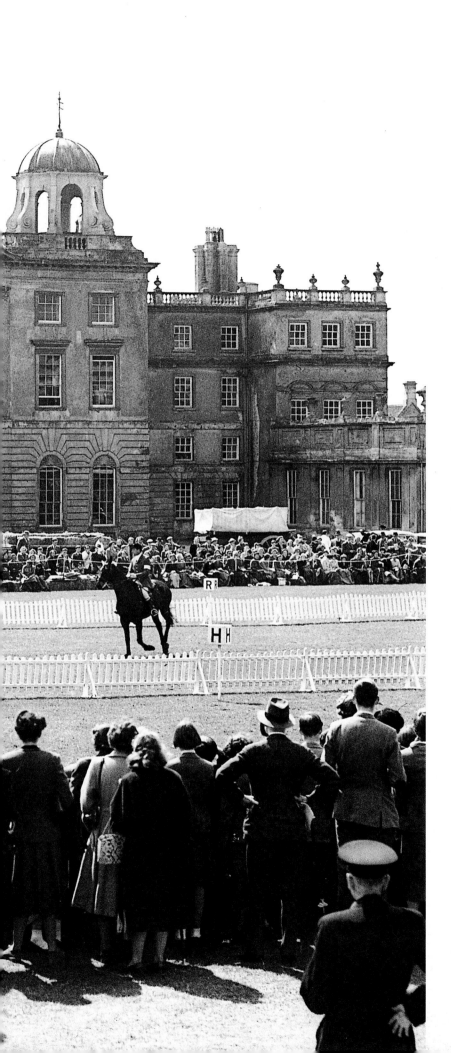

The 1950s

# 1950

# Team trainer leads the way

Dudgeon. The course now covered four miles and included twenty-eight fences. In this year the Irish Bank proved particularly troublesome – it was topped with cinders rather than grass, and this seemed to worry some horses as to whether it was safe to land on, or whether they should jump right over it. Golden Willow came over it successfully, but Neptune lost Miss

**Captain Tony Collings** and **Remus** were popular winners in 1950. An inspirational man, he was a great team trainer, and it was one of his ideas that led to the creation of London's Horse of the Year Show

**Isobel Reid** (née Touche) riding **Hunting Stuart** show fine style across country. Today Isobel is better known as a dressage rider and judge. Note the lack of protection worn by horse and rider – no chin strap, no body protector, no boots or bandages

Pages 22–3: During the early years the dressage took place in front of Badminton House. The open wagon to the right of the photograph, just behind the rider, served as the royal box

Captain Tony Collings was a popular Badminton winner in 1950 on the kind and consistent Remus, owned by Miss G. Chrystal. Their names were the first to be engraved on the newly presented Daily Telegraph Challenge Cup, and Miss Chrystal received £150. The second running of the Badminton Three Days' Event enjoyed fine spring weather and a growing number of spectators: an estimated 3,000 watched the dressage, 10,000 the cross-country, and 6,000 the showjumping.

Amongst the thirty starters were the two leading riders of the previous year: John Shedden with two rides, and Ireland's Ian

Machin Goodall here, as he did again at the Coffin where he tried to jump from slope to slope instead of proceeding down the incline to the ditch and up the other side. They eventually incurred 367.75 penalties in total, but still finished eighteenth!

John Shedden raised an objection in defence of his title after a fast clear on Golden Willow failed to achieve the number of bonus marks for speed that he expected. His objection was overruled, and undoubtedly few begrudged Tony Collings his win. For the second year running Remus had led the dressage, but this year he was able to gain thirty bonus marks on the cross-country; moreover his lead was sufficient to allow him the error of one showjump down on the final day. John Shedden and Mrs Fanshawe's Kingpin managed to atone for their poor dressage score by gaining seventy speed bonus points, but two showjumps down prevented them from dislodging Remus. Third place went to Captain P. Arkwright and Lady Leigh's Minster Green.

The competition was not without its amusing moments: Major Dick Hern, the recently retired racehorse trainer, was riding at his first Badminton on Millfield School's King Willow and unfortunately they fell at the penultimate fence. King Willow lost his bridle, but Major Hern put it back on, remounted and finished the course with both reins on one side of the

**Timeless timekeeping** For the 1950 event, the watchmakers Omega kindly tested and supplied a number of stopwatches to allow for accurate time-keeping. In the 1990s Omega returned to Badminton as official timekeepers and sponsors.

horse's neck – and still gained forty-five speed bonus points! They finished eleventh, a pleasing result for the Major, who was an instructor at Tony Collings' Porlock Vale Riding School. Eighteen of the thirty starters completed the event.

The triumphant Remus was bought by Miss Chrystal as a six-year-old from the Mill Hill Riding Establishment. His breeding was

**Isobel Reid's early memories** The now renowned dressage rider and judge Isobel Reid (née Touche) rode at Badminton as a nineteen-year-old in 1950. Riding her own horse Balalaika, Isobel recalls that before the Badminton three-day event she had never ridden in an adult dressage or showjumping competition – and it was her first cross-country experience! 'I had been point-to-pointing with my horse where the fences were 4ft high. When I saw in the Badminton schedule that the fences there were only 3ft 11in I decided we ought to be able to manage it.'

'Brigadier Lyndon Bolton told me that the only preparation you needed for the cross-country was half a bottle of champagne. I mentioned this to a friend, who duly had a bottle delivered to Badminton House for me! The event was incredibly friendly and informal because there were so few of us; Mary Beaufort, the Duchess, would invite all the female riders in for afternoon tea! There was very little fuel to spare for horseboxes so most people sent their horses by train and we hacked up from Badminton station to the stableyard. I was billeted in the sanatorium at Westonbirt girls' school, and can clearly remember the very short, very hard iron beds!

'In the early years the course wasn't roped off at all, and serious competitors like Sheila Willcox and Frank Weldon would take shortcuts through the car parks. However, as more and more people came to watch on cross-country day, it became harder and harder for riders to have a clear view of the next fence.

'The roads and tracks covered a much greater distance in those days – when the event moved to Windsor in 1955 there was something horrendous, like eighteen miles, to cover. Nor were there any markers to tell you how far you had gone, so it was much more about horsemanship and true judgement of pace then. I can't remember anyone wearing a stopwatch, but we all used to have a "friend" stationed half-way round the steeplechase course, who would cough loudly if we needed to go faster to make the time!'

Isobel rode for both Colonel Horn and his successor Colonel Cox-Cox, and she remembers how, as excitement about the sport grew, every owner hoped that their 'hunter' would make a Badminton winner; for instance: 'Colonel Cox-Cox had a lovely hunter which we were all convinced would take to eventing. He sent him to Robert Hall to introduce him to dressage, but the horse really hated it; he became so nappy that he wouldn't do anything he was asked, and was sent back to Gordon Cox-Cox as not only unsuitable for eventing but for just about anything else, too! Poor Colonel Cox-Cox was mortified and wondered what on earth he could do now with what had been such a lovely horse. But a local horseman, Willy Donaldson, advised him not to worry: "Just turn him away until hounds are meeting locally, and then get on him and go hunting." And it worked, because the horse hadn't forgotten the joy of hunting.'

unknown, but he was a thoroughly kind, reliable horse, very typical of the Irish hunter type. Remus was ten when he won Badminton, which in those days was considered too old to be an Olympic hopeful. However, he enjoyed several seasons hunting before he was retired to grass.

## Tony Collings: team trainer

Captain Tony Collings is credited with being the driving force behind Britain's successful introduction to international three-day eventing. He had seen active service during World War II with the North Somerset Yeomanry, the last mounted regiment; they went into action on horseback against the Vichy French in 1942. After the war he returned to run the Porlock Vale Riding School, where general equitation was taught to a great many pupils.

He was in his late forties when he won at Badminton, and as a 'professional' would not have been eligible to ride at the Olympics himself. But he was a wonderful trainer, quick to discover his pupils' strengths and weaknesses, just as he was his own. Even before his Badminton victory, he had been asked to take the Olympic riders for concentrated team training. He knew that his own knowledge of dressage was not good enough for international success and so he employed the German trainer Herr Richard Waetjen to teach the subtleties of this fine art. He had a remarkable talent for matching the right rider to the right horse, and also in 'charming suitable horses out of unsuspecting owners' so that they might be taken to Porlock Vale to form part of his Olympic armoury.

Indeed it was Tony Collings who converted Bertie Hill to eventing, and who was responsible for the successes of the 1950s: European team champions in 1953, team and individual gold at the 1954 World Championships, team gold at the 1956 Olympics. Of the riders he trained, Laurence Rook won Badminton in 1953, and John Oram was second in 1955 (at Windsor) where Bertie Hill also finished third.

Tragically, Tony Collings was killed in the 1954 Comet 1 air crash.

# The Badminton Olympic Horse Trials

Whilst the Badminton Three Days' Event was gradually becoming a well known feature on the horseman's calendar, Badminton House itself was already better known to the public as the place where the game of badminton (that of shuttlecocks and rackets) had been invented in l863. To avoid any confusion as to what the paying public might be expecting to see when they arrived, the horse event was renamed the Badminton Olympic Horse Trials; and with

Although the crowds may be as plentiful, the early Lake fence was nothing like as imposing as it is today, but, as has been proved over the years, the bigger the timber the better the fence is to jump. This one may be small, but is not particularly inviting

growing confidence, in 1951 the Badminton committee invited the world to compete. Ireland, Switzerland and Holland sent teams, and in all there were thirty-eight starters. As the 1952 Helsinki Olympics drew ever closer, the British Horse Society had made the Badminton committee responsible for selecting the Olympic three-day event team, and so the event's new name was particularly appropriate.

Dreadful weather almost brought about the cancellation of the event; as it was, Colonel Horn and his team ended up building three different courses in an effort to find the best ground on which to run. Phase C (the second roads and tracks) was shortened – but the cross-country course was lengthened by 1,000m to 7,500m!

## The Continental riders prove superior

The dressage marking in this year appeared to be stricter, resulting in a much greater difference in scores and revealing only too clearly the Continental riders' superiority in this phase. The British were still quietly confident; they knew that the Swiss horses had never been asked to jump across country, and because of their cold climate most of their training took place in indoor schools. But the Swiss were equally confident, knowing that what their horses lacked in experience and fitness they would make up for in obedience, balance and suppleness.

The Coffin was the downfall of many riders, and unfortunately that of most of the British. The Swiss and Dutch horses, for the most part, just listened to their riders and jumped when they were told, regardless of the size or complexity of the obstacle in front of them. *Horse and Hound*'s correspondent noted that 'of the British horses that stopped at the Coffin, only one rider, Mr R. Hall, was able to persuade his horse finally to jump it; the rest were eliminated or retired. The Swiss riders adopted a far quieter and neater approach and their horses responded obediently.' The suggestion was that perhaps the British were spending too much time galloping around and jumping, instead of concentrating on obedience and suppleness. Ironically the accusation thrown at British team riders during the early nineties was that they were losing competitions by playing safe – meaning that it was no good going out and doing a pretty dressage test if you couldn't show fighting spirit across country! Reg Hindley and Stealaway, who had put up the best British dressage performance, fell at the Coffin and then had a refusal in the showjumping arena; but an indication of the trouble the course caused was that they still finished thirteenth.

The Swiss took first and second places in the team competition, with Ireland third; in the individual placings Switzerland took first, fourth, sixth and ninth places. Captain Hans Schwarzenbach and Vae Victis were the winners. Britain did not lose face completely as Jane Drummond-Hay rode her own Happy Knight into second place. The Dutch rider, Mr Van Loon, riding his mare Narantsoula, was third; he had led after the speed and endurance phases, but four showjumps down lost him the title.

## Vae Victis: the unwanted horse that found victory

Captain Hans Schwarzenbach was first introduced to Vae Victis when a fellow Swiss cavalry officer tried to sell him the horse. Hans was not particularly impressed by him and walked away – but on returning home that night he found the horse had been ensconced in his yard with the message that he had bought him! Despite letters and telegrams asking the 'owner' to remove the horse, he refused to take him back. The situation finally came to a head when Vae Victis fell down while being exercised and broke his knees. Feeling responsible for the horse's well-being, Hans telephoned his fellow officer and negotiated a low price for him.

To Hans' pleasure and surprise he was soon able to get some good work out of Vae Victis, the key to his good behaviour being that he hated to be interfered with: if you rode him on a long rein and let him make his own decisions when jumping, he was more than happy to oblige. They won an event at Lucerne, and the horse attracted much interest from potential buyers. Then to Hans' horror the original 'owner' reappeared, claiming he still owned the horse – and before anyone could stop him, he moved Vae Victis to Italy and sold him to the Italian team! Luckily the president of the Swiss Federation was able to intervene, and Vae Victis was reunited with Hans. As a nine-year-old he carried his master to victory at Badminton, and returned again in 1953 to finish third behind Laurence Rook and Frank Weldon.

Hans' son, Anton, who is currently chef d'équipe of the Swiss three-day event team, recalls his father's account of their adventurous

**Friends in high places** In 1964 both Hans Schwarzenbach and his son Anton were at Badminton, Hans as the owner of Kipling and Anton as his jockey. They brought with them their groom, who in the evenings got into the habit of going for a quiet wander around Badminton House. One night he met a very pleasant lady feeding the dogs: 'Hello,' he says, 'I'm so glad to see you're still working here'; and they passed a pleasant hour chatting about the merits of their respective 'jobs'. The following day the Duchess of Beaufort was delighted to be able to tell Hans and Anton about her new-found friend!

trip to Badminton: 'About seven Swiss cavalry officers ventured over to Badminton in 1951 just to see what all the fuss was about. They soon found out that the English did not really know anything about dressage, and having performed a good test my father knew that he just had to produce a good clear round to succeed. Vae Victis was not fast enough to gain many bonus points, but neither did he make any mistakes to incur penalties; even a showjump down on the last day left him nearly twenty points ahead of Jane Drummond-Hay.

'There was always great rivalry between the army contingents of different countries, and so my father was absolutely delighted when he took on Burnt Trout, a horse deemed too difficult for eventing by Frank Weldon, and won the European Championships at Harewood in 1959, leaving Frank in second place!

'In 1955 my father was too busy to come over to England to compete, but he allowed a less experienced officer, Lt Zindel, to ride Vae Victis at the European Championships held at Windsor (in place of Badminton). As we have indicated, Vae Victis hated being interfered with – but this rider kept him on tight rein, and he fell twice at the Sandpit. After that he did not event again at international level, but concentrated on showjumping up until his retirement. I had also been introduced to eventing on Vae Victis, and I can vouch for the fact that he had to be ridden on a long rein!'

Anton also rode at Badminton himself, in 1964, 1968 and 1972, and he recalls his record as being three rides and five falls! Despite this, his daughters Michelle and Annette would both love to carry on the family tradition and compete at Badminton.

1951 winners **Captain Hans Schwarzenbach** and **Vae Victis** proved that obedience and trust were as important as sheer courage in an eventing partnership

# The 1950s

## The lady saves the day: Jane Drummond-Hay

**Jane Drummond-Hay** upheld British pride at Badminton's first 'Open Championship' by finishing second in 1951 on Happy Knight. She is pictured here in 1952 on **Abbeyfeale**

Riding at her first Badminton in 1951, Jane Drummond-Hay (now Mrs Timmy Whiteley) and Happy Knight saved the day for Britain by finishing second.

'Having failed my Pony Club A test my mother had been told by Colonel Cubitt – at that time in charge of the Pony Club – that I needed sending off somewhere to be taught to ride properly!' recalls Jane. 'So I was sent to Colonel Hume Dudgeon's yard in Ireland, which

£250 for him, which was a lot of money then, as much as a tractor!

'Our partnership continued successfully. Along with my sister, Anneli, we qualified with the Scottish Pony Club team to go down to Newmarket for the combined training championships; it was a very exciting competition – we had to ride off twice – but Happy Knight and I won it. Colonel Cubitt wrote and congratulated me, and by now I was thinking we could tackle anything – and Badminton seemed a natural progression.

'I went back to Colonel Dudgeon's that

was great fun. I made a good friend there, Sylvia Dallas, and in 1950, when we were still in our teens, we went to visit Badminton together, staying at The Bell Hotel at Malmesbury. I was really inspired by the likes of John Shedden and Tony Collings – but I can also clearly remember a great friend of mine, Alec Cubitt, falling flat on his face somewhere!

'Back home in Scotland I had been jumping at a junior class at a local show when a man came up and asked if I would ride his horse in the Open class. It was a great big animal called Happy Knight and we never did find out why the owner didn't like riding him! Anyway, the horse won the class, and we were then offered the chance to buy him. My mother had to pay

autumn to prepare for the great event. By that time Happy Knight was a grade A showjumper, but he had never gone across country. Nevertheless I had enormous trust in him, and it never occured to me that he wouldn't jump anything I asked! Our preparation in Ireland centred mainly on getting us both really fit. We were set schedules of roadwork and hillwork, as well as galloping on the beaches and in the sea. We had heard that we might have to jump into water, and so we practised jumping into a few ponds, and also went round the Irish Grand National course. Happy Knight was a truly lovely horse but quite an excitable character; he was also quite spooky, and hated having to walk. I remember Ian Dudgeon telling me there was no point going to Badminton unless I could make my horse walk instead of jog – the walk was a whole movement in the dressage test, and he warned me I would get nought! I practised for hours alone in the mountains, trying to persuade Happy that he could walk. Then on one of our hacks Happy Knight shied at a cement mixer and slipped on the road, cutting both his knees; because of this he had to have three weeks off. However, this didn't prove to be as much of a setback as everyone had told me it would be.

'At Badminton I was accommodated at the Westonbirt girls' school sanitorium, along with Isobel Reid and Penny Moreton. I remember watching the Swiss riders in their uniforms riding their well trained little horses and thinking how handsome they looked. I tried to imagine that I was one of the Swiss soldiers, and it must have worked as we rode a far better test than anyone expected – despite this being the first test I had had to ride in a double bridle! We ended up lying thirteenth after the dressage.

'Cross-country day was lovely and sunny; I remember Mother giving me a glass of orange juice and glucose, and then we were off. Happy Knight wasn't a Thoroughbred, and so didn't have that inexorable, easy gallop that a blood horse has, and so I had worked out our times very carefully, even allowing for some time penalties on the steeplechase – where, by the way, we had to jump a post and rail and a wall! On the cross-country course the only fence I had been really worried about was Tom Smith's Walls as I had never jumped anything quite as solid as concrete before. However, all went well until we arrived at the Coffin. There were no crowds to speak of and my mother chose this moment to step forward and shout "Hello darling!". It was enough to break our concentration, and Happy Knight stopped. He then turned and jumped it perfectly happily the second time – and without that interruption he would have won, as he showjumped clear the next day! The Coffin did cause a lot of trouble; Reg Hindley jumped straight into the ditch and lay as if for dead, which scared everyone.

'At that time women weren't allowed to ride at the Olympics. The British team had asked if they could borrow Happy Knight, but as he was my only horse and had cost us a lot of money we said no. Then the Irish team asked if they could lease him for £1,000 per year and this was a proposition we couldn't afford to refuse. We were just finalising the details of a contract when I was asked to ride at Wellesbourne – it was a team of Olympic possibles against a team of "impossibles", and Happy Knight slipped coming into what was really a tiny fence and broke his knee. We tried everything to keep him alive, but eventually had to concede defeat and have him put down. Happy Knight was by Merely-a-Minor, who was the sire of Merely-a-Monarch's dam. My sister Anneli rode Merely-a-Monarch to victory at Badminton in 1962.'

Jane rode at Badminton again the following year on Colonel Hume Dudgeon's Abbeyfeale. They led the dressage by twenty penalties, but cross-country day was a disaster. As Jane relates: 'We knew Abbeyfeale had a stop in him, so when I felt him hestitate on the approach to the first water I gave him a good smack. He jumped it, but then bolted with me, straight over a wire fence which we then had to jump again in order to get back onto the course. He careered over the next few fences until we came to the second water where he stopped dead, and I sailed headfirst into it. I clambered back on board with my boots full of water, and after that he jumped without a hitch – including a clear showjumping round – to finish thirteenth. I gave up competing after that as I was engaged to be married and planning to move to Rhodesia.'

Family connections with Badminton did not finish there, because Jane's brother-in-law, Martin Whiteley, won Little Badminton in 1960 on Peggotty, and on The Poacher in 1965; this horse won Badminton again in 1970 when ridden by Richard Meade. Martin's mother had also been affected by the family enthusiasm for eventing, and she had bought a potential team horse called Foxdor. He achieved third place at Badminton in 1968 with Sergeant Ben Jones and was shortlisted for the Mexico Olympics, but he died from a heart attack after a training gallop. Sgt Jones took over the ride on Martin Whiteley's The Poacher and won Olympic team gold (see 1960).

# 1952

# Dress rehearsal for Helsinki

Above: A 'vintage crop' – the car park in 1952

Left: A farm wagon was brought into use as a royal box

Below and margin: Princess Margaret and Queen Elizabeth. The royal family were free to mingle closely with the general public. Growing crowd numbers and the increased threat of terrorism meant that this charming intimacy was short-lived

Badminton in 1952 was designed very much as a practice run for the forthcoming Olympics. The course was made noticeably more difficult, with more combination fences such as the Quarry, a post-and-rail drop into a natural hollow, followed by a right-angled turn in the bottom hollow to jump a tree trunk out. Another test of good riding and ability was a big hazelwood fence with a drop sited at an awkward angle; so too was the penultimate fence, two sets of post and rails divided by a ream (ditch) – a warning to riders of the need to 'keep some petrol in the tank' towards the end of the course. The cross-country course itself had been lengthened to four and a half miles, and included thirty-four fences.

## The Queen attends

The sport of eventing was beginning to take off in Britain, with the first one-day events being organised in various parts of the country; these served as practice and preparation for Badminton. At the end of May, 5,000

spectators attended the one-day event at Sherbourne Park. In 1952 the sport's profile was raised further still by the presence of the young Queen Elizabeth, her husband and her sister, as guests of the Duke of Beaufort at the Badminton Olympic Horse Trials. A farm wagon was used as a royal box, and the number of spectators rose dramatically to approximately 50,000. Fine weather and perfect going made this a particularly enjoyable event.

## Mixed fortunes

Twenty-six horses came under the starter's orders, and problems were spread fairly evenly around the upgraded course. The Coffin – fence no 13! – caused almost as much trouble as it had the previous year, with four eliminations. One of the few to jump it really well was the six-year-old novice showjumper Lionheart, owned by Lt Col Harry Lewellyn and ridden by Lifeguards officer Lt Thompson. Several riders tipped up at the Luckington Lane crossings, and the new

**Olympic training** The determination of the Duke of Beaufort that Britain should succeed at the Olympics was more than matched by that of Tony Collings, the team trainer; the Olympic hopefuls – seven riders and twelve horses – were sent for six months' intensive training at Porlock Vale. They worked six days a week, their daily programme starting at 8.30am with physical training exercises on horseback, and dressage and jump training continued throughout the day until tea-time. At some stage each rider would have ridden every Olympic horse and they also rode the riding school horses; these less highly trained animals enabled Tony Collings to evaluate how his riders coped with refusals and other misdemeanours.

Reg Hindley (a joint master of the Pendle Forest and Craven Harriers) was team captain, and the others in training were Major Laurence Rook, Bertie Hill, Lt Cdr John Oram, John Miller, Captain Michael Naylor Leyland, and Angus McCance. The team spent a week at Badminton prior to the 1952 event.

The British Horse Society sponsored the training at Porlock Vale with money raised through the Olympic Equestrian Fund. Badminton was to act as a trial for the team, although because they were riding strictly to orders and in some cases missing out certain elements of the competition, they were to ride *hors concours*.

Newspapers at the time reported that no other sport was applying the same concentrated gravity to its preparation for the 1952 Helsinki Olympics.

After their determined and meticulous training, the team of three for Helsinki was finally named: Reg Hindley with Speculator and Bertie Hill on Countryman became the first civilians to represent their country in the Olympic three-day event, and the third team member was Major Lawrence Rook and Starlight; he was a last-minute replacement for Captain Michael Naylor Leyland who had succumbed to chickenpox.

Hopes were high, and towards the end of the cross-country day, it looked as if the Duke of Beaufort's endeavours to secure Olympic success for Britain would be amply rewarded. Laurence Rook was the last team member to go for Britain; Bertie and Reg had gone well and as Starlight came storming into view he was clear and well up on the clock – it seemed the British team promised to take the lead after the speed and endurance test. But as Starlight rounded the last corner to approach the final fence, he put his foot in a drainage ditch and fell. Laurence Rook was badly concussed, but was carried to his horse and pushed back on board. They successfully jumped the last fence but on the run-in of Phase E, a disorientated Rook rode the wrong side of a marker flag and this eliminated the team.

In spite of this disappointment, however, it was clear to all true sportsmen that the path to Olympic gold was quite attainable.

# The 1950s

Despite her diminutive size, **Emily Little** became the first mare to win Badminton, ridden by **Captain Mark Darley** in 1952

angled hazelwood fence saw a crashing fall for Major Frank Weldon who was riding at his first Badminton on Liza Mandy. He ended up in Tetbury hospital, much to the amusement of the two young officers he had brought with him, who completed the course safely on their government chargers!

Olympic hopeful John Oram was riding *hors concours* on Bambi and his own Philippa. He went clear on Bambi, but at the very moment the Queen was watching, Philippa

stopped at the rails in front of the water, decanting her rider who was completely submerged in its murky depths! The Queen kindly retrieved his stick, and the combination continued without further mishap.

Major Rook and Starlight, also riding 'HC', were excused the steeplechase but recorded a magnificent cross-country performance to finish five minutes inside the time!

The dressage leader, Jane Drummond-Hay, had been lost with a ducking at the water, so the field was open to a number of contenders. At the end of the cross-country, Brigadier Lyndon Bolton led from Ireland's Penny Moreton and Vigilante, and Brian Young and Captain Mark Darley were third and fourth. The showjumping phase was most influential, and caused a turnaround in fortunes: Brigadier Bolton hit three showjumps to drop to third, and Penny Moreton dropped to fifth; Brian

Young, an instructor at Porlock Vale riding the seven-year-old half-Exmoor pony, Dandy, made only two mistakes to move up to second place; but a clear round clinched victory for Captain Mark Darley and the mare Emily Little. Only 2½ penalties separated these three.

## Victorious little lady

Emily Little was the first, and one of only three mares, ever to win at Badminton. A 15.3hh chestnut mare by Satrap, Mark Darley had bought her as a five-year-old from her breeder, Miss Smith from Nettle Hall, in Warwickshire. He took her to Germany where he was stationed with the Royal Horse Guards and gave her a careful, thorough training. She competed in some showjumping competitions, and the week before Badminton was second in a combined training class in Dorset; this was her first appearance in a dressage arena. The pair then spent four days at Porlock Vale before tackling Badminton. At the time of her victory she was still only seven years old.

The Darley family was famous for bringing the Arabian horse to England – the Darley Arabian – and were therefore responsible for the birth of the English Thoroughbred; the late Colonel Mark Darley was himself a great amateur rider. Fellow Irishman Ian Dudgeon recalls how they had to seek the Queen's permission for him to have leave of duty to train for the Irish Olympic teams. He evented and showjumped with enthusiasm, and twice won the King's Cup at the Royal Tournament with Emily Little.

Colonel Darley was a close friend of Major Laurence Rook, and at the end of her illustrious career, Emily Little was retired to spend the rest of her days on the Rooks' farm as a broodmare.

> **Leading ladies** Only three mares have won at Badminton:
> Emily Little:  Badminton 1952
> Bambi V:  Badminton 1954
> Peggotty:  Little Badminton 1960

# Team reject wins European honours

In 1953 Badminton hosted the European Championships, the first official international three-day event to be held under the auspices of the FEI. There were individual entries from seven countries, and teams from England, Ireland and Switzerland. The overall winner was Major Laurence Rook riding Mrs J. R. Baker's Starlight XV, a horse of stunning looks and paces. Sadly he did not have the temperament to match, and due to his erratic dressage performances had been dropped from

Once partnered by **Major Laurence Rook, Starlight XV**'s performances improved tremendously. But in 1956 he 'blew up' in the dressage and was withdrawn. This ended his eventing career

the British team; this now comprised Major Frank Weldon on Kilbarry, Bertie Hill on Bambi V and Reg Hindley on Speculation – and on this occasion the team won gold!

Ironically Starlight was on his best behaviour and finished joint second after the dressage; a typically impressive cross-country round then gave him a three-fence lead. He used up one of his chances in the showjumping arena but secured victory with a rare plus score of 5.3, as opposed to a penalty score; in fact Major Rook became the first British rider, and the only rider since 1948, to finish a three-day event on a plus score.

Starlight XV was another classy Thoroughbred in the same mould as the inaugural winner Golden Willow, with enormous ability but a tricky temperament. He was by Trappeur II out of a mare called Dawn, and had been bred in South Devon by Mr Congden. He was bought by Mr Jack Baker of Ivybridge, Devon, as a wedding present for his wife. Mr Baker already owned a high class steeplechaser, Torhill, who had been bred in South Devon and was by Trappeur II. He was willing to chance his luck twice. Sadly Torhill broke down during training for the Grand National.

Starlight did not take to life as a racehorse, and his trainer, Gerald Balding, suggested he might be better suited to three-day eventing. He was sent to Porlock Vale in June 1950, and four months later was ridden at his

*Continued on page 39*

**Major Laurence Rook** Laurence Rook was born and brought up at Edwarlton House in Nottinghamshire. He loved horses and hunting, and as a boy would beg, borrow or steal anything to hunt. He joined the army, and while with the Royal Horse Guards (the Blues) had the chance to compete a great deal when stationed in Germany. Irishman Captain Mark Darley (the 1952 winner) was a great friend and fellow competitor. Laurence was a member of the first British team since the war to win a Nations Cup (at Rotterdam) and showjumped at the White City. His widow Jane recalls that when he was persuaded to take up eventing he was delighted to find that it meant he could get more leave from the army to go hunting, since hunting was considered a good 'preparation'!

Jane and Laurence were married in 1953. Although Laurence had been left off the British team for Badminton's European Championships in this year, he was feeling sufficiently confident to forecast privately to friends the margin by which he would win – and he did!

After the disappointment of the Helsinki Olympics in 1952 (see p33) British fortunes – and in particular the partnership of Laurence and Starlight – entered a golden era. The team of Laurence Rook, Bertie Hill and Frank Weldon won European team gold at Basle in 1954, and the following year the same team won European gold at Windsor, with Frank Weldon taking individual gold and Bertie Hill the bronze.

Badminton 1956 was the final trial for the Stockholm Olympics, and Starlight blew up in the dressage to the point that Laurence took him out of the arena without completing the test. Jane well remembers her husband disappearing over the horizon with his disgraced horse. Feeling desperately sorry for him, and not really knowing what to do, she followed the example of so many at Badminton and went 'shopping'. A pair of very trendy dark glasses from Aspreys cheered her up enormously, and it wasn't long before the ever-sporting Laurence

Opposite: Starlight's erratic temperament meant that his potentially brilliant career was relatively short-lived

reappeared clutching a cine-camera with which to terrorise his team-mates. He promised John Oram he would be there to film him if he fell off – and he was! After Badminton the team continued in training for Stockholm, but this time without Starlight, who would never again be asked to represent his country or Major Rook. Michael Naylor Leyland had been given the ride on High and Mighty (who had been bought from Sheila Willcox by the great team supporter Ted Marsh), but the horse went lame. Laurence was then offered the team place on Ted Marsh's Wild Venture. At Stockholm the team won Olympic gold, with Laurence sixth individually.

It was only after Stockholm that Jane had the chance to see the cine-film that Laurie had taken at Badminton: about 90 per cent of the footage was of Wild Venture, and when Jane asked him why, Laurie announced that, after Starlight, the only horse in England that he had ever wanted to ride was Wild Venture – prophetically, as it turned out!

Laurie gave up competition riding in 1956, although he continued to go hunting, his foremost love. He was Joint Master of the Eridge Foxhounds until he and Jane moved from Sussex to Beverston Castle in Gloucestershire in 1959; from there he hunted with the Beaufort.

From being a great competitor, Laurie turned his attention to horse trials' administration: he was FEI technical delegate at two Olympic games, a European Championship and the Pan-American games in Chicago. He was a member of the official British Horse Trials committee from 1956, and was made chairman in 1972, and he was a member of the Badminton committee until the day he died. He was also a dressage judge and the dressage steward at Badminton for many years. It was Laurie who was responsible for ensuring the change to a more simplified scoring system for three-day eventing, an improvement precipitated by the delay when, at the Pan American Games, it had taken ten hours to sort out the speed and endurance scores because someone had written a plus instead of a minus!

Laurence Rook died in 1989.

**Horse and Hound** correspondent: 'King Willow became the first horse to take Major Dick Hern round Badminton without him "buying a bit of the park". They finished fourteenth.' The pair are pictured left showing flamboyant style!

first one-day event by Major Dick Hern. He won at his first outing, and he looked set to win again at Larkhill, but his rider missed a flag and they were eliminated; ironically he and Laurence Rook had been eliminated at the 1952 Olympics for exactly the same sort of error.

The incident at Larkhill marked the start of a bout of bad luck for the horse. He was ridden at Badminton in 1951 by Colonel Duggie Stewart, and unfortunately Colonel Stewart only had leave to ride the horse for four days prior to Badminton; a poor cross-country and showjumping performance showed that this horse needed time to get to know his rider. In October 1951 he was partnered by Laurence Rook for the Great Auclum one-day event. Again they looked set to win, but turned too sharply to a gate and jumped the gatepost on the wrong side of the flag. Despite having to turn back and retake the gate between the flags they still finished third. It was a fitting reward for the pair to eventually win at Badminton after their unfortunate experience in Helsinki.

## The Colonel's cross-country course

This was Colonel Trevor Horn's last year as director and he made sure that he left his stamp on the course. Two new fences appeared in front of Badminton House, a post and rails and a pair of banks surmounted by rails; also new was fence no 29, a 3ft wall landing into rising ground; fence no 30, a 'stop gap'; fence no 31, the Park Paling at 3ft 9in; and the imaginative fence no 33, a bridge under repair. The Quarry and the Coffin were made more difficult by repositioning the various elements, and the Water Splash was approached from the opposite side, which necessitated a right-angled

# The 1950s

Brigadier Lyndon Bolton to his groom, who asked if he would like his horse washed down before the start of Phase D: 'Wash him down! Certainly not! He wouldn't get that out hunting, would he?' The horse in question was Flanagan (above), who became a successful showjumper with Pat Smythe.

turn to jump it. The Quarry caused the greatest share of problems: the 1952 winner Emily Little stopped here, as did Diana Mason and Tramella, and a Dutch horse fell on his rider, Mr E. Van Loon, who suffered a broken thigh; the Queen enquired at the Bristol Royal Infirmary as to his well-being! Bambi V and Bertie Hill also had a surprisingly disappointing round, with a refusal at the 'stop gap', and two at the unpopularly revamped Water Splash.

The warm weather effectively showed up any lack of fitness – or perhaps it was poor horsemanship? – and many horses were looking very tired. Significantly, only twenty-six out of the forty who started went through to the showjumping phase – and for the first time the press talked of the need for some sort of qualification to compete at Badminton, so that novice horses did not risk being overfaced.

Clear showjumping rounds were at a pre-mium: Captain Schwarzenbach and Vae Victis, the 1951 winners, produced one to finish third, and only three others jumped clear: Miss Machin-Goodall and Neptune (fifth), Lt C. Morgan and the King's Troop's Heavy Weather (ninth), and Bertie Hill and Bambi V (seven-teenth). Major Frank Weldon and Kilbarry fin-ished second – and from this time onwards, the Major continued to make his mark on Badminton in more ways than one (see pp48–9).

The big-jumping **Neptune** and his courageous rider Miss **Vivienne Machin-Goodall** were regular competitors during Badminton's first decade

Opposite: An immaculate combination: **Major Frank Weldon** and **Kilbarry**

# 1954

# Victory all round for the ladies

be allowed to beat a horse that was clear across country, but had had two showjumps down (Kilbarry). Either way, it must be remembered that the three-day event is about all-round horsemanship – and in the course of this toughest of tests, who can really adjudicate as to which is the less forgivable: a cross-country stop, or a careless showjumping round? This debate continues into the modern day, in fact

A year for the ladies: the 1954 winners were **Margaret Hough** and her mare **Bambi V**. Bambi had been loaned to the Olympic team prior to this and was renowned for attacking her fences with her ears flat back

Margaret Hough (now Mrs Gleave) and Miss Diana Mason took first and third places at Badminton, and they were riding mares, too: Bambi V and Tramella. For the second year in succession Major Frank Weldon and Kilbarry finished second – although it was generally felt that they had been mistimed on the steeplechase as they were not awarded the expected number of speed bonuses; he was the overnight leader going into the showjumping phase, but then two fences down dropped him below Margaret and Bambi who jumped clear.

The final result prompted some debate as to whether the showjumping was beginning to have too great an influence on the competition. It was suggested that the number of penalties for a fence down should be reduced. Cross-country enthusiasts would certainly argue that a horse which had actually stopped on the cross-country (Bambi V) should never

for the fiftieth anniversary Badminton in 1999 it was decided that a new scoring system should be adopted in a further attempt to get this balance right.

## The first female victors

In 1951 a very inexperienced Margaret Hough and Bambi V achieved third place at the Gisbourne event, which was only the second outing for the mare. The host at Gisbourne was Olympic team hopeful Reg Hindley, and he and Tony Collings were very quick to approach Margaret about whether she would loan her mare to the British team. 'I had very mixed feelings about the idea,' recalls Margaret. 'At the time girls were not allowed to ride in international competitions, and so it was tempting to think that your horse might achieve something like that, even if you couldn't. I did eventually agree to them having her, on the condition that if she went to Helsinki then I would go as her groom. She spent about five months at Porlock, which included being given a "training" run around Badminton, ridden by Bertie Hill, in 1952. In the end we did both go to Helsinki, but Bambi was the reserve horse and did not have to run. However, she stayed with the team throughout 1953 as well, and was in the gold medal-winning British team at Badminton's European Championship.'

Bambi came back to Margaret after that, and with a good idea of what to expect, they entered for Badminton in 1954: 'I was determined to do my best, though never really believed that that would be good enough to win. However, we led after the dressage, and I well remember how fit and strong Bambi felt on the cross-country. She had a stop at the Luckington Lane crossing – a cut-and-laid drop fence followed by a stone-faced bank with a post and rail on top – but she ran on well after that; at the Water Splash she was still full of running and was pulling my arms out! She tried to clear the pond in one, grazing her knee quite badly because she landed on the gravelly bank instead of in the water.

'I was nervous going into the showjumping arena because although we ran in numerical order, I did know by then that we could win if we jumped clear – and we did!'

As a result of her Badminton victory, Margaret was invited to compete at the Basle European Championships later that year, as was the third-placed Diana Mason. This was the first time that women were allowed to compete in an international three-day event (although they were still barred from the Olympics), and so Margaret and Diana became the first of the fairer sex to represent their country in a three-day event. Margaret recalls: 'As it turned out, Diana won the team place and I was sent as an individual, though I don't know why – you weren't told in those days why you didn't make the team, and you certainly didn't ask.'

Basle proved to be a shock to everybody in terms of the size and difficulty of the cross-country; Diana Mason recalls that the second fence measured 5ft 4in, and it was only after several appeals by all the different teams that it was eventually lowered by 4in. Both remember the course as being 'very long, very big and very difficult', and one water complex had to be altered part-way through the competition because it flooded; as competitors approached the fence, spectators rushed towards them waving and shouting to try to show them that the flags had been moved. Margaret finished sixth individually, while Diana, who was unseated twice, was one place below in seventh; she was also, of course, a part of the gold medal-winning team along with Frank Weldon, Bertie Hill and Laurence Rook.

Bambi was retired the following year, and Margaret bred nine good foals from her. She had originally acquired the mare by swapping a 14.2hh show pony that she had broken in herself, for Bambi, who was too big for what her owner wanted to do – so she must surely feel that she made a good deal that day! Bambi V was by Long Walk out of Dark Secret.

Today Margaret lives in Cheshire; she still has two of Bambi's great-great-grandchildren, including the stallion Gems Bok who was paraded at the 1998 Badminton Horse Trials.

---

**Thoughts on Basle** This tribute to Diana Mason and Margaret Hough appeared in *Horse and Hound* following their achievements at the European Championships in l954:

Now who'd have thought such modest charm
was hiding nerves so strong and calm
not ONLY found in She Who Rides!
And who'd have thought an English Miss
could stimulate the stolid Swiss —
(I mean could stimulate to cheers)
and bring the Germans near to tears.
So who'd have thought that we'd have TWO
who this, and doubtless more, could do.
But that we had, there was no doubt and,
being British, blushed about.
But now who dares the sombre thought
that at this three-day equine sport
the aids required to set the pace
are nerves, and curves and a pretty face!

J.A.L.

## Colonel Gordon Cox-Cox, director 1954–1964

While Colonel Horn was director of Badminton his brother-in-law Colonel Cox-Cox had been responsible for running the middle day. When Trevor Horn retired 'Master', the Duke, of Beaufort, asked Gordon Cox-Cox to take over with Colonel Babe Moseley as his assistant. All these had been regular cavalry officers and as such had an instinctive 'feel' for what a horse could be expected to jump safely.

The late Gordon Cox-Cox's daughter, Mrs Bridget Joynson, relates her father's story; it is typical both of the times and of the character that saw the birth of Badminton.

'My father was born near Dundee in 1898. When he was four Invertrossachs, the house in which the family was living, was burnt down and he had to escape from a first floor window down a chain of sheets tied together. His father having died before, my grandmother bought a house called Wooden outside Kelso.

'His brother, Thomas, fourteen years older, was responsible for most of my father's sporting up-bringing. He went to Eton where in due course my father became Master of the Beagles with the Duke of Beaufort as his first whipper-in. This started a friendship that lasted all their lives. The Duke always maintained that it was my father who taught him how to hunt hounds. Uncle Thomas was a great sportsman who taught my father to ride, shoot and fish, at all of which he excelled.

'In 1916 my father left Eton and after Sandhurst joined the 16th Lancers on the Western Front. He was wounded quite severely and took several months to recover.

'After the war the 16th were posted to India where my father learned the art, and joy, of playing polo. It was while he was in India that he met my mother. She had gone out to stay with her sister who was married to the then Captain Trevor Horn, and in 1924 she married my father. Sometime after this the regiment returned to this country and two or three years later my father was sent to the Staffordshire Yeomanry as the regular adjutant. When this appointment was finished he retired from the regular army and joined the Staffordshire Yeomanry as a territorial officer. Colonel Horn retired from the army in about 1930 and purchased Hyam near Malmesbury. It was in the thirties that his wife died and

Colonel Horn did not wish to stay in Hyam so sold it to my father in the spring of 1939. In August that year my father, like all territorials, was called up and in the spring of 1940 the Staffordshire Yeomanry were sent to the Middle East with the 1st Cavalry Division. They took part in a cavalry charge at Habbaniya against the rebel Iraqis, probably the last charge by the British Cavalry. By this time my father was commanding the regiment. It was then that they lost their horses and became an armoured regiment.

'The division was transferred to Egypt and took part in the battle of Alam Halfa where Rommel suffered a decided reverse. After this it became obvious that the 8th Army were going to launch a concerted attack. During the army's build up Field Marshall Montgomery witnessed an exercise in which the Staffordshire Yeomanry took part. After the exercise Montgomery especially congratulated my father on the performance of his regiment. My father handed over command of the regiment before the battle of El Alamein and was flown back to this country to take command of the Armoured Corps Depot at Catterick. He remained in this position until the war ended.

'After the war he returned to Hyam and when Master decided to hold a three-day event at Badminton he was one of the first to be drawn in. He loved being involved and was delighted when later he was asked to become director. In those days everything was far less formal but everyone involved was expected to give of their best. In this atmosphere my father excelled and was very popular with both officials and participants. He worked very closely with Charlie Chappell, the head forester at Badminton, who built the fences in those days.

'The spring of 1963 was particularly wet which made for the greatest difficulties. It caused a very large amount of work and worry for my father who was most upset about the state the park was left in after the event. It made him really ill for the first time I had ever known. It was at this time that he was diagnosed as having cancer of the throat and he decided in 1964 he must retire from being director. The treatment for the cancer affected his heart and in 1969 he died of heart failure.

'Had he lived another twenty years he would have been thrilled when Sir Wattie ridden by Ian Stark won Badminton as his niece, Mrs Susan Luczye Wyhowska, had bred and part-owned the horse.'

Opposite: Badminton's second director, Colonel Gordon Cox-Cox (right), with his good colleague Charlie Chappell (the Estate's head forester), who was also Badminton's first course builder

## The troublesome Tramella makes good

When Diana Mason saw the four-year-old, 15hh Tramella she was not particularly impressed. Tramella was a naughty young horse and looked very nappy – but for some reason Diana's father had taken a real shine to her, and was convinced that this was the horse for his daughter. Like many fathers, he had a great deal of influence on his daughter, and when Diana left school he thought she should go and study sewing and cooking. Fortunately for the animal-loving Diana, the domestic science and equine course that she had to attend was run by a certain John Shedden and his wife – and Diana 'had a lovely stay, riding horses the whole time'. She was able to ride both Golden Willow and Kingpin, and of course heard in great detail all about the challenge of Badminton.

When she turned her attentions to her own young horse, however, it seemed Tramella had entirely different aspirations. 'I knew she was going to be difficult,' recalls Diana. 'When we went to try her out she was so nappy that I had to be led to the bottom of the field where we were duly released and able to gallop back up to the gate; I couldn't imagine how I was ever going to be able to take her for a ride! Worse, we had only had her a few days when she jumped out of the field, landed in the road and slipped and cut her herself – and after she recovered from that she was even more determined not to leave the yard. I used to just sit it out; there was no point in hitting her, because then she just reared higher and higher. After about an hour and a half she would obviously be bored of that game, and would set off for her ride and never even look back! She was a very pretty horse with four white socks, and we showed her with great success; at one Horse of the Year Show she was second in the small hack class, third in the small hunter, second in the working hunter and she won the combined training.

'As a five-year-old she went eventing, winning on her second outing at Epperstone ahead of John Oram on his two Olympic shortlisted horses. In 1953, when she was seven and I was nineteen, we went to Badminton for the first time. She had always been hot-headed and I worked her in for five hours before the dressage, but then she took a dislike to the grand-stand behind the judges' box and would only work in two-thirds of the arena! Nevertheless we completed the event and were nineteenth.

'The following year Tramella was second after the dressage. With a good cross-country result and a clear showjumping round, we finished third, our best three-day event result to date. We were selected for the European Championship team in Basle later that year where we won team gold and were seventh individually. In 1955 we rejoined our Basle team-mates to contest the European Championships at Windsor, which replaced Badminton that year. Tramella led the dressage, but she lost her nerve completely on the cross-country: she slipped and fell on the flat after one fence and that really frightened her; she was later eliminated. I rode her at Badminton the following year, but again she was eliminated. She was only 15hh and had to carry the minimum weight of 11 stone 11lb so she was always being stretched to the limit, and finally she had had enough. We turned to dressage after that, and won team gold at the 1963 Copenhagen European Championships, and finished second in the Rotterdam Grand Prix. As far as I know Tramella is the only horse to have won European team gold medals in the disciplines of both dressage and three-day eventing.'

Out of a Welsh pony mare and believed to be by the Thoroughbred Tramail, Tramella was a little horse with a lot of character. Diana had taught her to bow, which she did beautifully for the Queen and Queen Mother when they visited the stables at Badminton, and also to rear – although this trick she was only too keen to offer unsolicited! Tramella was retired at the age of eighteen, and was finally put down when she was twenty-eight.

Diana Mason became one of Britain's best dressage riders. She competed at both the Montreal and Seoul Olympics, chaired the Dressage Group for seventeen years, and is now a dressage judge and the manager of the British paralympic dressage team.

**Major Frank Weldon, eventing's guiding light** Frank Weldon's involvement with eventing began at Badminton in 1952, when his competition ended with a crashing fall. He became a highly successful international competitor, and went on to become Badminton's most influential director to date. He guided both the Badminton event, and cross-country course design in general, to greater heights than had ever been known before.

Born in 1913 in India, Frank Weldon's childhood sounded idyllic: his family returned to England after the Great War, when his barrister father retired, and Frank hunted in the winter with the Taunton Vale and gymkhana'd in the summer. He was educated at Wellington, and when he left school, he joined the army. His Royal Artillery regiment was sent to France, but it wasn't long before he was taken prisoner. In his own words he 'was not a good prisoner', and after escaping three times and being labelled 'difficult', he was incarcerated in Colditz for three years. He was released in 1945 when the camp was liberated by the Americans.

He returned to his mother's house, which had been turned over to a convalescent home. The quartermaster was a young lady called Diana Anderson, and she was shortly to become Mrs Weldon.

'We were posted to Malta,' recalls Diana Weldon, 'and then to St John's Wood in London; here Frank achieved all that he had hoped for when in 1949 he was given command of the King's Troop, the Royal Horse Artillery. Although it was here that he started eventing, Frank's first love had always been racing. When he first joined the army he was stationed at Catterick. He used to work-ride – and then race-ride – for a trainer at nearby Middleham, and with racing still in mind, he bought Kilbarry as a five-year-old for £750. That was a great deal of money in 1952, although it was obvious from the outset that this was a very special horse.'

Frank's objective was to win the 'Gunners' Gold Cup' and when Kilbarry easily won his first point-to-point, it looked as if his ambition would be realised. But Kilbarry contracted equine flu and had to be hobdayed, and this meant that his racing career was over. Having ridden at Badminton in 1952

on Liza Mandy – and having ended up in Tetbury hospital with concussion and cracked ribs – Frank was quick to 'convert' his racehorse to eventing. When he arrived to ride at Badminton in 1953, Tony Collings asked him if he would ride as part of the British team, even though he had not been involved in the 'official' team training at Porlock Vale. He replaced Laurence Rook and Starlight – who then proceeded to confound everybody except themselves by winning the competition! But Frank and Kilbarry helped to win the team championship for Britain, and finished second individually. They finished second again in 1954, and then won the event in 1955 and 1956, by which time Frank was a lieutenant colonel in the army.

After the death of Tony Collings in 1954, Frank was asked to act as team captain; he was therefore responsible for the training and administration of the team. The British team won the European Championships in 1953, 1954 and 1955.

During 1955 Frank was granted a year's leave from the army to prepare for the Olympics in Stockholm. With his beloved horse Kilbarry he won team gold and individual bronze, and Diana Weldon clearly remembers the result of that:

'The army featured Frank in their magazine *The Soldier*. There was a double-page spread showing him winning his medals at the Stockholm Olympics with the caption "Look what you can achieve when you join the army". Soon after this he was called up in front of his superior who told him that they wanted to post him to Camberley – but he would have to give up his horses and competing. We had about three weeks to decide what to do. The army posting would obviously secure our future, but horses were Frank's life, and finally he decided to stick with horses. We then had to search for a new home; luckily some friends of ours, the Lowsley-Williams who lived near Tetbury, told us about a house to rent in Didmarton. We moved in, and it was here that Frank met the present Duke of Beaufort, David Somerset; they became great friends, and the Duke allowed him to continue to exercise and train his horses in Badminton Park as he had previously done due to the generosity of the late Duke.'

As a rider, Frank's hopes and aspirations came crashing back down to earth in 1957 when Kilbarry fell at the first fence at the Cottesbrook Horse Trials and broke his neck. It was a 3ft brush fence and appeared to be quite straightforward, but it had a solid rail behind it which Kilbarry obviously didn't see. Kilbarry was only ten and Frank was devastated. But something positive came of this tragedy, in that when Frank turned his attention to course design, his first priority was always that the fence was fair to the horse.

Whilst preparing for the 1960 Olympics, where he rode Anne Marshall's Samuel Johnson, Frank had an accident which very nearly curtailed his riding career, though in quite a different way: always a keen carpenter, he had bought himself a circular saw, but managed to slice off a couple of fingers and his thumb. He thought he would lose his hand, but that was saved – and with it his riding career. Some photographers had booked to come and take pictures of the team in training, and with a heavily bandaged hand and typical fortitude, Frank got on his horse and led from the front.

Frank did return to ride at Badminton again, finishing second in 1962 on Neil Gardiner's Young Pretender. However, later that year he retired from competition riding, and for a couple of years concentrated on bringing on and selling young horses. In 1964 the family moved to their own home in Wickwar. (Sadly for the whole family, a burglary in 1980 saw the theft of both Frank's Olympic medals, and also the unique silver cup presented to him by the Queen for the 1955 European Championships at Windsor, as well as the trophy he had set his heart on – the Gunner's Gold Cup.)

Following the retirement of Colonel Gordon Cox-Cox after the 1964 Badminton, the present Duke of Beaufort asked Frank Weldon if he would design the course for the following year; and when riders arrived for the 1965 Badminton they found the cross-country track bigger and bolder than ever before. Wherever possible Frank had increased the size of the fences within the maximum dimensions allowed, and had lived by his dictum of 'frightening the life out of the riders but not hurting the horses'. As Diana explained:

'The accident that killed Kilbarry made Frank determined to get his fences right and to make them fair to the horse. He didn't mind how much he terrified the riders because they had chosen to be there, but the horse was co-opted into the game, and so he was adamant that every question had to be one that the horse could answer safely. This need had been further impressed upon him when he competed at the 1960 Rome Olympics where the cross-country caused far too much grief as far as the horses were concerned. He was the first to appreciate that the bigger the timber, the better the

fence jumped; and he also introduced the idea of roping fences together so that they could be quickly dismantled if a horse got stuck in one.'

In 1967 Frank Weldon was appointed director of Badminton, and immediately began to restyle the event's finances as well as its fences. He knew that if Badminton and the whole sport of eventing were to survive, they had to be commercially viable, and this meant making them attractive to spectators and sponsors. As you progress through this book you will see the changes that Frank Weldon imposed upon Badminton, and enthusiasts of the sport will appreciate how Badminton's growth has fuelled the development of eventing both nationally and internationally.

Diana Weldon recalls that '...at any event we travelled to abroad, Frank would disappear onto the course with his notebook and tape measure, meticulously recording the vital statistics of any fence that interested him. He was never afraid to take other people's ideas and to adapt them for his own courses. Frank was called upon regularly to lecture on course design and course building. He was also one of the team of three asked by the FEI to write the first full set of official rules for three-day eventing; it took them seven months to complete!'

The directorship of Badminton gave Frank the chance to fulfil his own hopes and ambitions for the sport of eventing. In much the same way that 'Master', the 10th Duke of Beaufort, had been keen to give Britain every chance to succeed in the sport of eventing, Frank had his own convictions which influenced everything he did in terms of course design at Badminton. Basically, he was absolutely determined that British riders should never go abroad to compete and be frightened by what they found; thus he was equally determined that if they competed at Badminton, they would face some of the most difficult questions the sport could ever throw at them. That he has succeeded in this is evidenced in the way that the Badminton title is coveted by riders from all over the world. It may only be won by a select few, but to win it is the dream of everyone that competes.

Colonel Frank Weldon retired from Badminton in 1988; he died in September 1993. He succeeded in becoming a legend in his own lifetime, and he achieved this distinction with such integrity and dignity that it is rare indeed to find anyone with a word to say against him.

# 1955

# Badminton moves to Windsor

**How things change** The Irish Bank in 1955, negotiated by Major Derrick Dyson and Water Gypsy; and the 1991 version, tackled by Alison Brook and Kingscourt. The addition of a solid upright gives the horse a far better chance of landing safely well up the bank.

Great Britain hosted the European Championships in 1955, and the Queen offered Windsor Great Park as a venue instead of Badminton. Nine different countries were represented, and there were teams from Ireland, Switzerland, Sweden, Italy and Great Britain. A total of fifty-four starters meant that for the first time the dressage phase had to be run over two days. A measure of how standards had improved in the host country was indicated by the eighty-two point lead that the British team held after the dressage phase.

The new cross-country course designed for the occasion caused an exceptional amount of trouble. The situation was not helped by the fact that many horses were tired before they even started the cross-country, the long sections of roads and tracks evidently stressing them unduly instead of acting as warm-up and recovery phases for the steeplechase, as they were intended.

## The new cross-country course

The course started near Cumberland Lodge: fence no 2, the Trakhener, resembled a huge cavalletti over a ditch (3ft 6in high with an 8ft spread) and caused four refusals, a fall and an elimination. A big but innocuous-looking gorse and birch fence brought down both Starlight and Tramella (both members of the British team). Twelve horses, including Tramella, took a dislike to the Culvert, a concrete tank with 9in of water in the bottom. But it was the notorious Sandpit which took the greatest toll: this consisted of a 2ft 9in set of rails positioned at the top of a short but steep incline down into the pit; then there were two steps up, with a rail on the edge of the second, giving it a 5ft 6in drop. The first rail caused eighteen horses to stop, including Countryman, and it was here that poor Vae Victis fell with Lt Zindel; he remounted, only to fall again at the second set of rails (see 1951). A Swedish horse also fell at the second rail, and eight others refused.

The next fence was a hedge with a ditch on the landing side, a spread of 12ft in total. Six horses fell here, including Tramella: a badly shaken Diana Mason bravely remounted, but

Tramella had clearly had enough and was eliminated three fences later at the Irish Bank.

Devious use of the terrain was employed at the 'Into Space' jump, a horizontally laid birch fence sited twenty yards in front of a deep pit. To the horse it appeared that he was being asked to jump into a bottomless pit, when in fact the fence was quite small with only a little drop on landing. Two Swedish horses went the wrong side of a flag here and were eliminated.

Only ten horses managed to complete the cross-country without jumping penalties.

Good showjumping performances from the British team secured them the gold medal, with Switzerland, the only other team still in contention, taking silver. The enormously popular individual winner was Major Frank Weldon and Kilbarry. He was the only team member to jump clear across country, and he finished on a plus score, some forty marks ahead of second

placed Lt Cdr John Oram and Miss J. Johnson's Radar. Bertie Hill and Countryman III made up for their stop at the Sandpit with a fast time and finished third.

## Bertie Hill, horseman supreme

Bertie Hill was part of the team that enjoyed such great success during the l950s: team gold at the l953, 1954 and l955 European Championships, European individual gold in l954, and team gold at the l956 Olympics. He also trained the British team for the 1968 Mexico Olympics where they won team gold and individual silver. Bertie is generally acknowledged as one of the best riders this country has ever seen, but in spite of this accolade, ultimate success at Badminton always eluded him; his best placing was third with Countryman in 1955. 'I rode at Badminton many times, sometimes com-

Badminton moved to Windsor in 1955 for the European Championships. **Major Frank Weldon** and **Kilbarry** took individual and team gold medals

# The 1950s

petitively and sometimes as a team trial, but bad luck always seemed to follow me,' he says wistfully. Bertie was another whose first love had been racing, but who had been converted to eventing by Tony Collings; and it was Collings who invited him to take part in team training for the 1952 Olympics.

Bertie's greatest success was team gold at the 1956 Olympics where he rode his own Countryman. He recalls their first meeting:

'I had gone to a yard in Exeter to look at a

**Bertie Hill**, one of the world's greatest horsemen, finished third on **Countryman III**

showjumper for my sister,' recounts Bertie. 'As I looked around the yard I was watched the whole time by a horse with a lovely head. When I asked about him I was told he would be of no use to me: the owner had seen him "jump the moon" in Ireland bareback and, duly impressed, had bought him – only to find out that he couldn't saddle him. He had tried to get on him once, and had ended up on crutches. Nevertheless I was still interested, but offered £90, not the £250 that was being asked for him. I was turned down, but later that night received a phone call telling me to bring my £90 and to take the horse away. It

took me a while to get him to accept a saddle, but after a season's hunting, he won his first point-to-point. Within a year he had become a very successful event horse and was in the British team.'

After Windsor, Countryman was bought by a syndicate of HM the Queen, the Queen Mother, the 10th Duke of Beaufort, and Colonel V.D.S. Williams. Bertie kept the ride, and the pair rewarded everyone's faith in them by helping to win team gold at the 1956 Stockholm Olympics, having finished fourth at Badminton earlier in the year. Soon after this, the ownership of Countryman passed to David Somerset, the present Duke of Beaufort; he rode him into second place at Badminton in 1959. Countryman hunted with the Duke of Beaufort's foxhounds until he was eighteen, when he was retired. He spent the rest of his days at Badminton, where he was finally put down.

Bertie continued to compete, riding at the notorious 1960 Rome Olympics on Wild Venture. After that he set up the Rapscott School of Equitation at his farm in Devon and concentrated on training others; his own competition career he kept to the national circuit. His final three-day event was at Badminton in 1970 where he rode Chicago.

'Chicago was a terrific horse,' recalls Bertie. 'He was by a Dartmoor pony colt out of an eventing mare, and when I saw him I needed another horse like a hole in the head! However, I have always been a firm believer that when you see a horse that you think has got what it takes, you just have to buy it. At Badminton in 1970 I was lying second behind Richard Meade after the cross-country. My mind was so taken up with helping the ten students I had taken with me that when I went in to ride my own round I managed to jump a wrong fence and was eliminated – I knew as soon as we were in mid-air what I had done, but it was too late. That year Chicago was ridden by my son Tony in the Junior three-day event championship, by me at Badminton, and by Captain Mark Phillips at the Punchestown World Championships where he won team gold. Not a bad record for one horse for one year!'

# Sheila Willcox challenges Frank Weldon

Badminton 1956 recorded another well deserved win for Frank Weldon and Kilbarry, but it was a young lady, Sheila Willcox, who was really beginning to excite the attention of the crowds. Having come quietly onto the scene the previous year when she finished thirteenth in the European Championships at Windsor, her determined and professional approach at Badminton 1956 was to establish her position at the top of an increasingly competitive field.

Riding the same horse, High and Mighty, Sheila rode a beautiful test to take the lead. But then Frank Weldon, the reigning 'king' of the eventing circuit, entered the arena and produced the test of his life from Kilbarry to beat her by 1.56 penalties. Undaunted, young Sheila dared to throw down the gauntlet with a fast performance throughout all the speed and endurances phases. But Weldon was not to be outdone, and both riders finished the day with maximum bonus scores for their efforts, which meant that Weldon still had his 1.56 penalties in hand. On the third day both remained ice-cool, refusing to give in to the pressure, and both jumped clear showjumping rounds.

In third place was a rider from another country which was also just beginning to make its intentions known: Laurie Morgan had come over to England as part of the Australian team which was preparing for the Stockholm Olympics. Although on this occasion he was more than fifty points behind the victorious British riders, it would not be long before he, too, was challenging the leaders. Although Frank Weldon took victory this time, it was obvious that it was becoming a little harder to keep his place at the top!

**Sheila Willcox** and **High and Mighty** who were second in 1956 and went on to win Badminton in 1957 and 1958

# The 1950s

## Badminton is brought up to date

To cater for the growing number of enthusiastic spectators, the course and general layout at Badminton was largely redesigned in 1956. The event also changed its name because it was felt that the title 'Olympic Horse Trials' might conflict with that of the actual Olympic three-day event; in this year it therefore became known as the Badminton Horse Trials.

Another significant change was the re-siting of the steeplechase course, from Didmarton to a new site on The Slaits, a large field situated to the north of Castle Barn and the Quarry; more significantly, it was within walking distance of the car parks. The start and finish of the cross-country had also been moved so that it, too, was situated conveniently close to the main arena.

Of the thirty-five fences, the first big question came at no 4, a post and rails set on a bank with an awkward dip on the approach. Diana Mason's faithful little mare Tramella stopped here, and was then eliminated at the next fence, the big parallel bars over the Vicarage Ditch, indicating conclusively to Diana that she really had lost her nerve after

Opposite: **Sheila Willcox**, a rider who was ahead of her time in terms of talent, sheer dedication and professionalism. Here, she receives her rosette for second place from the Queen with Gordon Cox-Cox also present

---

**Sheila's challenge** Born in 1937, Sheila Willcox adopted a completely professional approach to her riding career from childhood. She learnt as much as she could through the Pony Club, and when that failed to sate her appetite for knowledge and self improvement she read, studied and questioned anyone or anything 'equestrian' in a quest for perfection which was to last throughout her life.

She rode at her first three-day event in 1955, with High and Mighty, the 16hh Irish-bred part Arab, part pony. The following year, aged nineteen, she challenged the well-established eventing élite at Badminton; charming as they all were, it must have been quite a shock to the likes of Frank Weldon to find themselves so ably challenged by someone not only so young, but also female! There were already plenty of good female event riders – Badminton had been claimed in 1954 by Margaret Hough – but Sheila was determined to be the best, and was totally dedicated to the cause. But on this occasion Frank Weldon won, and Sheila would have been desperately disappointed with her second place. She simply went away and worked even harder at the sport she cherished, and in 1957 she led from start to finish with High and Mighty to take the Badminton title. The following year an even more impressive dressage performance put them in the lead by over 22 penalties. Despite a showjump down on the last day, they took the title by a margin of 47 points.

With High and Mighty she also won the team and individual gold medals at the 1957 Copenhagen European Championships, and team gold in the 1959 Europeans at Harewood. Despite her success, it was still against the rules for women to ride in an Olympic three-day event. Ted Marsh, a great supporter of the British team effort, bought High and Mighty to add strength to the British challenge, but in the end the horse was not selected for the Olympics. Ted Marsh enjoyed many seasons hunting on his Olympic 'hopeful' before High and Mighty was put down at the age of twenty-two.

But the eventing world had not escaped from the challenge of Sheila Willcox; married and riding as Sheila Waddington, she came back to Badminton in 1959 with the inexperienced Airs and Graces. Having led the dressage she had to concede to the appalling ground conditions on cross-country day and go a little slower than she would have liked. David Somerset overtook her riding the inexperienced Countryman, but a showjump down on the final day dropped him back to second place. Sheila remains the only person to have won Badminton three years running, and in 1964, riding Glenamoy, she won Little Badminton.

In all she won eight major three-day events as well as being consistently successful on the one-day circuit. But in 1971 she suffered a dreadul fall at the Tidworth Horse Trials which left her partially paralysed. Never one to give up easily, Sheila resumed her riding career and concentrated on pure dressage, competing successfully at Grand Prix level on Son and Heir.

So many other riders of her era went on to become very involved in either training or the administration of the sport but Sheila has, for whatever reason, largely kept her own counsel. Perhaps she was simply born ahead of her time.

her experiences at Windsor the previous year (see p50) Another popular horse whose international career ended here at Badminton in 1956 was Starlight XV, the ride of Laurence Rook: Starlight became so out of hand in the dressage arena that Rook gave up halfway through his test.

Competitors then tackled the Irish Bank and the 12ft wide Open Water. The Luckington Road crossing included a rail and a bank onto the road, and a ditch and a hedge off it. There were then two galloping cut-and-laid fences either side of Centre Walk. The second Luckington Lane crossing was a hedge and ditch followed by a slightly offset ditch and post-and-rail fence on the other side. The Coffin, for the first time in the history of the event, caused absolutely no trouble at all!

After the Coffin, the course turned away over the Little Badminton Road, then ran back round towards the Quarry. Frank Weldon, Sheila Willcox and Anneli Drummond-Hay all spotted a short-cut here which must have saved them at least two hundred yards. Back over Little Badminton Road competitors jumped a hogsback over a wall into the caravan site, then went through the Sheep Pen and over a bullfinch to re-enter the main park. The last fence was a small rail of no more than 2ft 9in on the edge of the pond, which meant the horse had to land in the water; this was an innovative fence.

Although the course was considered significantly more difficult than in the preceding years, it rode particularly well. Seven horses were eliminated or withdrawn, but of the twenty-seven remaining, only nine refusals were recorded amongst them.

In the showjumping phase the fences and course design were starting to look more like the sort of track we are familiar with today. It was still nothing like as imposing and elaborate, but it was certainly a step forward from the simple, rustic fences used in the early years. Only seven horses managed clear rounds on the final day; with two fences down Laurie Morgan and Gold Ross kept third place, and one mistake by Countryman and Bertie Hill meant they remained in fourth place.

# 1957

# Success for long-standing supporters

The tragic loss of Frank Weldon's Kilbarry at a one-day event earlier in the year left the way wide open for Sheila Willcox and High and Mighty, and they did not disappoint, setting the standard with a dressage score of 24.33. To put this in perspective, Frank Weldon's winning dressage score the year before had been 56.22. A fast clear cross-country performance and a faultless showjumping round confirmed their victory.

Second and third places were taken by Ireland's Penny Moreton and Great Britain's Ted Marsh, and these were popular successes for long-standing supporters of Badminton. Penny Moreton was riding Joe Hume Dudgeon's Red Sea, and Joe's connection with Badminton could be traced right back to its inaugural year when his son Ian was second. Penny Moreton was a regular competitor at Badminton and it is indicative of the friendly atmosphere that prevailed at the time that everyone seemed to know everyone else. All those who have been asked to recall the early days at Badminton seem to hold affectionate memories of their fellow competitors.

Ted Marsh had always been a tremendous supporter of the British team; his practice was to buy and bring on his own young horses, and if they were needed he was always happy to loan them to the team for international competitions. This time, however, riding Wild Venture, the glory was all his own. This was the horse that so attracted Laurence Rook after Starlight's fall from grace, and the one that he rode in the gold medal-winning team at the Stockholm Olympics the previous year.

## England's loss is Ireland's gain

Penny Moreton carried out several successful 'raids' on Badminton from her base across the Irish sea. From an English family but brought up in Scotland, Penny had 'messed around with ponies' for as long as she can remember. She knew she wanted to work with horses and decided she had better gain some sort of qualification. Her brother had been over to Ireland and suggested she should go to Lt Col Hume Dudgeon's riding establishment. She based herself there in the early 1950s and her employer

obviously thought highly of her riding ability as, from her arrival onwards, he allowed her to compete at Badminton whenever he had a suitable 'spare' horse. His son, Ian Dudgeon also had great enthusiasm for the new sport of eventing (see 1949).

Penny had been a spectator at the first few Badmintons – her uncle Captain P. Arkwright had finished third in 1950, riding Lady Leigh's Minster Green. As Penny puts it, 'I had "dreamed" my way round Badminton several times before I actually rode there. My first ride was in 1952. At Lt Col Hume Dudgeon's I had been assigned one of his riding school horses, called Vigilant. He was a French-bred Anglo Arab and was actually owned by a French lady who loaned him to the riding school.

'It was at the time that Jane Drummond-Hay was over here training for Badminton and I used to join in her lessons on Vigilant. It gradually dawned on Lt Col Dudgeon that Vigilant was a very capable little horse. Somebody mentioned the possibility that I might ride him at Badminton and I made sure I kept pushing the point until I was allowed to enter. Vigilant was then "loaned" to me by his owner – I paid for his keep and looked after him during the preparations for Badminton and so he was entered as my horse. No one expected anything of us – neither of us had been to a show of any kind until Badminton – we were second after the dressage and cross-country phases but had three showjumps down to finish fourth. My horses were usually sold on after a short while and so each time I got to Badminton it was generally on a young horse so nobody expected too much of us. I rode Copper Coin, who was owned by Lt Col Dudgeon, in 1956 and finished fifth. He was only six years old and, along with another horse, Louchlin, was the best I ever rode. He went on to compete at three Olympics – once for Ireland and twice for America where he was renamed Grasshopper.

'My best result was in 1957 riding a last minute replacement after the horse I should have been riding went lame. Lt Col Dudgeon was away teaching in South Africa at the time and he telephoned and said I would just have to take his showjumper, Red Sea, instead. He said he didn't know how the horse would go

cross country but he promised me that my ride would look after me: he would either stop or jump, but he wouldn't do anything stupid. Red Sea was a huge horse but we got on well and finished second. He was then sold to America although I don't think he went on to do anything spectacular over there. In 1964 I rode Lough Druid, another six year old, into second place in the Little Badminton event.'

Having based herself for so long in Ireland, and in deference to the fact that she was generally riding Irish-owned horses, Penny took Irish nationality – aided by the fact that her grandparents were half Irish. She completed Badminton five times and was awarded the Armada Dish in 1965. (Armada Dishes are presented to all riders who complete Badminton five times.) Like Sheila Willcox, Penny had to live with the frustration of knowing she was as good, if not better, than many of her male competitors but because she was a woman she was still barred from riding in the Olympic three-day event. However, unlike Sheila, Penny did finally get her chance when a change in the rules allowed her to represent Ireland at the 1968 Mexico Olympics.

Penny rode Louchlin at the 1968 Games, a horse she had never ridden, but it was all to end in tragedy when he died on the cross-country course, having slipped and fallen at one of the smallest fences. That was Penny's last major competition. She married Frank McAuley, an Irish eye surgeon, and they live in Dublin.

**Penny Moreton** took second place on **Red Sea**, who was owned by Lt Col Hume Dudgeon, and was a last minute replacement for her own horse

Opposite: The great British team supporter **Ted Marsh** had a taste of personal glory when he finished third on **Wild Venture**. They were third again in 1959

# 1958

# Badminton breaks all records

her rivals, and she capitalised on the greater freedom inherent in the new test to show off High and Mighty to his very best. Her score of thirty-seven put her twenty-two marks ahead of Ted Marsh and Wild Venture, and she added to this lead with maximum bonuses on the speed and endurance phases; this meant that she could afford far more than her eventual one

A late convert to eventing, **Major Derek Allhusen** on **Laurien** took second place in 1958

Opposite: A classic example of **Sheila Willcox**'s fluent style

This was a record-breaking Badminton, for the number of entries and starters, the number of cars and spectators, and for the margin by which Sheila Willcox, the current British and European champion, won the competition. Riding High and Mighty once again, her final score was forty-seven points clear of Major Derek Allhusen and his mare Laurien, in second place.

A new FEI three-day event dressage test was used in this year, and it allowed for a much more flowing performance. Sheila's dressage capabilities were already well ahead of many of

showjump down on the last day. Derek Allhusen moved up to second place with a clear showjumping round, and in third place was another young lady quietly making her presence felt: Anneli Drummond-Hay, on this occasion riding Mr R.T. Whiteley's Pluto.

## From pentathlete to event rider

Major Derek Allhusen's interest in eventing was aroused by what he saw at the 1948 Olympic three-day event at Aldershot. He was an Olympic pentathlete, but he adapted his

skills to eventing with great success. Riding his mare Laurien, he had won team gold at the 1957 European Championships in Copenhagen; in 1958 they were second at Badminton; and in the following year they won team gold and individual bronze at the Harewood European Championships. Laurien was then retired to become a broodmare, and in 1964 produced Laurieston; this horse remained in the ownership of Derek and Claude Allhusen, and was ridden by Richard Meade. In 1972 the partnership finished second at Badminton, and then achieved the yet-to-be-repeated success of winning an Olympic individual gold medal for Great Britain at the Munich Olympics.

Major Derek Allhusen also evented at Olympic level: he went to the 1968 Mexico Olympics, and was nicknamed the 'galloping grandad' alongside the 'galloping nurse' Jane Holderness-Roddam (née Bullen), the first female member of a British Olympic three-day event team. But the galloping grandad, riding Lochinvar, came home with the team gold and individual silver medals!

**Facts and figures: Badminton 1958**

First prize was £150 plus the Daily Telegraph Challenge Cup.

Every competitor who completed the event received £10.

Plaques were presented to the owners of all horses completing the event.

The entry fee in 1958 was £3.

QUALIFICATIONS

For the first time horses and riders had to meet certain criteria regarding experience and achievements in order to compete at Badminton. Over the previous few years there had been some disquiet regarding the number of inexperienced horses being asked to tackle such a difficult course. These criteria were as follows:

* Riders had to be members of the British Horse Society.
* Riders had to be over seventeen on January 1st.
* Horses had to have been born in or before 1952.
* Both horse and rider had to have completed the cross-country phase in at least two one-day events, or have been placed in the first five at a one-day event.

Other conditions were:

* A double bridle was still compulsory for the dressage test.
* A minimum weight of 165lb (to include rider and saddle) had to be carried by every horse.

# 1959

## Mud, monsoons and a mammoth entry

Torrential rain in the spring of 1959 turned Badminton's green and pleasant lands into a sea of mud. To make matters worse, in this year the Badminton committee had accepted the highest number of entries ever. To cater for the 103 hopeful entrants it had been decided to divide the competitors into two groups, and so for the first time a 'Little Badminton Event' was held for novice horses, specifically those which had not won more than £30 in horse trials. The more advanced horses competed for the Great Badminton Championship.

It rained continuously throughout the dressage phase and the arena was reduced to a series of deep muddy tracks. Laurence Rook was one of the dressage judges, and his wife Jane remembers how they could barely keep from laughing when Norman Arthur asked his horse to perform the halt and rein-back movement, and the mud was so deep that, having halted, it simply could not extricate its legs to step backwards: for that particular movement he remained glued to the spot! In this phase Sheila Willcox remained unbeatable: riding the inexperienced seven-year-old Airs and Graces, she demonstrated in no uncertain manner how correct training could pay off no matter what the conditions. They gave a smooth, polished performance, and took the lead in the Great Badminton Championship.

The cross-country course was examined again that night and it was decided to continue, but with a drastically modified course: five fences were taken out altogether, and a further four reduced in complexity to try and accommodate the dreadful conditions. Unwilling to press the inexperienced Airs and Graces too hard in the deep and slippery conditions, Sheila Willcox was overtaken on speed and endurance day by Badminton's present host, David Somerset. He had bought Bertie Hill's former ride Countryman, and knowing the horse's experience, gave it his all across country to pick up 94 speed bonuses compared with Sheila's 34.

The conditions in the showjumping arena for the final phase were as appalling as they had been for the other two phases. Since the first Badminton in 1949 BSJA showjumping competitions were occasionally held in the main arena

when it was not in use for the three-day event, and despite the dreadful weather one such competition had been held earlier, leaving the ground in a sorry state to begin with.

With less than the cost of a showjump between the overnight leader David Somerset and the fiercely competitive Sheila Willcox, there was still everything to play for. The excitement was all the greater as those connected with the Badminton estate waited to see if 'their' horse and rider could pull off victory. But it wasn't to be, as Countryman, always prone to the odd showjumping error, had a

fence down whilst the young Sheila kept her composure to jump clear. Thus she won for the third year in succession (now married, it was as a Waddington this time, rather than a Willcox), and to date she remains the only rider to have won the event three years running. Ted Marsh was third on Wild Venture.

Little Badminton was won by Shelagh Kesler on Miss Shaw's Double Diamond, thanks to a clear showjumping round. The cross-country leader, Mrs McMillen on J. Crofts' Robinwood, had four of the last five showjumps down – but still finished second.

HM the Queen – dressed for the weather in 1959

The present Duke, **David Somerset**, competed at Badminton regularly in the late fifties, always partnered by **Countryman III** (see opposite and overleaf)

**David Somerset** spent his childhood in Cornwall. 'I came to Badminton House in 1945; my cousin the 10th Duke of Beaufort was childless, and my elder brother had been killed during the war. The Duke very kindly asked me if I would like to make Badminton my home, which meant I would succeed to his title.' In 1984 David Somerset inherited his title, 11th Duke of Beaufort, following the death of his cousin at the age of eighty-three. He had become a master of the Beaufort Hunt in 1974 and despite giving up riding completely by 1990 he remains as interested and enthusiastic as ever about the Duke of Beaufort's foxhounds and the Badminton three-day event.

David Somerset was responsible for appointing Frank Weldon to take over from Colonel Gordon Cox-Cox in 1965. As he recalls, not everyone agreed with his decision: 'Any number of terribly important people telephoned me to say that Frank would wreck the whole sport, but I think he proved them all wrong. He was a very special man, but for some reason a number of people were against him in those early days. He used to like to think that the younger generation of riders were terrifed of him, but they were all enormously fond of him. It was Frank who made Badminton the spectacle it is today. My cousin had never been keen on it growing too big as he didn't like having too many people on the place. In fact, during the sixties he changed cross-country day to a Friday in an effort to cut down the number of people who might attend – but they still came! Frank, quite rightly, could see that Badminton had to pay its own way if it was to survive. He understood about siting fences so that spectators (and TV cameras) could see four or five fences from one spot. He just seemed to have a feel for what was wanted, and yet he never lost sight of his first responsibility – to build courses which tested the rider but which were fair to the horse.

'When Frank retired I was delighted to have Hugh Thomas take his place. There was an attempt to persuade me to have someone else, but I held out for who I believed was the right man. Hugh not only has riding experience but he is also a good businessman. Our next major hurdle was when Whitbreads decided to end their sponsorship. Hugh rang me to say that we had been invited to lunch at Whitbreads in London, and I remember remarking that I didn't like the sound of this – something must be wrong. But Hugh was sure it was an innocent enough invitation. However, a few days later I had a call from Sam Whitbread saying that he was really sorry but they were pulling out of nearly all sporting sponsorships. It was during the recession, and despite the brave face we put on at the time, it was very hard to find sponsorship. Again, when Mitsubishi stepped in there was some local ill feeling about the idea of a Japanese company taking over such a British event, but it must be remembered that the Colt Car Company is the British arm of Mitsubishi. The Badminton three-day event has continued to improve and Mitsubishi have extended their sponsorship again, but you can never be confident about how long anything will last.

'The three-day event is a wonderful thing for the whole estate; it brings a good deal of prosperity to the surrounding area. Timber from our woods is used to make the fences, and local people do bed-and-breakfast. We don't have a village pub, but the Badminton Club does very well. There are many other spin-offs and, in addition, it is a good excuse for us to tidy the whole place up each year.'

The Duke's whole family is enthusiastic about the horse trials, although sadly the Duchesss of Beaufort died in 1995; their eldest son, the Marquis of Worcester, is on the Badminton Committee. Anyone who loves the event can rest assured that Badminton's future is certainly safe as far as its host is concerned. The Duke of Beaufort's parting words will be echoed by many: 'I enjoy it immensely and hope it goes on forever.'

Andy Crofts recalls his first sight of Robinwood: 'He was standing in a field near Bristol, covered in snow. I bought him as a four-year-old and he went on to win in the showring, run in a point-to-point, and complete Badminton five times. I owned him in partnership with Mrs J. McMillen (the sister of Colonel 'Monkey' Blacker), who rode him at Little Badminton three times, finishing second in 1959 and 1960, after which he was ridden by Jeremy Beale. At his first Badminton [1959] he was sixteenth after the dressage – he never did like it very much – but ended up in the lead after the speed and endurance phase. He was as brave as a lion across country but could be a little careless in the showjumping. You wouldn't get away with that today, but in those days a clear, fast cross-country round kept you in the picture. Although we ran a dealing business Robinwood was never for sale. He lived to the age of twenty-eight.'

Following the competition in 1959, the beautiful Badminton Park was left in a heartbreaking state, and many found it hard to believe that the Duke would ever again be prepared to sacrifice his grounds. But one coach driver was quick to put things in perspective and to set people's minds at rest – as far as he was concerned it was simple: 'The Duke's such a sportsman he'll think nothing of it – you'll see!' What the Duke really thought that night is probably unprintable, but he was indeed a sportsman and at the prize-giving there was a collective sigh of relief when he announced that he looked forward to welcoming everyone back the following year!

## Badminton's heir settles for second

Despite the possible advantage of competing on home ground, the heir to the Badminton estate, David Somerset, had to settle for second place. A daring performance across country, resulting from the combination of Countryman's experience and his rider's determined courage, earned them enough bonus points to wipe out the disadvantage of their fifteenth placing after the dressage, and put them into the lead.

David Somerset, now the 11th Duke of Beaufort, recalls with endearing modesty his surprise at finding himself in this position. 'I was very much an amateur rider compared with my nearest rival, Sheila Willcox, and I knew only too well that Countryman wasn't the easiest horse to showjump. We had one pole down which in those days cost 10 penalties and, as it turned out for me personally, the Badminton title as well! I was still very happy to finish second and, although it is a prize I would love to have won, I had to accept that I was never able to dedicate enough time to the sport to hope to come out on top. Sheila was a professional competitor and the reigning European Champion, so she certainly deserved to win.

'I had ridden and hunted horses for as long as I could remember, but was inspired to take up eventing by a wonderful Hungarian who worked at Badminton. He had escaped to England during the war and helped me enormously with the intricacies of dressage and jumping. After the war I did my national service and came out not really knowing what I wanted to do. I started an art gallery with a couple of people I met at a party, and this developed into an international company. My work kept me in London most of the week so I only had the weekends to train and compete.

'Countryman had been bought from his rider, Bertie Hill, by a syndicate [see 1955] which included my cousin [the 10th Duke of Beaufort]. After the 1956 Stockholm Olympics (where Countryman won team gold) no one was sure what to do with the horse, as he would be too old for the 1960 Olympics. He was offered to me as I was keen to further my eventing experience and I paid something like £800 for him. It was a lot on money then, but even so would probably not convert to the equivalent fortunes that Olympic horses are sold for today! He was the most wonderful horse and I had a great time with him. Our second place at Badminton was our best result – we were seventh in 1958 – and after that my work began to take up too much of my time. I gave up competing but carried on hunting as this doesn't need the same amount of personal preparation as eventing! I hunted Countryman until he was eighteen; he had a few years' retirement, and was put down in his twenties.'

# The 1960s

# 1960

# Australia sets the pace

After the devastation caused by the weather in 1959, Badminton in 1960 enjoyed warm, sunny conditions. About the only concession made to avoid the scars of the previous year was that the dressage and showjumping arena was moved from its site in front of the house to a position near the Lake. The Olympic prospects, the overseas visitors, and the biggest prize-

Despite a five-week journey by sea from Australia, **Bill Roycroft** and **Our Solo** took the title ahead of fellow countryman Laurie Morgan

Pages 64–5: **Ginny Freeman-Jackson** and **Liscarroll** at full stretch over open water, an apparently simple obstacle when compared with water combinations of more recent years

With the 1960 Olympics imminent, Badminton was used as an Olympic trial and it certainly provided an accurate pointer as to who would be in contention for gold in Rome: Australian riders took first, second, fourth, tenth and eleventh places – and sure enough they won team gold in Rome! The winning rider at Badminton was Bill Roycroft: a tall, lean dairy farmer from New South Wales, he rode the 15hh ex-polo pony, Our Solo. (A partnership of the eighties which bore an uncanny resemblance to these two was New Zealand's Mark Todd and the dimunitive Charisma.)

winners from the national entry were put in the Great Badminton Championship; the remainder competed in the Little Badminton Event. Martin Whiteley and Peggoty won Little Badminton (later in his career, Martin became chairman of the Selection Committee and the Horse Trials Support Group).

To qualify to take part, each competitor had to have completed two Open or Intermediate one-day events.

It was estimated that twice as many people visited Badminton as in previous years, and the growing number of spectators was beginning to cause problems. For instance, Captain Norman

**Leather gloves and a lost Olympic ticket**   Like so many of his generation, Martin Whiteley had joined the regular army; he was in the Rifle Brigade, and during his career with them he was asked to run the army corps at Eton. This led to his appointment as a house master, and he was remembered at the school as a particularly kind and conscientious master – and it was precisely this considerate nature which perhaps prevented him from achieving his ultimate ambition as an event rider. His godfather, who was an MFH in Ireland, had given him a good horse, St Nicholas, and it was this horse which brought him into eventing. He then bought Peggoty (see below), with whom he won Little

Badminton in 1960. She was followed by The Poacher, bought in 1964, and it was in the following year that they claimed another Little Badminton title. In 1966 they finished fifth in the inaugural World Championships at Burghley, and in 1967 they won team gold and individual silver at the Punchestown European Championships. But Martin's greatest ambition was to ride at the Olympics, and many would have thought this record good enough to earn them a ticket. In 1968 potential Olympic horses were excused Badminton, but they had to run at Burghley to prove their fitness for the Mexico Olympics which followed just a few weeks later.

To this day it has always been reported that Martin Whiteley lost his Olympic ticket because of a recurring back problem and subsequent lack of fitness at the final trial at Burghley. But Jane Whiteley (née Drummond-Hay), his sister-in-law, recalls things differently: 'Martin made the mistake of wearing leather gloves at Burghley, and of course they very quickly became wet with sweat – and as many a rider has found to his cost, leather gloves offer no grip at all once they are wet. He was therefore unable to keep a tight hold on the reins and so could not control The Poacher properly during their ride at Burghley. The selectors immediately assumed this apparent 'weakness' was a result of his bad back, and told him very publically that he would not be selected because he was not fit enough. To a conscientious man like Martin who had made sure that, despite his back problems, he jolly well was fit and strong, this condemnation cut very deep; he was dreadfully hurt, but he was far too polite to argue the true case, which was simply that he had made the mistake of wearing leather gloves.'

So The Poacher was ridden by Ben Jones in Mexico, and helped win the team gold medal (ironically, Ben Jones' potential Olympic mount Foxdor was owned by Martin's mother; tragically the horse had suffered a heart attack after a training gallop). Even then, the late Martin Whiteley was far too much a gentleman to bear a grudge, and having given The Poacher a season's hunting with the Grafton, he continued to allow his horse to be at the disposal of the combined training committee (the selection committee). With Ben Jones again in the saddle he won team gold at the 1969 Haras du Pin European Championships.

In 1970 the ride was given to Richard Meade, who won Badminton with him that year, making The Poacher the only horse to have won both Little Badminton and the main Badminton Championship. This new partnership went on to win individual silver at the Punchestown World Championships in 1970, and team gold at the 1971 European Championships. The Poacher was then retired to enjoy more hunting with the Grafton; he died in 1977.

His owner, Martin Whiteley, continued to make a tremendous contribution to the sport of eventing in his role as chairman of the Horse Trials Support Group; a title which he held from 1960 until his death in 1984.

Arthur and Blue Jeans were enjoying a faultless round when a child ran straight into them and was knocked down. Captain Arthur pulled up to see if the child was all right, which it was, but this lost him valuable time and affected his final placing. He finished fifth.

## Bill Roycroft

Bill Roycroft was a late starter as far as eventing was concerned; he was already in his forties when he set his sights on Olympic success and began to think about selecting a couple of what he hoped would be suitable horses to train. But he had the enormous advantage of being a natural horseman, brought up in an age when the horse was vital to survival:

'My equestrian background was quite simply that we rode to school, we rode to work and we rode to dances,' says Bill. 'Horses were my transport right up until the war. I then spent five years in the war when they were also essential, and when I returned they were still my transport. I used to do a bit of competing on my work horses, though I suppose it was only when the 1956 Olympics came to Melbourne that my interest was really aroused. Our own horsemen had to go to Stockholm for their "Olympics" because quarantine regulations didn't allow other horses to come to Australia to compete; but after those games I told my wife that we were going to try for the 1960 Rome Olympics.

'We were dairy farmers, and I tell you, it was hard work training and preparing horses either before or after the day's farmwork had been dealt with! Australia had a few one- and three-day events of its own by this time, which I entered. People kept telling me, "Bill, you're too old!" – but we kept on winning! Because of the quarantine regulations we had to leave Australia six months before the Olympics, so it seemed a good idea to prepare in England and to take in Badminton as part of our preparation. The horse I had been planning to ride had a bruised foot so I took the little ex-polo pony Our Solo.

'We went by cargo boat and the journey took five weeks. We were delayed a week as we had to go via Italy to offload wool which had been brought from Sydney. The horses were stabled below deck, but we had tons of sand put down on an outer deck so that we had somewhere to work them – and Our Solo was so small that I could ride him round below deck as well! We docked at Liverpool and then went by train to Aldershot where we were to be based.

'Our "Olympic" team went to its first one-day event in England seven weeks later. Word had gone ahead of us that, being Australian, we wouldn't have a clue about dressage, and we were given some terrible scores. But our trainer, Franz Mairinger, wasn't worried, and assured us that the Continental judges would judge us differently – and he was right, because at Badminton and at the Olympics the Continental judges gave us much better scores.

'At Badminton I was the first to go. On the cross-country there was a really big brush fence on the far side of the Vicarage Ditch which they thought would stop everyone, but Our Solo, who was only 15hh, batted on in there and did it! He had been eighth after the dressage, but he went clear across country and in the showjumping to win. The British girl, Anneli Drummond-Hay, was ahead of me after the cross-country, but her horse Perhaps hit the gate and put a foot in the water. My team-mate Laurie Morgan was second, and the British girl dropped to third.'

The Badminton result prompted *Horse and Hound*'s correspondent to note that, 'We need to find three good big 'uns because the Aussies have got the three best little 'uns that ever looked through a bridle!'

## Olympic success

Bill recalls, 'Our Olympic preparation continued at Aldershot, and then we flew to Rome for the Olympics. I had a fall on the cross-country at the notorious concrete Drainpipe fence, but completed the course before being taken to hospital with a broken collar bone and damaged shoulder. There I learned that another member of our team had had to withdraw when his horse broke down after the cross-country, but that if my score could count, we were in with a chance of gold. So I discharged myself from hospital the next morning and

The stylish **Anneli Drummond-Hay** and **Perhaps** were best of the British to finish third in 1960

managed a clear showjumping round: and as you know, Australia won the gold!

'From then on it was a case of going home, preparing more horses for the next Olympics, then going into quarantine for six months in England each time and so competing in England as well. People kept telling me I was too old, but I kept on winning! During 1964-65 we were in England again, serving our quarantine period. I hunted my horses so that I could qualify them for hunter chases, which gave us something else to do, and then in the spring of 1965 I rode three horses round Badminton to finish second and sixth in the Big Badminton competition, and second in Little Badminton. For the rest of the season I concentrated on showjumping them, finishing third in the Nations' Cup at the White City, and third in the Agha Khan Cup in Dublin.

'I rode at the Mexico Olympics so was back in England for quarantine after that; so at the l969 Badminton I finished third and fourth. In that particular year I consider I should really have won: one of the horses I was riding, Warrathoola, hesitated fleetingly at the Gravel Pit. The fence judge had marked my sheet clear, but Colonel Babe Moseley, the head of the Ground Jury, had been watching my round on the television screen and he decided that I should be penalised. The fact that he had not watched every other horse on the screen, or all the fences, didn't come into it: if he said you had a stop, then you had a stop – and clearly Colonel Moseley didn't want Australia to win again if he could possibly help it! I remember a previous occasion too, in 1965, when I achieved two seconds and a sixth at Badminton, and there was a special prize for the best British performance. At that time I held a British passport, and many of the national papers questioned why I wasn't given the prize!

'I rode again at Munich, and then at the Montreal Olympics. In Mexico in 1968 and at Montreal in 1976 we took team bronze, and on both occasions my son Wayne was in the team with me – I was well into my sixties by then! Wayne is now the Australian team coach, and my other two sons, Barry and Clarke, have both represented Australia.'

Bill Roycroft had a reputation for succeeding against all the odds. He suffered a rare ducking in the Badminton Lake one year, and as he waded after his horse who had gone for a swim, an Australian voice bellowed 'Don't tell me – he can walk on water as well!'

# Brewers back Badminton

Opposite: A more
popular sight than any
motor vehicle – the
magnificent **Whitbread
Shires** lead the parade
of competitors

Below: The coveted
**Whitbread Trophy** –
a symbol of one of the
longest running sporting
sponsorships
(1961–1991)

Part of Badminton's early charm was the relatively inobtrusive, but essential, support of Whitbreads. The Whitbread/Badminton partnership began in 1961; the late Colonel Bill Whitbread and the then Duke of Beaufort (cousin of the present Duke) were great friends, sharing in particular a love of horses and hunting. Colonel Bill Whitbread hunted regularly with the Beaufort hounds and his company's sponsorship of Badminton was the result of a chat on the subject whilst out hunting one day. It started as a gentlemen's agreement between good friends and remained so until 1984. Then a new marketing team took over with the aim of making the arrangement more lucrative to Whitbread, and a more commercial approach was adopted.

John Fox, who handled Whitbread's press and publicity, recalls how, having already supported the first ever sponsored National Hunt Race – the Whitbread Gold Cup at Sandown – it was a natural progression to then sponsor the event run by his great friend.

'We were never keen to push the commercial aspect of it all,' says John Fox, emphasising the easy-going nature of the early agreement. 'As far as we were concerned the horse trials belonged to Badminton and to the Duke of Beaufort. So it was only right that the name should reflect this. In the early years our name did not even appear on the programme cover. And when it did, it was known as the Badminton Horse Trials for the Whitbread Trophy. The winner received the Whitbread Trophy and, in the days of Little Badminton, that winner received the Whitbread Tankard. What with that and the various fences on the course such as the Whitbread Bar and the Whitbread Barrels, our involvement was obvious enough without overdoing it. The most popular attraction of all, apart from the real Whitbread Bar, was the Whitbread Shire horses, which headed the parade of competitors. It was only in the final years of our association that the programme was changed to read "The Whitbread Championships – Badminton".

'There was always a very friendly and sociable atmosphere. We used to produce a film about the horse trials which was shown in the village hall. One film was actually given the general release! As well as the famous cocktail party we also used to arrange a special evening for all the grooms. All of us involved at the time still look back on those days with affection and a great feeling of nostalgia.'

When Whitbread's Badminton association finally ended after the 1991 event, it marked one of the longest running sporting sponsorships of all time. Time waits for no one and Badminton forged a new and successful partnership with Mitsubishi Motors. The Mitsubishi Motors Badminton Horse Trials, as it then became known, achieves greater heights of perfection each year. But the Whitbread years remain a happy and enduring memory.

# 1961
# Australia dominates again

**Laurie Morgan to Salad Days**, who had landed in the middle of a set of big parallel bars: 'You got yourself into this mess, now you get yourself out of it!' He did, and went on to win Badminton. Salad Days could have been forgiven for saying the same thing to his rider for learning the wrong dressage test and losing marks for errors of course...

By the end of Badminton 1961 the Duke of Beaufort could be forgiven for beginning to wonder if the Badminton three-day event was actually serving the purpose for which it had been created. The Duke's aim had been to see British riders succeed in the sport of eventing at international level, but the growth in Badminton's popularity and prestige had done much to promote the sport in other countries as well as in Britain, and Badminton was fast becoming the event to try and win. This fact was quickly recognised by Whitbread Breweries who decided to sponsor the Badminton Horse Trials, an association which continued for the next thirty years.

Australian riders had dominated at Badminton the previous year and had gone on to win Olympic gold in Rome. In 1961 Laurie Morgan, a member of that gold-medal winning team, returned to Badminton to claim this title for his own as well, having finished second to Bill Roycroft in 1960. Ireland's Captain Harry Freeman-Jackson, a regular visitor, earned his best Badminton result by taking second place on St Finbarr. British honour was duly upheld by Michael Bullen who, despite a fall on each of his horses, finished third and fourth with Cottage Romance and Sea Breeze, both owned by Colonel V.D.S. Williams. The Little Badminton Event was won by Captain J. Welch riding his own Mr Wilson; he had been tenth after the dressage, but he earned a good speed bonus and was clear in the showjumping to come out the winner.

Once more the ground was a bog on cross-country day. The course was beginning to take on a more modern look, with the start and finish contained in a boxed area – but the qualities needed for victory were still the old-fashioned ones of stamina and guts, particularly when the conditions were bad.

The eventual winner, Laurie Morgan, started out at a disadvantage, having discovered the day before the dressage phase that he had in fact learnt the wrong test! He managed to get 'lost' in it two or three times, which cost him a few penalties, but clean performances in the speed and endurance and the showjumping moved him up from tenth place after the dressage to the winner's spot. His horse, Salad Days, was a worthy partner: in his career he was first and second at Badminton, he won Olympic gold, and he also competed in a number of hunter chases between the Olympics and his Badminton victory. He was a brown gelding by Hunter's Moon and was foaled in 1951. He thoroughly deserved the fabulous retirement he was given at Badminton as the Duchess of Beaufort's hunter. Laurie was also a top-class race rider; his wins included the Foxhunters' Chase at Aintree and at Cheltenham on College Master. He died in 1997.

## Captain Harry Freeman-Jackson

Captain Harry Freeman-Jackson had competed regularly at Badminton since 1952, and although never far down the line, this was his best result. He was another old-fashioned hero about whom a bad word is rarely uttered.

His daughter Ginny (now Vicountess Petersham) recalls her mother's description of the day Captain Harry went off to war: 'He was with the Kent Yeomanry, and the day he was called up he set off on his motorbike wearing a pair of dungarees, a tin hat with a sprig of holly in it, and his guitar slung over his shoulder. His war was shortlived, because when his regiment landed in St Valerie they discovered it had already fallen to the Germans. He and a couple of other soldiers tried to escape in a small boat, which unfortunately had no oars; they somehow manoeuvred it down the river and out into the Channel under cover of fog, but about a mile out to sea the fog lifted and they immediately came under fire. My father was hit, but managed to swim ashore where he was captured and held prisoner for six years.

'Father returned to England after the war, but had always wanted to settle in Ireland – so when the chance came, he took it. He represented Ireland at two Olympics, and he was a keen race rider, but his greatest love was hunting; he was a Master of Foxhounds for many years. He would have loved to have gone round Badminton with his pipe in his mouth, which is what he did out hunting!'

Fellow Irish Olympic rider, Tony Cameron, also remembers Harry Freeman-Jackson with great affection: 'I knew him because he had been to school with my father, and I went to two Olympics with him – in fact he lent me one of his horses, Sonnet, to ride in Rome. He was a wonderfully patient, kind man, and totally honest. He was second in the Irish Grand National on a horse he trained and rode himself while he was still eventing. He won a great many point-to-points and had won the Galway Plate in 1949.'

Harry was unlucky not to win Badminton in 1961. Riding St Finbarr, a ten-year-old

chestnut gelding by Sandyman, he was sixth after the dressage, and as the poor conditions caused many to fall by the wayside, he had every chance of overtaking Laurie Morgan's score. He was making very good time on the cross-country when a woman and a dog crossed the course in front of him: the woman tried to run one way, but the dog decided to run the other, so they effectively blocked his path, forcing him to stop while they sorted themselves out.

He rode St Finbarr again at Badminton in 1964 to take fourth place; his friend and fellow countryman Tony Cameron was third that year. Quite apart from his own successes at Badminton, Harry would also have taken great pleasure in the many occasions that he com-

Opposite: Despite learning the wrong dressage test, **Laurie Morgan** made up for this early setback to take the 1961 Whitbread Trophy

**Photographing Badminton** Tetbury photographer **Peter Harding** visited Badminton every year to record the highs and lows of its gallant competitors: 'There were only a few of us photographers in the early years, and I can remember how the others would laugh at me as I ran round the course trying to capture every rider at a different fence. My "colleagues" would stand at one fence all day, but I liked to get some variety – it didn't always pay off: the year Laurie Morgan won I was sprinting towards the next fence when he galloped

flat out past me! But I was always happier with the collection of photographs I ended up with by doing it the "hard way".

'I used to have a stand at Badminton, and would rush home and develop my pictures so that I could display them for sale the next day. One year I remember Harry Freeman-Jackson came storming up to me demanding to see the photograph I had taken of him. I pointed it out to him, and he promptly took hold of it and ripped it up in front of me, exclaiming, "I'm fed up with people coming up to me laughing because they have seen this picture, so this will put a stop to it!" The only thing wrong with it was that his horse had obviously jumped quite big, and instead of being in his usually immaculate position,

Harry's arms and legs were swinging out in all directions!'

These days, Somerset-based **Kit Houghton** acts as the official photographer for Mitsubishi Motors at the Badminton Horse Trials. But his first visit to Badminton was for quite a different reason: he was taken there as a five-year-old by his mother, who was determined to see the Queen. 'I remember my mother dragging me from pillar to post in an effort to see the Queen, who we never did manage to track down,' recalls Kit. 'I had no idea what the event itself was as we never seemed to stop to watch anything else!'

His official business as a photographer at Badminton can be equally frustrating. Kit was dispatched to take a photograph of the Labour politician Robin Cook, who any number of people insisted they had seen enjoying the sights. But just as his mother had searched in vain for the Queen, Robin Cook proved to be equally elusive.

Kit's early photographic career took him to London and Belfast where he worked for various magazines before deciding to specialise in equestrian photography. With his wife Kate he has attended Badminton each year since 1980 and was Whitbread's official photographer for the last few years of their sponsorship. When Mitsubishi took over in 1992 they retained Kit in the same role. 'Our main task is to produce good publicity pictures for them. Ideally they want "branded" pictures, ie a photograph with the name Mitsubishi featured somewhere in it. They have become more understanding about the difficulty of achieving this at a horse trial – it's not like motor racing where the car and driver are plastered in the name of their sponsor. At Badminton we only really have the option of featuring one of their cars in the picture, or capturing their name when it is on a feature fence. The rider's number on cross-country day has Mitsubishi written above it, but it is not always visible in a photograph. My main aim is still to take what I consider to be good action photography – the "branding" concept is something I have to keep in mind as I'm working.

'Our other main task is to produce pictures and text for the many regional newspapers who do not send an official reporter to the event. We send them news stories and photographs of their local riders and this really helps to increase the amount of media coverage Badminton receives.

'We're usually too busy over the dressage and cross-country days to get too excited about how the competition itself is going, but by Sunday afternoon when we're stationed in the main arena we get just as caught up in the atmosphere as everyone else.'

peted alongside his daughter Ginny, (see also 1962).

Harry Freeman-Jackson was from Mallow in County Cork. He died in 1994 having ridden until nine days before his death.

## Michael Bullen

Michael Bullen's versatile riding career – including ponies, hunting, hunter trialling, polo, and Western riding while working in Canada – contributed greatly to his success as an event rider, which requires all-round horse-manship. In 1958 he travelled a group of horses and ponies from Glasgow to New York, then made a second trip across America to the Duke of Windsor's ranch in Canada; when he returned to England, his mother sent him on a riding course run by Colonel Jack Hance. Hance recommended him to Colonel V.D.S. Williams, who took him on to compete his horses for him.

Michael remembers vividly being given Cottage Romance to ride. 'She was a beautiful grey mare who, like all ladies, was unpredictable, but in the nicest possible way. She looked after me through five Badmintons. I was never that good at dressage, but she usually managed well enough – except that her version of walk was to walk in front and trot behind, which failed to impress the judges! I was asked to ride her *hors concours* at the 1959 European Championships at Harewood so that our suitability as Olympic prospects could be assessed. We were chosen for the Rome Olympics, but very much as the combination not expected to finish! My team-mates were Norman Arthur, Bertie Hill and Frank Weldon, who told me to just go out and do the best I could! I managed to finish fourth, and the team missed out on the bronze medal by half a penalty.

'I had ridden at my first Badminton earlier that year where I finished ninth on Colonel Williams' Sea Breeze. I was third at Badminton the following year on Cottage Romance, and fourth on Sea Breeze. Unfortunately Cottage

**Photographing Badminton**

(opposite) One of Peter Harding's favourite shots, taken in 1953, shows Brigadier Darling on Trinity Point. (The pair did make it safely over the fence.) Brigadier Darling was killed in a hunting accident in 1978

(centre left) The Badminton photographers have to cope with all kinds of light and weather conditions

(left) Kit Houghton trying to get the best position for a dramatic shot at the Lake

# The 1960s

**Sea Breeze**, with whom **Mike Bullen** took third place in 1962, having been fourth in 1961

Opposite:
**Merely-a-Monarch** won Badminton at his first and only attempt in 1962. After that, he and **Anneli Drummond-Hay** enjoyed great success showjumping

Romance had frightened herself jumping into the deep water at the Rome Olympics, and after that she was never really sure how to tackle a water jump, whether she should jump in it or over it. When she was finally retired the Williams gave her to their groom who had always cared for her.

'At Badminton in 1962 Sea Breeze went one better to finish third, and in 1964 he finished fifth; he was also my ride at the 1964 Tokyo Olympics. On the steeplechase the footing was of chopped molten lava, and having been rained on, it meant that it was soggy and deep in places, and rock hard in others. Sea Breeze put his foot in a hole and fell, cutting his head badly and dislocating and breaking my shoulder; we held ourselves together well enough to jump twenty-eight of the thirty-two fences before finally grinding to a halt.

'After those Olympics it was time to decide whether to concentrate on riding or my work. I had met James Peden whilst travelling horses out to Canada – where I also met my future

wife Sally – and at the time we had both been keen to do something to improve the conditions under which horses travelled. James' grandfather ran a firm in Folkestone called Peden & Son, and out of this grew Peden Bloodstock, the business we are involved in today. I travelled the horses to the 1968 Mexico Olympics, where I was also in charge of looking after my little sister Jane who was in the gold-medal winning team there! We now move around 6,000 horses a year; we transported most of the European-based horses out to the 1996 Atlanta Olympics, and will be doing the same for the Sydney Olympics in 2000.'

Mike is still very much involved with horse trials; he is an FEI judge and steward, and he and his wife Sally run the Borough Court Horse Trials at their home in Hampshire. Sally also competes most successfully on the Advanced event stallion Rock King.

## A small price to pay

The Australian riders would sometimes stay at the Bullens' family home in Didmarton for the duration of their stay in England. Michael Bullen recalls how one year they were short of grazing for all the horses. The Bullens had approached the neighbouring farmer for a field but he wasn't prepared to rent it. Bill Roycroft paid him a visit, and seeing that he had about 600 ewes that would need shearing, offered to undertake the shearing in exchange for the use of the field. The farmer liked this idea far better and agreed. When the time came for the sheep to be sheared he thought he had a pretty good deal as he reckoned it would take three or four days to get through the flock. He told Bill he would get 200 in ready for him the next day, and then pull in another 200 the day after that until they were through. 'No, you won't,' said Bill, 'you get the whole damn lot in tomorrow and we'll get through them.' They started at 5am and were finished by lunchtime!

'They had a big party in the village when they left to return to Australia. It lasted three days – the local policeman mislaid his trousers three times and on each occasion had to cycle home trouserless to pick up another pair.'

# 1962

# Burghley winner takes Badminton crown

Anneli Drummond-Hay had been inspired to compete at Badminton after the success of her sister, Jane, who was second at her first attempt in 1951. Anneli is best known for her achievements with Merely-a-Monarch, winning the inaugural Burghley three-day event in 1961, Badminton in 1962 and then having considerable success in international showjumping. At this point in our story Anneli had been quietly making an impression at Badminton since the early fifties. As she recalls:

# The 1960s

'We lived in the north of Scotland, and really didn't see anything horsey apart from the Pony Club finals! So when my sister Jane went to Badminton in 1951 there was tremendous excitement! Then in 1955 she was offered the ride on our cousin Major Drummond Moray's horse, Freya, at the European Championships at Windsor, but it coincided with her marriage to Tim Whiteley so we asked if I could have the ride. I trained for a few months with Robert Hall as preparation, and finished seventeenth out of fifty-one starters.

old. Although he looked very nice, he was younger than I really wanted. But some time later his owners rang me to ask for their photo back, and as I still hadn't bought a horse and he would by then have been three, I decided to go and look at him. I fell in love with him immediately; he was three-quarter Thoroughbred cross Fell (by Happy Monarch out of a mare by Merely-a-Minor), but he had a great deal of quality and fantastic natural paces. I had to pay £300 for him, every penny of which I had to borrow, and repay in instalments!'

**Little Badminton** The Little Badminton Event brought another victory for Australia. Success on a 'last-minute ride' is usually more the stuff of dreams than of reality, but as the record will show, Badminton does sometimes allow such magic to work. Just before the start of the event, Australian rider Penny Crofts was given the ride on H. Graham-Clark's Priam. Although not right up with the leaders after the dressage, a fast cross-country performance and a clear showjumping round pulled them up into first place. In second place was Captain James Templer riding M'Lord Connelly; this combination went on to win the Great Badminton Championship in 1964.

'After that I rode a young horse called Trident that had been started off by my sister. We finished sixth in 1956, and then he was sold to the British team as a potential Olympic horse. At around this time I was advertising for a three- or four-year-old potential event horse – but more about that later! In 1958 I finished third with the six-year-old Pluto, and was twelfth with him in 1959.

'Apart from my win in 1962, my best memory of Badminton was from 1960 when I finished third, and best of the British, on Perhaps. I had saved Perhaps from the slaughterhouse, paying £15 for the privilege, and he rewarded me with a really brave performance at Badminton. He was then sold to the Swiss for their Olympic team.

'By this time I owned a young horse called Merely-a-Monarch. Amongst the many replies I had received from my advertisement for a potential event horse was a photo of a two-year-

'Monarch was a difficult youngster, naughty but also lacking confidence. He bucked me off regularly, but was very talented and had great presence. As a five-year-old he won the army horse trials at Tweseldown, and he also won the Foxhunter showjumping class, the show hunter class and the combined training championships at the Horse of the Year Show. My sister helped me tremendously with my training, especially as I started to prepare for Badminton. As a six-year-old he won the first Burghley three-day event – and by now everyone had noticed him.

'Monarch was seven when I rode him at Badminton; he was obviously very fit which meant he could boil a bit in the dressage, but he produced a lovely test. Just before Badminton he had a training gallop against a well-known racehorse, the champion two-mile chaser Flame Gun. Only race jockeys were allowed to use Ivor Herbert's gallop, and so a jockey rode Monarch – and they left Flame Gun standing! And Monarch was only three-quarter bred!

'When we came in off the roads and tracks we had a few minutes to spare to prepare for the cross-country. At this point my mother wanted to shovel some glucose down me: I was still puffing when she pushed a spoonful of dry glucose under my nose, and all of it seemed to go either up my nose or straight down my throat so that I was choking. A very good start! Across country Monarch found it all so easy; he never had to move up into top gear. He knocked a brick out of the wall in the showjumping, but still won with a 42-point lead over Frank Weldon and Young Pretender. Mike Bullen was third on Sea Breeze.

'I thought Monarch was so wonderful, and was so frightened about him getting hurt that I only did Badminton that one time with him. I had always wanted to showjump internationally, but had never had a horse good enough, and now was my chance. The fact that girls still weren't allowed to ride at the Olympic three-day event also swayed my decision. However, the bit of eventing that Monarch had done was the making of him as a showjumper. As a young horse he had always been a bit precious, but having had to kick him into his fences across country made him much bolder. He quickly grew up and just got on with the job.

'A few months after Badminton we won showjumping's Imperial Cup at the Royal International. The showjumping world could not believe its eyes when this skinny ex-event horse flew round – with me still riding as if I was going cross-country, dropping strides here and there! He was just an amazing horse and would have been a world-beater even by today's standards.

'I did have a few teething problems when I first converted from eventing to pure showjumping – and in this respect I will always remember how fickle the press could be. When I was third at Badminton on Perhaps there were a lot of very complimentary press cuttings saying I deserved a far better horse than the one I was on. But when I hit a few problems showjumping with Monarch there were more press cuttings declaring that this talented horse deserved a far better rider! In fact we were attracting criticism from all sides. I was very much frowned upon by the eventing world when I "moved camp" to showjumping, and I can clearly remember one very upper-class Army officer, with whom I had evented, asking me, "What on earth do you find to talk about when you have to speak to those people?!"

'During this time I had had to sell a share in Monarch in order to survive financially, and after the press reports criticising my riding, the other shareholders wanted him to be ridden by someone else. The whole affair was devastating and ended up in court. A friend, Colonel Tom Greenhalgh, helped me buy back the share which secured his future.

'We went on to represent Britain in five Nations Cups' teams, and we won many other major classes, including the Guinness Time Championships and the Sunday Times Cup at Wembley in 1963, the Queen's Cup and, after a year's break, we won the 1966 Grand Prix in Toronto and Grand Prix in Madrid and Geneva. At Monarch's last major competition he was second in the 1970 World Championships in Copenhagen.

'When Monarch was sixteen, in 1972, I retired him from competition and moved to South Africa with my husband. I left Monarch with Merlin Meakin, who used to work for me. She looked after him, and enjoyed hunting him for the next ten years.

'Then on one occasion when I was visiting England, I called Merlin as usual to see how Monarch was, and all was well. But the following morning she rang to tell me to come to the yard straightaway, because Monarch had fallen down while having his feet done and couldn't get back up. I went over immediately, and was able to say goodbye before having him put down. I was always grateful that he "waited" until I was home so that I could do that.'

Anneli is still enjoying her showjumping career. She left South Africa in 1994 to compete at the World Equestrian Games in the Hague. The quarantine procedure was so lengthy that she decided to stay in Holland and now teaches, trains and competes there.

# The 1960s

**Granite** – a wild little filly who didn't know what dressage was, but who pulled up to third place after making nothing of the bottomless ground in the cross-country

**Mercury** who 'was a very funny shape, built completely downhill and with a very short neck'

## A popular Badminton regular

The very popular Badminton regular, Ireland's Miss Ginny Freeman-Jackson, was fast emulating her father with good performances at this event; in this year she finished third on Granite, her best ever result. She first rode at Badminton in l957:

'I well remember my first Badminton,' says the now Vicountess Ginny Petersham. 'I was seventeen and had been away in Switzerland for six months; I got home in March, and my father announced that we were both going off to Badminton. He told me the horse had had forty-two days' hunting so it would be fit enough, but he then said he wasn't sure about me! So we went to Dublin en route to England and galloped on the beach – and that was the only bit of fast-work I did on Liscaroll, my Badminton horse! I hadn't much idea what I was letting myself in for, having never ridden at an event, but I had a wonderful time! The cross-country felt great – we had a run-out at the Coffin, but I think that was due to sheer exhaustion on my part – and we finished fifteenth out of thirty-eight starters. It was all such fun, and we never took it too seriously or prepared particularly well for it; it was simply a case of taking our hunters over there for an exciting ride.

'Our third place at Little Badminton in 1962 was our best result. I rode a wild little filly called Granite; her tail swished all the time, and she had no idea what dressage was. We gave her a sleeping pill the night before to see if that would calm her down, but it made absolutely no difference; and none of us had really thought about what effect it might have on cross-country day!

'We were pretty near last after the dressage, but she made up for that the next day; having hunted so much she made nothing of the bottomless ground, and pulled up to third.

'In 1964 I rode a horse called Mercury. He was a very funny shape, built completely downhill and with a very short neck. We had a trainer at the time called Brigadier Bolton who thought that with a bit of help, Mercury would be an Olympic prospect. He worked him in all kinds of gadgets to make him carry himself more 'uphill', and then announced that he was ready for his first preparatory event. We had an amazing thirty-two refusals and four falls, but completed eventually! However, it was fairly obvious that "going correctly" didn't suit Mercury at all, so we let him revert to his downhill shape, and he finished twelfth at Badminton.

'The following year I rode Sam Weller, who had been given to me by fellow Irish rider Tony Cameron. Sam Weller had spent the first year of his life in a stable, and had learnt that if he got his front legs over the door then he could see out. He developed into a very funny shape as a result, but he had a heart like a lion. I was selected as reserve for the Tokyo Olympics in l964, and on the way back, received a telegram from Tony Cameron saying that Sam Weller was mine. We finished ninth at Badminton in 1965; that was the last year I rode at Badminton. But I still look back on every occasion as having been the greatest fun. Badminton was always like a lovely day's hunting to me, and I certainly didn't prepare for it specifically. But I knew I was riding good hunters who were unlikely to fall or do anything too stupid, so I just went out and had a wonderful time.'

**Eventing on a shoestring** The modern eventing world is very much more 'professional' than it was in the days of the sport's infancy, both in terms of its organisation and in the status of its competitors. Whilst still remaining in theory an amateur sport, there are a good many competitors today who make their living (directly or indirectly) from competing. But alongside the 'professional' with his string of horses there is, and always has been, the dedicated 'one-horse' amateur whose heart is just as firmly fixed on success.

Worcestershire-based rider Jo Challens competed at Badminton in the sixties on her best horse, Stranger V:

Badminton still offers a chance of greater glory for the 'one-horse' amateur: **Jo Challens** and **Stranger V**. Note again the small timbers used in the fence construction at that time (far right)

This impressive fall in 1964 (right), featured in a good many newspapers. They still finished fifteenth

would have a holiday and then go to Colonel Cockburn to be his hunter.

'Our Badminton preparation consisted of jumping anything I could find around the farm, and galloping him in our water meadows. I could usually only afford to ride at one preparatory event plus Badminton each season. To put things in context, it was such a struggle for us to keep one horse going that when I got to an event and saw a rider there with two horses of his own, it just seemed unreal!

'We went to Badminton for the first time in 1963 when it was reduced to a one-day event because of the dreadful

'We bought Stranger as a five-year-old from Althea Gifford's parents. He had been hunted and had won some hunter trials, but he had turned out to be pretty wild and not really cut out to be a showjumper, which is what the Giffords had wanted, so we bought him. Mum had to sell her jewellery to pay for him! I had always wanted to event, but finding the money to do it was a constant problem. My parents farmed and loved horses, though Dad would rather I had gone point-to-pointing and showing. But at the time there weren't many ladies' races, so I wasn't that keen – though if I had known then that one day I would have been allowed to ride in the Grand National, I might have thought differently.

'I spent three months at Edy Goldman's as a working pupil, although in those days, generally, there wasn't the amount of instruction and encouragement that there is today. To support my competing we had hunter liveries on the farm in the winter, and I worked on the farm in the summer. Even Stranger had to pay his way – I could not afford to compete him for the whole season, so after Badminton he

weather. The first two fences were brush fences, but the second one had a big ditch on the landing side. Everyone seemed to be "popping" over both and landing in the ditch at the second one, and of course no one had had the benefit of the steeplechase to get them going. So when it was my turn I set off like the clappers and cleared this bogey fence. Despite several stops we finished sixth – as only six of us completed!

'In 1964 we had quite an impressive fall which split my breeches! I had to borrow the money to buy another pair to wear in the showjumping the next day! We finished fifteenth.

'Our last Badminton was in 1965 where we finished twelfth – Stranger was usually handicapped by a pretty appalling dressage mark! I also took him to Wylye that autumn, but he started to refuse when he was asked to jump downhill, so I retired him to the hunting field. Colonel Cockburn hunted him for some years and then, when he needed an even gentler life, he went to a friend in the Berkley country.'

Jo still events, but as is the case with so many riders, has to sell on her horses to help pay the way.

# 1963

# A winter washout

**Susan Fleet** and **The Gladiator** hold the unique record of winning Badminton's only 'one-day-event'

Struck once more by appalling weather conditions, for the first time Badminton could not go on, or at least not as planned. Rather than cancelling the event altogether, however, it was decided to run it as a one-day horse trials; this meant the steeplechase and roads and tracks phases were cut out completely, and competitors performed their dressage, followed by showjumping and then a shortened cross-country course. Susan Fleet and The Gladiator won the main section, with the Junior Stakes (Little Badminton) going to Sergeant Ben Jones and Master Bernard.

## Taking care of the horses

Right from the very beginning, the welfare of the horse has been paramount in the sport of eventing. In 1949, at the very first Badminton, horses were assessed for their physical fitness before the first phase, the dressage, and again before the final showjumping phase. Until 1973 the first horse inspection was carried out at the end of the first day of dressage, which meant that when the dressage ran over two days, some horses had already started the competition whilst others were due to start the following day. In 1973 the first horse inspection was moved to Wednesday evening, before any horse had started the dressage phase.

At the inspection each horse is led up in hand in front of a specially appointed committee; in those days the committee consisted of two members, one of which had to be a veterinary officer. In 1949 the 'horse examiners' were Colonel C. Townsend CBE, MC, FRCVS, and Lt Col the Hon Guy Cubitt DSO, TD; the inspection was held in the stable yard at Badminton. At the second inspection the committee is obliged to exclude from continuing in the competition any horse which is obviously exhausted or lame, or which has been treated during the competition with anti-tetanus drugs, sedatives or stimulants.

Today, the same horse inspections are carried out, but they are undertaken by the ground jury, comprising three members, and a veterinary delegate. In the ten-minute box each horse is checked for soundness, his heart and respiration rates are monitored, and his temperature is taken; as long as the readings drop to an acceptable level during the ten-minute halt, horse and rider may continue onto the cross-country phase. The final horse inspection on the morning of the showjumping phase is to ensure that the horse is fit enough to carry out the final test without damaging himself.

By 1984 the horse inspections had become almost an event in their own right, with many people making the most of the chance to see so many of the world's top event horses at such close quarters. Moreover, by moving the venue from the stable yard to the front of Badminton House, far larger numbers of spectators could be catered for. Nowadays, each horse is trotted up in front of the Ground Jury. Up until 1996 'the voice of Badminton', Major Ronnie Dallas, announced solemnly whether the horse had passed or failed, this task is now undertaken by Mike Tucker.

One year Lucinda Green tripped up as she trotted her horse past the jury; after announcing that the horse had passed, Major Dallas quickly added 'Lucinda Green – failed!'

**The ten-minute halt** In 1963, the year the Badminton Three-Day Event was cancelled, a new initiative had been introduced: this was the 'ten-minute halt'. After completing the first three sections of the speed and endurance test – Phases A, B and C – there would be a compulsory ten-minute 'halt' or rest, in a marked-out enclosure known as the ten-minute box; here the horse would be checked over by a committee of two judges and a veterinary official. At the same time he might be washed down and refreshed by his rider and groom, and adjustments to tack and equipment could be made. However, if the panel deemed the horse unfit to continue, he would not be allowed to start the cross-country phase.

**Colonel Babe Moseley** The larger-than-life figure of 'Babe' Moseley was a familiar one at Badminton right from its inception. He assisted both Colonel Trevor Horn and Colonel Gordon Cox-Cox with their directorship of the event and the design of the cross-country course until 1964, when he and Gordon Cox-Cox both retired.

On leaving school the young Moseley had desperately wanted to go to sea. He started his naval training at Dartmouth, but suffered so badly from sea sickness that he had to 'change course', and switched to the army. He was adjutant to the Somerset Yeomanry who were sent out to Palestine during the war as a mounted regiment.

**Colonel 'Babe' Moseley** with **Colonel Gordon Cox-Cox**

He was appointed senior liaison officer between Montgomery and the commander of the fleet, Cunningham. One of the 'small tasks' allotted him was to get the Greek Prime Minister into Cairo and back for a meeting without the Germans finding out! After this sort of responsibility the organisational skills needed for Badminton must have seemed very easy indeed!

Babe Moseley was born and brought up in Anglesey, in Wales; his family was famous for the Moseley mackintosh. Babe was a keen race-rider, and rode for Derbyshire's 'Ma Hollands'; he became champion amateur jockey before a bad fall at Cheltenham broke his back and ended his race-riding career. It was only then that he began to develop the rotund figure by which he was so easily recognised – although it has been noted that 'he remained a wonderful dancer!'

After the Helsinki Games of 1952, 'Babe' surprised his many friends who always thought of him as the 'eternal batchelor' by announcing he was to marry Kay Green. It was Kay who encouraged his continuing interest in eventing.

Babe was a great supporter of young event riders, and chaired the Junior Selection Committee for many years.

# 1964

# The curious thing about M'Lord Connelly

Victory in 1964 went to Captain James Templer and M'Lord Connelly who in the course of their career together saw their fair share of eventing's highs and lows. The problem with M'Lord Connelly was that although he could be stunning, he did have a stop in him, and no one ever knew when he might choose to produce it.

In January 1961 Captain Templer bought the 16.2hh Anglo Arab from a Mrs Bunney. However, when the horse arrived at his army base Captain Templer saw that he had two appalling curbs. He tried to return him to Mrs Bunney, but to no avail, but the outcome was one he was never to regret. Their first year was a great success: they won a point-to-point which was their first competitive outing together, and then won two Foxhunter showjumping classes and both Woburn and Tweseldown Horse Trials. The following year

M'Lord Connelly was second at Little Badminton but at the Fontainebleau CIC they were eliminated for three refusals. Later in 1962 they won the selection trial at Eridge for the Burghley European Championships, but were left off the team. However, entered as individuals they duly won the gold medal, and at the end of the season were presented with the Tony Collings Memorial Trophy and the Calcutta Light Horse Trophy for the horse and rider winning the most points.

Convinced that they would win Badminton in 1963 it was a major disappointment when it was reduced to a one-day event. But all was not lost, because they competed at the Munich three-day event where they won the team and individual gold medals. As James Templer recalls, 'It was the only time he really felt as if he would not put in a stop. Our next target was Badminton in 1964, and we confounded everyone by not having a single competitive outing prior to the event. I felt it was the right way to produce Connelly at his best, but the Badminton form pundits didn't like not knowing how we had "wintered!" However, it was the right approach, as we won with a 27-point margin over Jeremy Smith Bingham and By Golly.'

Like his horse, James Templer (now a Major-General) was something of an all-round athlete. Before concentrating on eventing, he was the British cross-country skiing champion, and at the time his general had given him the choice of taking part in the winter Olympics or joining the King's Troop. He opted for the King's Troop, having already successfully evented on 'his grand little military charger, Colleen'. It was soon after this that he bought M'Lord Connelly.

At Badminton in 1964 Captain Templar and Connelly gained maximum bonuses on the steeplechase and recorded the fastest cross-country round of the day; regarding speed, he made an interesting point: 'At Badminton, and indeed at any big three-day event, I always ran beside my horse for the entire length of the roads and tracks. It was quite common then, and it must make a huge difference to the horse in terms of saving his energy and strength, and yet today it is very rarely seen. I was also quite a specialist at going very fast and taking the shortest possible route. The course still wasn't roped in those days, and I made sure I stuck to the straightest possible line between fences. Having walked the course once, I always rewalked it from back to front, as this is the best way to ascertain the straightest line between two points. It was quite common for me to gallop straight at groups of spectators if they happened to have strayed onto the line I had in mind. They usually moved pretty quickly!

'That year we also won the Prince of Wales Cup and the King's Cup at the Royal Tournament. Not surprisingly there was great expectation hanging over us when we arrived for the 1964 Tokyo Olympics. We were fourth after the dressage, but were then eliminated at the third fence from home. Just before the Olympics I had put Connelly up for sale as I knew I was about to be posted for active service in Borneo, and this was hardly the situation in which to keep an event horse! The American Mike Plumb bought him, after some stiff negotiating. The American team vet said that Connelly was blind in one eye. Peter Scott Dunn was asked for a second opinion and said the horse was fine, but it had put a doubt in Mike's mind and so I had to drop the price to secure the deal.

'I only found out recently that there had been a terrible furore at home about my selling Connelly, and specifically about how unpatriotic I was to have sold the horse. I was stuck in Borneo and knew nothing about the fuss, but as usual it was a case of people thinking the worst, rather than asking why I had to sell him. Connelly was very successful in America; he won the US Championships three times with three different riders, and was reserve for the Mexico Olympics. But the most curious thing of all about him came to light some years later, when I met Mike Plumb at Princess Anne and Captain Mark Phillips' engagement party; I remember saying that I presumed dear M'Lord Connelly was long gone, but he told me that in fact he had only been put down two weeks previously and he was blind in both eyes!

'Connelly really was an extremely able horse, and there never was another to match him.' James Templer retired from the army in 1991.

## Fun and fisticuffs!

Irish Olympic rider Tony Cameron finished third with Black Salmon at Badminton in this year. Cameron first rode at Badminton in 1960, of which attempt he observed: 'I think I broke the record for the highest number of penalties, because I fell at least five times and had no end of refusals. My uncle gave me a tenner for getting round! My own background was racing and hunting, but during the sixties any Irishman with a half-decent horse was welcome to prepare for the Olympics, and after that first Badminton I was selected as "cannon fodder" to go into training for the Olympics. I rode at Rome where the Irish team came sixth; we could have done far better but we all went off to see the Pope and missed the chance to walk the showjumping course – we were too late even to see the course plan! Dear Harry Freeman-Jackson missed a turning flag, which you had to pass in order to cover the right distance, so he was eliminated which dropped our overall score. However, as he had lent me his horse, Sonnet, to ride at the Games I really wasn't in any position to bear him any hard feelings!

'Throughout my competitive career I was always very torn between eventing and racing and of course when I went off eventing I always lost the good race rides I had been promised and could never get them back! I rode a horse called Dignity in 1962 who was

# The 1960s

**Black Salmon** and **Tony Cameron**, third in 1964

fourth at Badminton and had also been fourth in the Grand National.

'Black Salmon was a home-bred, broken-down racehorse, but took to eventing incredibly well. He was a 16.1hh black gelding by Papist, and was ten the year we went to Badminton; later that year at the Tokyo

Olympics he was fourth. His success meant that a lot of people were interested in buying him. Then someone took him out of his stable the day after the Olympic three-day event to try him as a showjumper and he broke down again. He came back to fitness and was ridden at one more event by my brother-in-law, but then he broke down a third time.

'Badminton itself was always wonderfully entertaining. Major Laurence Rook and his wife Jane were always very kind to the Irish. The sport as a whole did not get too serious until sponsorship came in. When I was third in 1964 I won enough money to buy a new saddle; nowadays it would be enough to buy a new car.

'We were perhaps spoilt in Ireland as there were so few of us eventing then. If you went into training you knew you would get into a team, so there was never too much rivalry to worry about. But the English always kept us greatly amused; the competition was so much fiercer between the different English "camps" that there was always plenty of fighting, both physical and verbal!'

## End of another era

Badminton 1964 marked the end of the enduring partnership of Colonel Gordon Cox-Cox and Colonel Babe Moseley. Gordon Cox-Cox had been director of Badminton for the previous ten years, and Babe Moseley had assisted both Gordon and the previous director, Colonel Trevor Horn. All three are remembered by those who knew them as the most marvellous and kind men. It is worth bearing in mind that their successor, Colonel Frank Weldon, had such an enormous impact on the event when he took over, that it is all too easy for the memory of the early Badminton management to fade. But his predecessors were undoubtedly the men 'for the moment' – right for that particular stage in the development of both Badminton and the sport as a whole.

---

### Facts and figures 1964

First prize: The Whitbread Trophy and £400.

Little Badminton: The Whitbread Tankard and £150.

£10 to each rider completing the event.

£5 to each groom whose horse completed the event.

**Entry fee:** £5 if qualified and entered before 1 March 1964; £10 if qualified and entered by 5 April 1964.

**Qualifications:** Riders had to be members of the BHS and seventeen years or over on 16 April 1964.

Horses had to be registered, and must have been foaled in or before 1958. They had to have won at least £15 in horse trials, and to have completed at least two qualifying competitions, ie an Intermediate/Open horse trials or a three-day event. To qualify to start, they must have completed a qualifying competition since the start of the 1963 season.

# Dissent in the camp

The fact that Badminton was evolved originally to help train and prepare riders to achieve success at the Olympic Games means that the two are forever linked in people's minds; indeed, over the years Badminton has become a major trial for potential Olympic riders from many different countries. It is probably not so evident today, but certainly in the past it was felt that the 'post-Olympic' Badminton should be, and usually was, quite a kind course, with the severity gradually increasing over the following three years so that the course was at its most difficult in the Olympic year. For many years the prize money also increased or decreased depending on the four-yearly 'Olympic cycle'.

Every sport seems to attract its own 'armchair brigade' – those that sit and watch and criticise. Conveniently forgetting that they have the benefit of hindsight, they tell you that obviously the wrong team was chosen for this Olympics or that. The British team had failed to complete at the Tokyo Olympics in 1964, and so the build-up to Badminton 1965 brought with it a flurry of letters in the press about how useless our riders were! In more recent years, the failure of Britain to win a medal at the Barcelona Olympics in 1992 brought a similar outpouring of scorn on the luckless riders who represented us, and the system that selected them – perhaps some comfort may be taken from the fact that complaining after the event is a scourge that has always been with us!

Another subject that quite possibly had some tongues wagging was the decision of the present Duke of Beaufort, who had taken over as director of Badminton after the retirement of Gordon Cox-Cox, to ask Frank Weldon to design the cross-country course. Frank attracted criticism because not only had he been chef d'équipe of the medal-less Tokyo Olympic team, but in a post-Olympic year when everyone was expecting a relatively easy course, he actually increased the dimensions of nearly every single fence! However, the cross-country route which he produced has been broadly used ever since, although he kept the Lake as the final fence, which it no longer is today. But its dimensions under Frank's rule came much closer to that which

we expect nowadays: for instance, whereas in the fifties the competitors had to jump a 2ft 9in rail into water, in 1965 Frank put a 3ft 8in log in front of it!

## Another win for Ireland

In 1965 Eddie Boylan won Badminton, riding Durlas Eile. Despite always sending over a strong contingent to contest Badminton, Ireland had not produced an overall winner since Mark Darley's victory with Emily Little in 1952.

Major Eddie Boylan had finished tenth at the first Badminton in 1949, but in 1965 it was a first visit for the 17hh Durlas Eile. This big brown gelding by Artist's Son out of Royal Cob had been bought by the Irish army, but was put up for sale when they decided his showjumping was not good enough. However, Eddie Boylan bought him and got on suffi-

Having won Little Badminton the previous year, **Sheila Waddington** (née Willcox) was third with **Glenamoy** in the 1965 Great Badminton Championship

# The 1960s

ciently well with him to finish fourth at Burghley in l964. At Badminton they took the lead in the dressage and gave a fluent performance across country, exhibiting their genuine enjoyment and mastery of this phase. Two showjumps down was disappointing, but not so bad as to lose them the top slot.

bother about Phase E, the run in – I headed off for my breakfast instead!' recalls Eddie. 'I was riding down Constitutional Hill one morning when suddenly I remembered I had an important appointment to keep. The quickest way back to base was to ride up the steps and through the Duke of Wellington monument.

**Major Eddie Boylan**, seen here winning Badminton in 1965 with **Durlas Eile**, is a member of the Ground Jury for Badminton's fiftieth anniversary three-day event. He also rode at the very first Badminton

Eddie Boylan had found himself based in London while he was preparing for the first Badminton Three-Day Event in 1949. 'I made the most of my situation by doing all my training in Hyde Park! The hack to the park counted as Phase A, then there was a good piece of ground I used to gallop on for the same distance as the steeplechase, then it was another hack around the edge of the park for Phase C before cantering at "cross-country speed" through the park until I had covered the necessary distance for that phase. I didn't

As we clattered up the steps my horse decided to go to the loo – which must have left a few people scratching their heads as to how on earth a load of horse droppings came to be deposited on the monument steps!

'I was twenty-four when I rode at the first Badminton and so I kept my mouth firmly shut as I walked the course and listened to the likes of John Shedden and Tony Collings. My horse, Cool Star, was a middleweight hunter type, but proved to be an excellent all-rounder. In 1949 he did Badminton, showjumped in the King's

Cup at the Royal International, and we did our first Prix St George dressage competition.

'I had been worried about his stamina – or lack of it – all along, hence the long treks around Hyde Park. He seemed to be going well on the cross-country until we slipped on landing over one fence and he went down on his knees. I was still on board and he tried to get up, but his legs slipped from under him again. I thought he must be exhausted so I stepped off to make it easier for him; he jumped up happily and we carried on to finish tenth. Afterwards I confided to Brigadier Lyndon Bolton that I was really fed up with my performance; I felt that I could have gone faster as my horse finished the course quite happily. He looked at me and said. "The day you complete a three-day event to your entire satisfaction is the day you should retire." I was horrified – here I was just starting out in a sport I was determined to perfect, and someone was telling me that when I achieved perfection I should give up! Lyndon Bolton obviously spotted my disappointment because he countered it with the comment "Don't worry, Eddie, no one ever completes a three-day event to their complete satisfaction!"

'He was right of course. Even when I won in 1965 on Durlas Eile there were things I would have liked to have done better. For instance, we had a showjump down and a foot in the water to incur twenty penalties on the last day. Only a clear round would have completely satisfied me. We led after the dressage, and a fast clear cross-country round put us far enough ahead to get away with the mistakes this time. Luck must have been on our side because there was some stiff opposition, with Bill Roycroft and Eldorado taking second, and Sheila Willcox and Glenamoy third.

'Durlas Eile had originally been bought by the Irish army, but they sold him because of his poor showjumping ability. But I got on well with him; he turned out to be a fabulous horse who always tried his best for you. We were second at Badminton in 1967. When he was thirteen I sold him to Canada for £19,000, which was an awful lot of money. I had estate duties to pay and couldn't afford to turn down such an offer. Barry Sushine rode him and they won

the Eastern Canadian Championships when Durlas Eile was seventeen. When they decided to retire him they offered him back to me, and a very generous benefactor paid his fare back home. He stayed with us until he had to be put down at the age of twenty-three.'

## The record-breaking Bill Roycroft

In 1965 the Australian Bill Roycroft became the first person to complete one Badminton on three horses (see also 1960). The only other to achieve this distinction was Lorna Clarke (née Sutherland) in 1970, although her placings were not as high as Bill's.

Bill's remarkable performance meant that he covered a total of forty-seven miles on speed and endurance day – and covered it well! In the Great Badminton Championship he was second with Eldorado: this twelve-year-old 16.2hh chestnut gelding was by Concise out of

The gallant **Stoney Crossing**, who was placed in the Cheltenham Gold Cup, the Aintree Foxhunter Steeplechase, and Badminton, all within a month

# The 1960s

a mare called Myntie; he had been seventh at the Tokyo Olympics with Bill the previous year, and at Badminton in this year he jumped the only clear showjumping round, which put him ahead of Sheila Waddington (née Willcox) and Glenamoy. Bill's other ride in the main competition was the magnificent Stoney Crossing, a 16.3hh, six-year-old brown race-horse by North Riding out of Sunlight Stream. Stoney Crossing had been lent to Australian Brian Cobcroft to ride at the Tokyo Olympics, and then with Bill in 1965 he was placed in both the Cheltenham Gold Cup and the Aintree Foxhunters' steeplechases, just a few weeks before Badminton. His racing background did not help him in the showjumping, however, where he had three fences down, causing him to drop to sixth place. In the Little Badminton Event Bill took second place on Avatar; this was the last year this competition was held. Avatar was a six-year-old grey gelding, just under 16hh, by Rawston Manor out of Avarice. Little Badminton in 1965 was won by Martin Whiteley and The Poacher.

## Bill Roycroft's horses

Our Solo was born in 1950 in Western Victoria, Australia. He was by the pony stallion Royal Welkin out of a Thoroughbred mare, and had been bred by Bill Henry who wanted a racing pony. He was only 15hh, but this was still too big for pony racing and so the wiry brown gelding was broken to ride and drive. He was bought by a friend of Bill Roycroft's for his children to ride, but as he soon began to get the better of the whole family, it was suggested that Bill should ride him. Bill liked him straightaway, and bought him to use for polocross; after two successful seasons they turned their attention to showjumping and eventing. In 1960 Our Solo won Badminton, and Olympic team gold in Rome; he was also a grade A showjumper and an excellent stock horse. He was retired from international event-ing when he was twelve, and Bill's children rode him at Pony Club events. He then went to a family friend, Joan Palmer, to play polocross again, and then to enjoy a quieter life as her hack. He was put down in 1975.

In 1965 Bill Roycroft rode Stoney Crossing into sixth place at Badminton. He had already made history by being the first — and only — man to complete a single Badminton on three horses, but his achievements with Stoney Crossing alone were quite exceptional. Having hunted him throughout the winter in England, Stoney Crossing was entered for the Cheltenham Gold Cup, where Bill rode him into third place behind Arkle and Mill House. Ten days later the intrepid pair took part in the Foxhunters' round Liverpool's Grand National course; they fell at the Chair, but Bill remounted and finished sixth. Ten days after that he rode three horses at Badminton: Stoney Crossing finished sixth, Eldorado was second, and Avatar was second in the Little Badminton Event.

Stoney Crossing (see p89) was actually given to Bill by Sir Alec Cressick who bred a lot of racehorses in Australia. As Bill recalls, 'At the Rome Olympics I had lent one of my horses, Sabre, to Brian Crago to ride in the team. Sabre broke down after the cross-coun-try, but Sir Alec promised me then that he would give me another horse to replace him. Anyway, years went by and I was never given another one or heard any more about it, until I saw him at a race meeting: he hadn't forgotten his promise, and showed me the horse he wanted me to have. It was Stoney Crossing. He asked what I would do with him, and I said we would go and win the Novice three-day event in Australia in six months' time — which we did. Then I took him to England for the 1965 season where he raced and came sixth at Badminton.

'We were staying at the Bullens' home in Didmarton at the time, and Stoney Crossing was turned out in a field there to rest. A chap from Doncaster came down to buy a show-jumping horse from me, and he asked what I was going to do with Stoney Crossing. When I said he would be for sale, he bought him then and there. Bearing in mind that he was fat and unfit having been turned away, we were all surprised to see him running in a steeplechase a fortnight later. He won the race, but did not race again after that — although I know he stayed sound enough for the man to hunt him a bit.'

**Eldorado** gave **Bill Roycroft** the best result from his three rides in 1965. They finished second

# Frank Weldon makes his mark

Having had two years to settle into his new role and to work out exactly what he wanted, competitors were greeted with a real taste of Frank Weldon's course-designing skills when they returned to Badminton in 1967. David Somerset (the present Duke of Beaufort) had also achieved what he had really wanted since the retirement of Gordon Cox-Cox in 1964, and that was to give Frank Weldon his own title of director of Badminton, and to take a step sideways himself, becoming chairman of the event.

Frank knew that he needed to make Badminton commercially viable: it was not going to be enough simply to be a good course designer – in order to survive, Badminton had to make money. Closed-circuit television was introduced for the first time so that spectators could see what was happening on different parts of the course; in fact this innovation proved the downfall of Bill Roycroft two years later when the head of the Ground Jury happened to see on the television screen his horse hesitate at the Gravel Pits, and decided to overrule the fence judge and give him twenty penalties for a refusal (see 1960, Bill Roycroft). Little Badminton and the many show classes that used to be held throughout the event had all gone: for maximum impact, Badminton needed to stand on its own two feet. To add excitement to the climax of the competiton, it was announced that the showjumping phase would be run in reverse order of merit, as it still is today.

The cross-country course provoked much discussion; an innovative new fence was the Shark's Teeth which, Frank Weldon assured readers of his regular articles, would ride better than it looked. There was a novel version of the Trakhener in the form of 'The Tripods', and the Quarry was now near the end of the course. Frank Weldon was already well into his enduring principle of building fences to frighten the riders rather than the horses. He put far greater emphasis on 'horsemanship', making the riders use their brains as well as raw courage to earn their rewards. Despite all this, the number of spectators was felt to have fallen. The weather turned out to be fair, but worse had been predicted, and this could have

discouraged many from coming; also the entry charge of £3 per car could well have put off even more. Those who arrived early enough (and whose conscience didn't trouble them) parked on the grass verges surrounding the Badminton estate and walked in!

## Celia Ross-Taylor

In 1967 the Badminton title was won by Celia Ross-Taylor and Johnathan. Even as a young girl, Celia Ross-Taylor was determined to achieve success with horses; whilst a member of the Staff College and Sandhurst Pony Club she was already buying cheap ponies to bring on and sell in order to finance her eventing career. Her talent and dedication were quickly recognised, and Celia and her family were more than grateful for the help and kindness shown to them by others. As Celia's mother recalls,

A clear showjumping performance moved **Celia Ross-Taylor** and **Johnathan** up from third place to victory

# The 1960s

**Building Badminton: The Willis Family** Much of the success or otherwise of a cross-country course depends not only on its design, but on how well it is built. When the Badminton course first took shape in 1949 the man charged with its building was the Duke of Beaufort's head forester, Charlie Chappell: it was Colonel Trevor Horn who came up with the ideas and designs, but he needed a 'craftsman' to bring them into being. Also employed was George Stoneham, whose building firm 'Edwards' worked under contract to the estate: they provided some of the more elaborate craftwork needed to give the fences their imposing, yet attractive appearance. The 'portable' brush fences which were put into place each year for Phase B, the steeplechase, were Stoneman's idea, too.

The **Willis family** team: Alan (left) with sons Tim (centre) and James (right). Family pet Alfie looks ready for action

George Stoneman was assisted by a young man called Alan Willis, one of four brothers whose father had his own hurdle-making and estate-fencing business. When George Stoneham retired, Alan Willis took on the course-building. The first Badminton course that the 'Willis Bros' built as a company was that of 1967. As their reputation grew, they took on more and more course-building and racecourse work, and now the company has world-wide contracts, such as the building of the Sydney Olympic three-day event course.

Whilst the skills required have remained much the same over the years, the size of the timber used has changed enormously – and therefore the machinery needed to handle and shape it. Photographs of the original fences show that one man could easily hold up a rail himself whilst bolting it into position; now, a tree trunk would probably be used, which might require a JCB to lift it. From a safety point of view the rails and uprights are now roped rather than bolted together so that they can be quickly dismantled should a horse get stuck in a fence. Another concern that has become of increasing priority over the years is that of the 'groundwork': the work done to ensure that take-off and landing areas remain reliable whatever the weather conditions.

'There was always someone willing to give her a lift to competitions, and a very dear friend, the late Joan Cross, gave her free lessons.' Celia had won the Pony Club Championships for two years running, and she rode at her first Badminton in 1959 when she was eighteen. Her horse was not really good enough for a course of this severity, but despite two falls they completed the event.

Her next horse, Johnathan, was to reward her with the ultimate prize. He was a 16.1½hh bay Anglo Arab gelding by Amigo out of My Fair Lady, and had been bred by Betty Keys. Celia recalls how she finally came to own him: 'I first saw him in the field, but could not try him as he had slipped on the lunge and hurt his back. Some time later I had a fall from another horse and was stuck on crutches with a broken femur. Betty Keys approached me again and said I could buy Johnathan quite cheaply as there was a 50/50 chance that his back injury would be a recurring problem. I paid £250 for him and turned him away for six months to give him time to strengthen up. When he came back into work he quickly took to eventing. In 1966, as a six-year-old, he won the points championship, having won Tidworth, Wylye and Chatsworth.

'Badminton was such good fun; the cross-country was pretty big, but we didn't find it too startling. There was a strange tripod fence, and an unusual Luckington Lane crossing with offset fences, but they all rode better than they walked. There were two walls which could be jumped individually or as a corner; Johnathan had always been a very accurate jumper so we were one of the few to jump the corner, but all the way to it I was still trying to decide if it was worth the risk!

'We were lying third at the end of cross-country day, and the thing I remember most was the amazing way in which we suddenly found ourselves moving up the leader board. We showjumped clear, which although I had quietly hoped we would, was still really more than I had dreamed of. Derek Allhusen came in with Lochinvar and had a disastrous round – five fences down – which dropped him to eleventh. Then almost unbelievably, Eddie Boylan and his 1965 winner Durlas Eile had

two fences down to drop to second place. We won £350 and a new saddle!

'After Badminton we were shortlisted for the European Championships in France, but Johnathan went lame with his old back trouble and had to have more time off. He was fit again in 1969 when he won Tidworth and was sixth at Badminton, but after that I didn't compete him very much, as it was obvious that his back would continue to trouble him. He was retired and then put down at the age of twenty-one. I still bring on and sell young horses, mainly abroad. I know it is unlikely ever to happen, but riding at Badminton was such a great thrill that I would be more than happy to do it again.'

**Count Jasper** (above) was bought for Polly Hely-Hutchinson as a four-year-old. He finished fifth at Burghley as a six-year-old, and went to Badminton in 1967 when he was eight. Despite being given twenty penalties for a 'hesitation' at the Quarry, they finished third — without the stop they would have won by a point! They were fifth at Badminton in 1969 and were part of the gold medal-winning team at the Haras du Pin European Championships in France. Polly married Hamish Lochore soon after this and Jasper was retired to act as a 'school master' for a young girl; her interest in him helped her to overcome anorexia. He died of a heart attack at the age of nineteen. Polly and her family run the Burgie Eventing Centre, and also the centre's three-day event, in Scotland.

**Major Ronnie Dallas** Those who attended the first and final horse inspections until 1996 will be familiar with the calm, level voice of Major Ronnie Dallas delivering the verdict of the veterinary panel – either pass or fail – and thereby announcing either the beginning or the end of so many hopes. As so many of the 'old guard' who have helped Badminton become the world-class event it is today, Major Dallas was brought up on the tough but enjoyable regime of horses, hounds and the army. Having ridden and hunted from the age of seven, it was surely only natural that on rejoining his regiment in Germany, he took a small pack of hounds with him – but before all that there was a war to fight!

He recalls: 'Having joined a squadron of my regiment (3rd The King's Own Hussars) in 1941 we were sent out to the Dutch East Indies. We landed in Sumatra the day that Singapore fell, and then went to Java which immediately surrendered to the Japanese. We spent three months trying to avoid capture and to find a ship to escape in, but then the natives, who were by that time terrified of the Japanese, turned us in. I spent three years building a railway across Sumatra as part of a POW work force. Sadly many of my fellow prisoners died of overwork and semi-starvation. But I was young, fit, and a lightweight, and this must have helped me survive. When we finally heard that the war was over, we took control of the camp and soon received medical help and proper rations. But this aid came too late for many of my comrades who were by that time desperately ill. It was truly heartbreaking that they should live to see the end of the war, but not survive to enjoy freedom.

'After the war I was with the North Somerset Yeomanry but living at Castle Coombe, and from there started hunting with the Duke of Beaufort. I rode at Badminton once, in 1951, on a hunter mare that had been kindly loaned to Captain Tony Collings by Ted Marsh. We did not get on very well together and had two falls, including one on the steeplechase. We finally got as far as the Coffin and my excuse is that, as crowd control wasn't very good in those days, she couldn't see where she had to go! Whatever the reason she wasn't to be persuaded to tackle the Coffin, and we had to retire. I was then asked by the Hunt secretary at that time, Colonel Scott, whether I would help with the many showjumping and showing classes that used to be held alongside the event. When he retired as Hunt secretary I was delighted to be invited to take over his role. I remained as the Beaufort Hunt secretary from 1957 to 1987. I also took over from Colonel Babe Moseley as Badminton's stable-yard manager, a post I held until 1996.

'Thanks to Badminton's stud groom, Brian Higham, the task of preparing and running the stable yard during the three-day event is not as complicated as one might expect. The yard is fully occupied with hunt horses until shortly before the event, so there is very little time in which to rough them all off, then scrub, whitewash and generally "spring clean" the whole place. But Brian always manages to run a very happy yard, and that is an essential part of the relaxed atmosphere that the event enjoys. Clearing up after it all is an equally mammoth task, especially as the temporary stable staff will have left by then and so it is the permanent faithfuls who have to see to it.

'Most competitors arrive on Tuesday or Wednesday of Badminton week, although a few overseas riders may arrive as early as the previous weekend. Before being stabled each horse is checked over by a vet, mainly to guard against any contagious illness. Once everyone has "put their horse to bed" everything settles down pretty quickly. We provide feed, forage and bedding for all the competitors, and work hard to ensure that everyone ends up with what they want. There is generally a very good atmosphere throughout, although some riders get a bit tight-lipped on cross-country morning and before the final horse inspection. Communications are generally much better now; for instance, there are loudspeakers in each yard connected to the stable manager's office so messages can be passed on quickly.'

Obviously Major Dallas has witnessed the growth of Badminton during his long involvement with the event, and for many years he was a mounted steward on speed and endurance day: 'Now that's a wonderful way to see the event and meet all your friends, as you are so visible to everyone! All the stewarding is done very efficiently these days. Mind you, the crowds are probably easier to control now since the drink-driving laws came in, and the officials and stewards are obviously very sober! Many years ago that was not always the case – having a job at Badminton was a very sociable affair, and the wine and the whisky flowed freely. Colonel Weldon was the first to really clamp down seriously on that side of things – and quite rightly. The sport today is very professional, and there is no room for avoidable errors.'

Sitting at home, having exercised his hunter already that morning, Major Ronnie Dallas looks and sounds very much like an error-free zone.

**Brian Higham Stud Groom** Brian first came to help out on the Badminton estate in 1959 and was 'promoted' to stud groom in 1966. His full-time responsibility is the care of the Duke of Beaufort's hunt horses, but by the time of the Badminton Three-Day Event the hunt horses are turned out, and the magnificent nineteenth-century stable yard is used to accommodate the horse trials' entrants. Even the most cos-

setted event horses would be unlikely to find better accommodation than that offered to them at Badminton. The large, airy internal stables have changed little from the day they were built in 1880; they even retain the original flagstone floors, although they have been updated with the installation of electricity and automatic water drinkers.

In the weeks before the event every stable is cleaned out and disinfected, and then each competitor's choice of bedding is put down ready for the arrival of the horses. 'Badminton is a very busy time for us, but also a special time,' recalls Brian. 'With so much going on you are on quite a "high" – and then when it's all over you feel almost jet-lagged!'

Brian is the first to acknowledge that the Badminton estate stable yard is probably one of the last big yards still to be run on traditional lines. Such large establishments are expensive to maintain, and many big estates have sold them off to be converted into apartments. But as Brian says, 'Living at Badminton is a bit like living in a cocoon, in that you are almost totally protected from what is going on in the "outside" world.'

Brian has a reputation of running a happy yard, and that has a lot to do with the relaxed atmosphere that prevails, even in the face of the tension that normally takes over at a three-day event competition: if you walked off the street into the stable yard you would never guess that these horses are in the middle of one of the toughest tests of their lives. And as long as you are willing to share a joke with Brian he would probably be delighted to show you round what is so evidently his pride and joy.

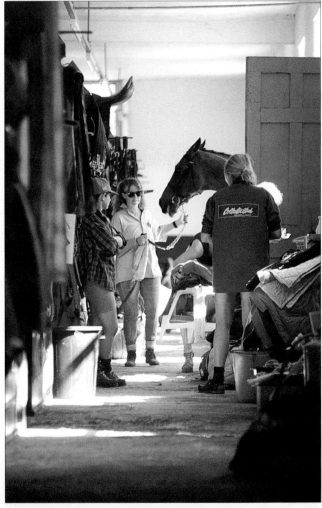

Left: Brian Higham on duty at the vet check in 1998
Top: Lucinda Green arrives at Badminton in 1985
Above: Always a buzz of activity in the stables on cross-country day
Opposite: Brian Higham: always ready with a fund of tales and terrible jokes!

# The 1960s

**Press and publicity** Under Frank Weldon's guidance, Badminton continued to try to increase its profile in order to guarantee the greatest publicity and ensure commercial viability. In the 1968 programme, drawings of the fences were included for the first time; these were produced by Caroline Bromley Gardiner who has produced the drawings ever since, right up until the present day (1999). Today we would probably be most surprised if magazines such as *Eventing* and *Horse and Hound* failed to provide us with a detailed preview of the fences to be featured at Badminton each year. So it is

Above: Badminton's press officer of thirty years, **Jim Gilmore** (far right) receives the British Equestrian Federation Medal of Honour from Princess Michael of Kent and Mr Stephen Dixon, Managing Director of the Colt Car Company in 1998
Badminton's press facilities are second to none: (right) Whitbreads' hospitality marquee in 1990

fascinating to note that during the fifties and sixties the equestrian and country press felt it would be most unfair to show their readers photographs of the Badminton course; they obviously considered that such a preview would be in breach of the rule which says competitors must not be allowed prior knowledge of the course to be jumped. Some would argue that this should be the case today, as more than one competitor has admitted to setting up at home a similar 'problem' to that posed by the course designer! However, since everyone has access to these preview pictures, it can probably be argued that it should have little outcome on the final result. And the publicity that previews create, in terms of attracting further press coverage and stimulating spectator interest, can only be to the good of the sport.

Publicity for the 1968 event was covered by the new press officer, Jim Gilmore, who still holds that post today. He had not been impressed by his visit to the first Badminton Three-Day Event in 1949: as a cub reporter for the *Wiltshire*

*Gazette,* he had to gather not only the results of the main event, but also of the numerous showing and showjumping classes that were held at the same time. 'I remember writing down the last lot of results late at night, using the headlights of my car,' recalls Jim, 'and I told everyone who cared to listen that I would never be visiting Badminton again. But something changed, because some years later I found myself taking a week of my holiday at Badminton so that I could concentrate on covering it, without the interruption of being called away to report on other things!'

When the late Colonel Frank Weldon took over as Badminton's director, one of the first things he did was to start to bring control of the event back to Badminton, and to the local community. He was keen to involve all those in the Beaufort Hunt country so that they would feel it was more than just *an* event – it was *their* event. At the time the press and publicity was handled by a London company, but in 1968, Frank Weldon asked Jim Gilmore to come in to see him. 'He asked me what I thought of the press facilities at Badminton,' says Jim, 'and I told him the truth ... they were pretty useless. The results were slow to get hold of, and there was always a queue to use the telephone; reporters often found it quicker to walk into the village and use a pay phone. So I was told to see if I could make a better job of it. I started on a year's trial, and I have been there ever since.

'The biggest overall change that I have witnessed has been in the standard of the press facilities. We used to have a canvas tent, a couple of trestle tables, a few telephones and a tea urn; now it is considered a premier media centre, and we have visitors from overseas coming to see how they should be organising things for their own events. In the early years there would be about forty press reporters – now we cater for about 500 media representatives. They are provided with food, drink, closed-circuit television, fax, modems, telephones and computers. The computers are pre-programmed with rider profiles, fence descriptions and so on, and the results are printed out several times a day as the competition progresses.

'It was in the early seventies that everything seemed to take off at once: the Princess Royal was competing and was romantically involved with fellow competitor Captain Mark Phillips, the motorway network was opening up at the same time, and suddenly Badminton just seemed the place to be. Our sponsors at the time, Whitbread Breweries, could see the huge potential of the event and they began to put more resources into it. Things have gone a step further with our current sponsors, Mitsubishi Motors, who took over in 1992.

'The build-up to Badminton is the most hectic time for me, and the major headache is checking the accreditation of all those applying for press passes. Once the event is under way, I have a wonderful team "behind the desk" who keep everything running smoothly. Daft as it sounds, one of the hardest jobs is getting the leading riders each day to come to the media centre to meet the press; quite understandably they want to be checking their horse, or walking the course. On the last day, however, they have no choice, and as soon as the prize-giving is over they are bundled into a vehicle and driven straight to the media centre!

'Generally things run very smoothly – I can only ever remember having to eject one photographer who was being just too much of a nuisance to the royal family. Another year the late Gypsy Joe, who was a wonderfully gifted photographer, got arrested. He had asked me if he could fix up a remote-control camera in a tree above the Ski Jump to get an interesting angle for his photographs. He had set it all up on the Friday night, but when the police discovered a contraption in the tree with wires attached to it, they decided it was a bomb and took action accordingly!

'Looking back, 1972 stands out as a great memory simply

Above: The late **Gypsy Joe** – a knight in shining armour for the rider of this horse in 1991!
Left: The 1992 winner **Mary Thomson** celebrates during a press interview
Below: **Radio Badminton** marked the start of a new concept in sports coverage

because Badminton received so much press coverage (the royal romance) and so many people attended (250,000 on cross-country day). At the opposite end of the scale, 1992 was probably the hardest year. It was bad enough explaining to the gathered media that three horses had had to be put down, but worst were the rumours that more had died – stories were being put about that five or six horses were dead, and nothing would convince them that this was not so.'

In 1998 Jim was awarded the British Equestrian Federation Medal of Honour for his thirty years of service at Badminton. He has also been the press officer at Cirencester Polo Club for twenty-five years.

Despite being privy to probably more inside information than anyone else at Badminton, he ruefully admits that he still invariably fails to predict the winner!

# 1968

## The smallest horse wins on the biggest course

This was an Olympic year, and with growing confidence in the task in hand, Frank Weldon produced what was considered to be Badminton's biggest cross-country course to date. Weldon assured competitors that it would be 'pleasant to ride – although there are, admittedly, a few places where it might be wise to approach with your eyes tight shut, on a loose rein, at about thirty miles per hour!' On the other hand, great control was needed at the Cat's Cradle, a collection of fences in Huntsman's Close. The Quarry was

looking more as it does today, with a stone wall in and the Giant Steps out. The Lake had a jetty for the first time, adding technicality to a fence which previously had required purely boldness. Fence no 12 was the one most feared by the majority of competitors: a 6ft wide ditch, followed 10ft away by a 3ft 9in post and rail — and their fears were justified, because all but one of the first fifteen contestants were eliminated here. The competitor who showed the way for the rest of the field was Lorna Clarke (née Sutherland) (see 1970).

## Our Nobby

In spite of the evident severity of the course, the eventual winner was 'the galloping nurse' Jane Bullen and the tiny Our Nobby. Officially standing at 15hh, the minimum requirement for an event horse, Jane confesses that it was quite difficult to get him to measure that height; she even admits to his having won classes for ponies 14.2hh and under! Our Nobby was a full Thoroughbred by Bewildered out of Lady Sicily, a Happy Landing mare, and he arrived on the Bullens' doorstep led by a farmer who thought Mrs Bullen might like him for her children. Jane's mother thought he might suit Frank Weldon's son George, but once Nobby had some good food inside him he became too difficult and nappy to sell on. Jane's older brother Mike and her sister Jennie (now Mrs Loriston-Clarke) did their best to 'sort him out', and eventually he was deemed suitable for Jane to ride.

At competitions his dressage always let him down, but his cross-country was so fast that he usually earned enough bonus marks to pull him up the placings. In 1967 he had been fifth at Badminton, and he had also been third at Burghley — but it was still a surprise to many that this partnership managed to win the Badminton Championship in the Olympic year. Jane was working in London as a nurse at the time, so despite the excitement of their victory, it was back to work as usual on Monday morning. In second place was Richard Meade on the nine-year-old Turnstone, owned by Lady Hugh Russell. The popular Sergeant Ben Jones had looked set to win until a showjump down

with Mrs Whiteley's Foxdor dropped him to third. Captain Mark Phillips and Rock On finished fourth. All four riders were selected for the Mexico Olympics, with Captain Phillips going as reserve and the extra team place being taken by Major Derek Allhusen. In atrocious conditions, where torrential rain had flooded much of the course, the British team won the gold medal. Derek Allhusen won individual silver. Jane and Our Nobby suffered two falls on the cross-country, each as a result of Nobby crumpling on landing when he was unable to pull his front feet out of the mud.

After Mexico Our Nobby, who was then thirteen years old, was retired to the hunting field, and Jane was glad she made this decision as he continued to be suspicious of water even out hunting, which he loved. At Badminton the following year Derek Allhusen's Olympic horse was eliminated, and Jane is convinced that this was a direct result of the stressful conditions in Mexico. Jane went on to win Badminton again in 1978, this time as Mrs Holderness-Roddam, riding Warrior (see 1978).

**Sergeant Ben Jones** achieved his best result at the great Badminton Championships when he finished third in 1968 on **Foxdor**

Opposite: Victory at Badminton earned **Jane Holderness-Roddam** (née Bullen) an Olympic ticket. They won team gold at the Mexico Olympics later that year

# 1969

# Badminton's youngest winner

**Richard Walker**, at eighteen, remains the youngest-ever winner of Badminton

Not only was the eighteen-year-old Richard Walker Badminton's youngest ever winner, he also beat one of the highest-class fields of competitors ever seen at the event. At the end of the dressage phase the top four places were held by four Olympic gold medallists: Bertie Hill, Richard Meade, Ben Jones and Bill Roycroft. Sitting happily in ninth place was Richard Walker and his 15.lhh Anglo Arab Pasha. But then cross-country day saw a complete turnaround in fortunes: Chicago fell with Bertie Hill on the steeplechase, and Barberry dropped Richard Meade in the water, lost his bridle and was retired. The Poacher was withdrawn by Ben Jones before the start of the cross-country, and fifth-placed Sheila Wilcox had a fall in Huntsman's Close – it seems that Fair and Square strained his tendons on landing over Huntsman's Leap but still tried to jump the next fence. Bill Roycroft, despite being given his questionable twenty penalties at the Quarry by Colonel Babe Moseley, moved up into second place. From amidst this catalogue of disasters,

Richard Walker produced a fast and faultless cross-country performance to take the lead, and on the next day maintained his position with a clear showjumping round. Also benefiting from a penalty-free showjumping performance was Angela Martin Bird and Grey Cloud, who moved to second place. Bill Roycroft dropped to third and fourth with Warrathoola and Furtive.

## Pasha

Pasha belonged to the Phillimores, old family friends of Richard's father. His usual jockey, Francis Phillimore, was away at Cambridge University and so Richard was lent him to ride. They won the 'boys' division' of the 1965 Pony Club Championships, and repeated this success the following year. At the suggestion of Jack and Margaret Hance, Richard spent a short time training at Waterstock with Lars and Diana Sederholm, who were to become his mentors in the eventing world. As Richard recalls, 'When you are involved in a sport which you know very little about, the direction you take is something that just happens – if you are lucky enough to be led by someone like Lars who does know the ropes there is more chance that you will make the right choices.

'As my partnership with Pasha continued to develop we felt obliged to buy him from the Phillimores so that our future together would be secure. In 1967 the inaugural Junior European Championships, which had been the brainchild of Colonel Babe Moseley, were held at Eridge, with only the British and French competing, and we won that. In 1968 it had developed into a fully fledged European Championships and was held in France, and again we won the title.

'By this time I had come to a bit of a crossroads; there had been an agreement with my parents that I could spend time as an equestrian apprentice instead of continuing my school education, but this agreement only lasted until the end of l968. So Pasha was put on the market in the spring of 1969 for the princely sum of £250. However, we were unable to find a buyer, and so he was entered for Badminton.

'We had only one hair-raising moment during our round, at the combination of fences in Huntsman's Close. Some very high deer-park paling was used to divide one option from the other, and as Pasha landed over the drop, the paling was the first thing to catch his eye. It wasn't designed to be jumped, but that made little difference to him. He hit the top of it, which luckily snapped so we stayed on our feet – and having passed legitimately between the red and the white flags, we were also unpenalised.

'Generally I was sufficiently over-awed and over-excited to remember anything very clearly about the whole occasion. I do remember returning to my bed that night, which was in the grooms' dormitory, and being asked by Mary Gordon Watson's groom if I knew anything about the very young man who was meant to be in the lead after the cross-country! I'm not sure he ever realised that I was there as a rider as well as a groom!

'Because of our success at Badminton, we were selected for the European Championships later that year in Haras du Pin. Britain won team gold, and Pasha and I took the individual silver – just beaten to the tape by Mary Gordon Watson and Cornishman V, who took the title!

'After that we felt that Pasha's success could never be bettered, and so he was retired from eventing at the age of fourteen. I continued to do some dressage and showjumping with him, and in 1970 he won the Spillers Combined Training Championship at the Horse of the Year Show. He was used at Waterstock as a schoolmaster, and then enjoyed a season's hunting with the Grafton – or at least, he enjoyed it! He proved to be a somewhat wild and eccentric hunter for Sue Watt, the very brave lady who partnered him. Eventually he returned to me again, and finally was put down in 1977.'

Since his win in 1969, Badminton has not been as successful for Richard as he would have liked. 'It is always a wonderful event to ride at, but things never seem to quite come off for me there. I was fourth in 1971 with Upper Strata – his owners, Mr and Mrs Compson Bracebridge, had "sponsored" Pasha's running costs for me for a few years and then bought me a couple more horses to ride, so that was a good result for them. My best chance after that was probably on The Accumulator. We were second to Lucinda Green after the dressage, but a stop at the Ski Jump due to his inexperience dropped us out of it. The following year he fell at the Bounce, which had been built for the first time into the Lake. Both my attempts at Badminton with Jacana involved an annoying and disappointing mistake, as did my round with him at the Barcelona Olympics in 1992,' confesses Richard. However, at the time of writing he has two young horses in his yard which he thinks are eminently suitable, so there is still time to reverse the trend.

## Grey Cloud

As a child, Angela, her brother Alistair and sister Tessa were all 'brought up on Badminton. We were taken there every year by our parents and, although in the beginning it did not occur to any of us that we would ride there, as the years went by you did start to hope that you might,' recalls Angela.

Angela's eventing career started in the Pony Club and suddenly she found herself with a nice horse which helped her to second place at Badminton. 'I had ridden there once before in 1967 on a horse called Leedora. We had 100 jumping penalties on the cross-country but we did complete. Grey Cloud was very much a fairy-tale happening. I had bought a horse which was really nappy when you tried to compete him. I had found a family in Scotland who were keen to have him as they only wanted to hack out and they offered to swap him for their horse. Grey Cloud had done a bit of everything but without any great success. He had a spavin which had worried me a bit but in the end I decided to accept the swap. We just clicked and went from there. When we found ourselves at Badminton in 1969 all I really hoped was that we would both enjoy our ride round. I was quite a long way down the field after the dressage but the cross country and showjumping caused quite a lot of trouble – we moved to fifth after the cross country and then into second with a clear showjumping round. We were asked to go on the team for the European Championships. I had to confess that Grey Cloud had a spavin and it was decided not to risk him as a team horse. As it turned out Badminton did takes its toll on Grey Cloud, and although we did a few more one-day events, he was retired soon after that.'

A fairy-tale ending for **Angela Martin-Bird** (now Craddock) and **Grey Cloud** when they took second place: 'He really was a horse of a lifetime – even though his competitive career proved to be so short.'

Pages 104–5: **HRH Princess Anne** and **Goodwill** clear the fence into the Lake in 1973

The 1970s

# 1970
# The legendary Lorna

**San Carlos** (pictured above) had been destined originally for the racetrack; bred by Charlie Bird, he was by Trueville out of Rough Silver, but didn't make it as a racehorse. He began a career in showing and before he was bought by the Irish army had won the ladies' sidesaddle championship at Dublin.

Colonel Ronnie McMahon (who at the time was a captain in the Irish army) was given the ride on him, and Badminton was their first three-day event. San Carlos with Ronnie McMahon won Punchestown and Fontainebleau, and represented Ireland at the Munich Olympics. When San Carlos died he was buried at the showjumping ground in his army barracks.

Testimony to the growing number of competitors wanting to ride at Badminton was the decision to run the dressage over two days. This arrangement continues to the present day and is commonplace at all modern three-day events.

In 1970 Badminton featured a greater number of combination fences than usual, changing the emphasis away from sheer speed and scope and more towards accuracy and control. The Normandy Bank produced a great many glum faces when it was first seen, as did the Ski Jump, a steep ramp ending with a big drop followed by a sharp turn to a spread fence on top of a steep rise. As it happened, the Vicarage Vee, the Cattle Crush and the Coffin caused more problems. Amongst the hard luck stories that occurred was that of Bar Hammond, whose horse Eagle Rock was so surprised by the starter dropping his hand to send them on their way that he reared up and deposited his rider on the floor. She was soon back on board and the pair jumped clear to finish eighteenth. In 1973, when ridden by Richard Meade, Eagle Rock finished second. Far worse was the mistake made by Bertie Hill and Chicago in the showjumping: Bertie jumped the tenth fence instead of the sixth and of course was immediately eliminated.

The victor finally emerged as Richard Meade (see 1972) riding The Poacher. Back in l965 The Poacher had won Little Badminton when ridden by his owner Martin Whiteley. Martin later gave the horse to the combined training committee, and Richard Meade was asked to take on the ride. The Poacher is the only horse to have won both Little Badminton and the main Badminton Championship. He was ridden at the Mexico Olympics by Ben Jones where they won team gold. With Richard Meade in the saddle they were second at the Punchestown World Championships later that year, and in 1971 won team gold at the Burghley European Championships. The Poacher was retired to the hunting field; he died in 1977.

In second place was Captain Ronnie McMahon riding the Irish army's San Carlos, whilst third place went to Mary Gordon Watson and Cornishman V (see 1971).

## Three times round the course for Lorna

Lorna Clarke, then Sutherland, made history when she became only the second person – and the only woman – to complete one Badminton with three horses. She also holds the record for completing Badminton the greatest number of times; she retired from competition riding after the l992 Badminton, having by then completed the event twenty-three times.

At Badminton in 1970 she covered 48 miles and jumped 132 fences with only 15 minutes' rest between each of her horses. Lorna had not planned to take on such a gruelling task at all when she realised that she had three horses all qualified for Badminton; she fully expected at least one of them to fall by the wayside before the actual event. As she explains: 'I owned one of my rides, Popadom, but The Dark Horse and Gypsy Flame were owned by other people, and all three of us wanted our particular horse to run at Badminton. I was not unduly worried, as I fully expected to have to drop one out – but when the day came, all three were fit and raring to go! I was most concerned about my prospects on Gypsy Flame, so I put her last of the three.

'I was drawn to go first, thirty-third and sixty-sixth; looking back it was a great achievement, but at the time it was no fun at all because if I wasn't actually riding a phase of the competition, I seemed to spend the rest of the time either working in for the dressage or walking the roads and tracks, steeplechase and cross-country courses. I had a "helper" but that wasn't the same as having a groom, and I did all the plaiting, tacking up and riding in, so it was pretty exhausting!

'Riding the roads and tracks three times was excessively boring, and by the third time, I was going over and over in my mind how on earth I was going to get round on Gypsy Flame. As it turned out she gave the best performance of all of them: she finished fourth, Popadom was twelfth and The Dark Horse fifteenth.

'It was the first year that Frank Weldon introduced his version of the Normandy Bank,

an obstacle he had seen at the European Championships at Haras du Pin, and everyone thought it was unjumpable. The prospect of having to get over it three times was pretty daunting, and I ended up jumping it three different ways: Popadom bounced on and off which was the correct thing to do, The Dark Horse fiddled his legs on top and skipped on and off, and Gypsy Flame put in a stride which was not a good thing to do – but we got away with it.'

1970 winner **Richard Meade** and **The Poacher**. The Poacher is the only horse to have won both Little Badminton (1965) and the main Badminton Championship

**Long leathers and long reins** Lorna first rode at Badminton in 1967, having previously concentrated on showjumping. 'I showjumped in Juniors until I was sixteen, and then had a spell in America; I brought back a Saddlebred horse from there which I took to Grade A level. However, he developed an arthritic problem in his shoulders and so we decided that perhaps he would find eventing less stressful – which just shows how little we knew about the sport then! I enjoyed eventing so much that I "converted" all my showjumpers to it. In those days I trained under Captain Edy Goldman, but when he heard I was planning to go to Badminton in 1967 he said he didn't wish to be held responsible for me and refused to train me any more! So Celia Ross Taylor, who also trained with him, helped me in turn. I arrived at my first Badminton with Nicholas Nickleby, a long-backed, broken-winded Thoroughbred whose theory when jumping was: "If in doubt, stand off a mile" – so our first Badminton was pretty exhilarating! I should have been second to go behind Sheila Willcox, but she withdrew so we had to go first. We finished eighth, and Capt Edy Goldman decided that perhaps I was capable of getting my act together, and helped me again.

'We all took our preparation as seriously as we do today, the difference being that we didn't really know what we should be doing; we were all so hungry for knowledge and advice that you ended up trying anything anyone suggested to you. I was riding each of my horses for three hours every day because that's what I thought they needed!

'In 1968 I rode "Nick" and Popadom. The course had been causing problems at one fence in particular, a wide shallow ditch a few yards from a post-and-rail fence. The first fifteen competitors failed to get over it because they had all been trying to jump the ditch and "bounce" over the post and rail. I hadn't realised this was a possibility, as I didn't know that a horse could "bounce" anything – this means jumping two obstacles without taking a stride in between them – you land over one and immediately take off over the second. My own interpretation had been to trot down into the ditch and up the other side, and then trot up to the rail to jump it. Popadom finished eighth and Nick was tenth.'

Lorna continued to compete at Badminton regularly throughout the seventies, eighties and early nineties. She was fourth in 1983 and 1984 on Danville, with whom she also won team silver at the 1983 Frauenfeld European Championships. Glentrool was another regular competitor, although he simply could not do dressage, and could rarely make up for that deficiency despite going well across country. He is remembered by the Glentrool Trophy, presented at Badminton to the rider who makes the most improvement on their dressage score.

With the endearing Fearliath Mor – whom Lorna admiringly describes as 'a common pony who stepped out of his class' – she really thought she might actually win the trophy she had competed for so often. 'Once we got his dressage up together I thought we might do better than my traditional fourth place!' recalls Lorna. 'But the one year he could have done it, I fell off him! I am happy to say I rarely simply "fall off", but that day I did, damn it!'

King's Jester gave Lorna the fourth of her fourth placings at Badminton, in 1991. She took both King's Jester and Fearliath Mor there in 1992, but Jester's recurring corn trouble meant he had to be withdrawn, and Fearliath Mor broke down on the steeplechase. It was an undeservedly sad end to Lorna's competitive career, which included two Burghley victories (Popadom in 1967 and Greco in 1978) and seven British team medals.

Lorna's style of cross-country riding was unique, but it worked well for her. She was renowned for her long

stirrup leathers and loose reins, but her logical explanation of why this technique worked for her is a good lesson for many:

'Firstly, I did not have any training in the early days so I was free to develop my own way of doing things. I always rode with long stirrups simply because having quite short legs I always felt safer the more leg I had wrapped around the horse. The long reins were a result of riding really bad pullers – it takes two to tango, so if you give the horse his head then he can't pull. It started when I rode a horse in a big Foxhunter showjumping class. Having fought and pulled all the way we incurred twenty-one faults, so the next time I had to jump this horse I said, "Fine, you do it your way" – and set off on a long rein and just kicked on into the fences. Previously he had fought against me and blundered into his fences; left to his own devices he soon learned to pay attention to what he was doing and to jump cleaner.

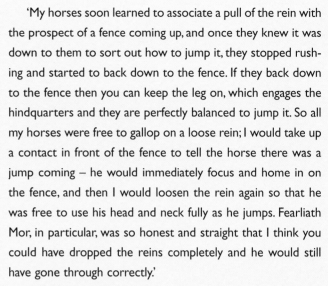

'My horses soon learned to associate a pull of the rein with the prospect of a fence coming up, and once they knew it was down to them to sort out how to jump it, they stopped rushing and started to back down to the fence. If they back down to the fence then you can keep the leg on, which engages the hindquarters and they are perfectly balanced to jump it. So all my horses were free to gallop on a loose rein; I would take up a contact in front of the fence to tell the horse there was a jump coming – he would immediately focus and home in on the fence, and then I would loosen the rein again so that he was free to use his head and neck fully as he jumps. Fearliath Mor, in particular, was so honest and straight that I think you could have dropped the reins completely and he would still have gone through correctly.'

Lorna's charismatic coloured cob Popadom (pictured left) earned affection wherever he went: 'He had huge feet, was only 15.3hh, with a big head and enormous ears. He could be very naughty in the dressage and needed 3½ hours riding before a test; he couldn't extend to save his life, but was very neat, active and accurate. He came from Jennifer Harrison in Kendal who had bought him and his mother for £40, beating Chipperfields Circus to it! The week before I took him to Burghley in 1967 I concentrated on his flatwork, as he had a habit of sticking his head in the air; so every time he did this I tapped him between the ears with my stick. It worked, as he led after the dressage, and won the event! After that I was offered every coloured horse in Ireland to ride. I thought I had written back to everybody politely refusing their offers, but one of my negative replies was obviously misinterpreted because Gypsy Flame, who belonged to the late Mrs Martin, arrived in my yard!

'After winning Burghley and going well at Badminton, Popadom was picked for the 1970 World Championships at Punchestown. The course caused all sorts of trouble – we had two falls and still finished twelfth. I took him to Wylye later that year and he fell at the sixth fence, and I realised that he had lost his nerve. So I took him back to Ireland the following year to do a smaller three-day event, where he went clear, and then retired him. He went to Gloucestershire to be hunted by the aunt of racehorse trainer David Nicholson. He allowed her to jump things she never thought she could, and all the masters used to doff their caps to him! He came back to us to be retired to grass, and was put down in his twenties.'

# 1971

# It's an ill wind...

**A right royal achievement** HM the Queen had been a loyal and enthusiastic supporter of Badminton since the 1950s, and in 1971 she had the pleasure and excitement of watching her daughter, Princess Anne, compete on a home-bred horse, Doublet. This was their first Badminton, and they were second after the dressage; moreover they achieved a clear round across country, although thirty-two time penalties on the steeplechase hindered them somewhat. On the final day Doublet performed very well in the showjumping until he came to the Open Water: neither horse nor rider had faced such a question before, and Doublet was obviously not sure whether to jump over it or in it. Unfortunately he opted for the latter, which in those days incurred another ten penalties. However, a fifth place at their first Badminton was a performance to be proud of. Later that year they won the individual gold medal at the Burghley European Championships.

Eventing has always been a comradely sport in that no matter how competitive the rider, no one likes to see anyone else in trouble. But its very nature means that often it is someone else's bad luck which proves to be another's good fortune.

At the 1971 Badminton, despite having led after the dressage, Lt Mark Phillips had set off on the cross-country with the intention of 'just getting round'. But he was held on the course down near the Vicarage Ditch because an Irish horse had had a bad fall at the Normandy Bank, and as he recalls, 'After a twenty-minute wait on the course I thought to myself that we had successfully jumped a third of the way round and now I would be restarting on what was a fresh, happy horse. So when they sent us on our way again I set off with my foot on the accelerator, posted a good time, showjumped clear the next day – and won. Which was a complete surprise!'

## Great Ovation

Mark Phillips' surprise can be better understood when it is appreciated that he came very close to selling Great Ovation the previous season. 'I had taken him to what is now the Boekelo three-day event and he had fallen in one of the big ditches there. I was all for selling him because I really didn't think he was going to make the grade. But as I was in the army and stationed at Catterick at the time, I knew I would have plenty of opportunities to go hunting through the winter, so I decided to hunt him hard and give him one more chance. He came out in the spring and won the Intermediate at Rushall, and was fourth in the Advanced at Liphook – so Badminton did not seem such an unrealistic aim after all. Throughout his career he was always a better horse in the spring than the autumn; by the time he had endured a summer of hard ground, flies and hot weather he was less than enthusiastic about the game.

'Great Ovation was never naturally brave, although that is perhaps a harsh thing to say about a horse which won Badminton two years running; but the fact remains that if you saw a long stride coming into a fence he would usu-

**An eventing partnership** Finishing in sixth place this year was a certain Mike Tucker riding Farmer Giles; less than a point behind him in seventh place was Angela Sowden and Mooncoin. These two happy competitors were soon to marry, and for a while both continued to compete regularly at Badminton. Now, Angela remains a successful competitor whilst Mike's career as an international course designer and BBC commentator has flourished (see 1983). Remaining cool, calm and detached, as would be expected by the BBC, has tested Mike's skills to the limits when he has found himself trying to give an unemotional commentary on Angela's performance as she progressed round the course!

ally stop rather than take the fence on. After winning Badminton for the second time in 1972 we were picked for the Munich Olympics, and this somewhat hesitant attitude caught up with him: I saw a long stride at the third fence, a very wide parallel, and Great Ovation did decide to have a go but without enough forward momentum, so he didn't quite make it and came down on the back rail. I was thrown off, and remounted in such a hurry that I didn't notice one rein was wrapped around his nose. With a shaken horse and ineffective steering and brakes, a few more stops and another fall were inevitable. The team won the gold medal but ours was the discard score.

'At Badminton in 1973 we led the dressage again, but Great Ovation went lame on the roads and tracks and had to be withdrawn. The following year he was eliminated at Centre Walk, and I knew then that he had clearly had enough. He was retired to the hunting field where my Aunt Flavia, who co-owned him, enjoyed many seasons hunting with him.'

Great Ovation was a dark bay Thoroughbred gelding by Three Cheers, a Cesarewitch winner. He was a good-looking horse and moved well, but proved too slow for racing. He had been bought as a four-year-old by Mark and his Aunt Flavia.

## Then and now: speed and endurance scoring

Up until this year, 1971, the scoring system for the speed and endurance phases was based on penalties being awarded for jumping errors, such as a fall or a refusal, as well as for exceeding the stated time for each phase. But equally, bonus points could be earned if a phase was completed faster than the stated time. This system made it possible for a competitor to make up for a bad dressage performance by going fast on the speed and endurance phases.

On Phases A and C (the roads and tracks) and Phase E (the run-in, which was abolished in 1967) five penalties were incurred for each commenced period of five seconds over the set time.

On the steeplechase it was possible to gain three bonus points for every commenced period of five seconds inside the set time, and to lose ten penalties for each commenced period of five seconds outside the set time.

Similarly on Phase D, the cross-country, there were three bonus points to be gained for each commenced period of ten seconds under the time, and ten penalties to be incurred for each commenced period of five seconds over the set time.

In 1971 this system was changed to a simplified one based on an optimum time, with penalty points incurred for being over that time. At Badminton the following penalty point system is used:

**Phases A and C (roads and tracks):** 1 penalty per each second over the optimum time.

**Phase B (steeplechase):** 0.8 penalties per second.

**Phase D (cross-country):** 0.4 penalties per second over the optimum time.

## Mary Gordon Watson and Cornishman V

The shy but popular Mary Gordon Watson and her father's impressive horse, Cornishman V, were asked to compete at Badminton in 1967, even though they were not qualified to do so, so that the selectors could consider them for the British team. Unfortunately Cornishman jumped the third from home awkwardly, and Mary was unseated. In 1971 the pair took second place at Badminton. He was considered to be one of the best three-day event horses ever seen: Richard Meade rode him at the 1968 Mexico Olympics and thought him very talented, and that was before he had realised his full potential; however, an outright win at Badminton eluded Mary and Cornishman. Their runner-up position in this year was their best result here – and that was despite a refusal at the rails out of the Coffin (fence no 3). In 1969 they had finished ninth, in 1970 third, in 1971 second, and in 1972, when they could really have hoped to go one better, a fall on the cross-country dropped them to fifteenth. They were sixth in 1973, even though they had a fall, because they were the only combination to finish inside the time and so avoided time penalties.

The following year Mary was hoping to earn an Olympic ticket to Mexico; however, bad luck was following her still, because she broke her leg – but as was the 'done thing' in those days, the selectors asked if they could still have the use of the horse. So Cornishman was ridden by Richard Meade in Mexico, where they won team gold.

In 1969 Mary and Cornishman took the European Championship title, and then in 1970 they won individual and team gold at the World Championships in Punchestown. In 1972 they were chosen for the Munich Olympics where they won team gold. In 1973 Cornishman V was retired to the hunting field, and was finally put down at the age of twenty-seven.

Mary continued to event for other people and was a successful point-to-point rider. She is a dressage and hunter judge, as well as being a member of the Jockey Club.

**Mary Gordon Watson** and **Cornishman V:** European Champions 1969, World Champions 1970, and second at Badminton in 1971. Cornishman was originally bought as a hunter for Mary's father, but when Mary came to take her Pony Club A test, he was the only horse available for her to ride. Although he was a difficult youngster, the two formed a good partnership and happily took to eventing, winning their first three-day event at Tidworth. Mary was eighteen and Cornishman was eight, and by the end of their first season he had upgraded to advanced

Page 110: The stylish combination of **HRH Princess Anne** and **Doublet**. They finished fifth in 1971 and went on to become European Champions later that year

Page 111: A 20-minute wait on the cross-country course gave **Captain Mark Phillips** and **Great Ovation** the chance to record a fast clear round to help them to victory

**Major Derrick Dyson**
*(Assistant Director and Treasurer 1971–1988)* Derrick Dyson was born in 1919 and was in the army at the beginning of World War II; he served in the Royal Artillery (The Gunners) for about twenty years, but it was a posting in the 1950s to the King's Troop which introduced him to Major Frank Weldon and to the sport of eventing:

'I was second-in-command to Frank Weldon at the King's Troop, and from the first day I served with him he was my greatest friend – on top of which I married his sister, too! I left the army in 1959, and then worked as a land agent in Herefordshire; I married Frank's sister in 1965 – much too late, but you don't realise these things at the time! – and we moved back to Warminster where I worked for the Country Landowners' Association.

'I was Frank's assistant from 1971 to 1988, when we both stepped down, but my involvement with Badminton began as a competitor in the 1950s. Whilst we were in the King's Troop, Frank rode at Badminton and came back with such enthusiasm for the event that we were all encouraged to aim for it. One of Frank's greatest gifts was that he was such an inspirational man – he had great ideas of his own, but he also inspired others to strive for greater things. So it was Frank who inspired us to make Badminton our aim. Today most of us would not even qualify to compete there, but at the time you just sent your entry in and they were probably jolly glad to have you. My best result was sixteenth in 1954 on the King's Troop's Officer's charger Water Gypsy. I also rode a horse of my own there, Henry Farman. He did well at one-day events, but had a fairly disastrous record at Badminton, which included putting me in hospital for several weeks!

'Henry Farman was bred by Henry Wynmalen who was a great dressage judge and trainer; he named the horse after the aviation pioneer who was a friend of his. Henry Wynmalen used to come to St John's Wood and advise us during our preparation for Badminton, and he gave the horse to me. When I left the army I handed him over to another officer, but shortly afterwards he had a crashing fall while jumping at the Royal Tournament. The vet said that he had intermittent heartbeats and should only do light work, but when a second opinion was asked for, that vet said there was nothing wrong with him. About a month later he went to camp with the King's Troop; a groom was hacking him out and popped him over a small log – and he dropped down dead.

'When I first took on the post at Badminton it did not take up too much of my time, but as the event grew – during the seventies the gates were increasing by 20-25 per cent per year – we all found ourselves getting more and more involved. I was in charge of all the accounts, the trade-stand area, admittance charges, car parking, loos, and so on and so forth! It seemed a big enough task then, but the event is vaster still now. After the finances of the event the trade-stands were my biggest responsibility – and the greatest nightmare was if the ground conditions were bad when they were setting up. In the early days it didn't seem to matter too much, but as the stands got bigger and more professional-looking, so too did the size of lorry that they arrived on! Time after time we remained convinced that the park would never recover, and it is a tribute to the estate staff, and the Duke's generosity, that it did. There was always a waiting list for trade-stand space, and as soon as anyone even hinted that they might be giving up we would be inundated with telephone calls from keen exhibitors, often offering us well over the going rate for space. I can assure you there was a civilised system for replacing people, and it wasn't bribery! Frank would, I am sure, join me in saying that we were so lucky to have the invaluable support of efficient and charming secretaries such as the late Victoria Sanford and Jane Tuckwell (née Gundry).

'I well remember making my customary inspection of the

Opposite: **Major Derrick Dyson**, seen here competing at Windsor
Above: The trade-stand village was expanded in the late eighties to cater for the growing number of visitors
Right: When the weather doesn't co-operate things can get complicated – and *extremely* muddy!

trade-stands once setting up was complete, and being horrified to see that we had allowed in a very scruffy-looking stand which appeared to be selling toys and jokes. I made a mental note to myself to make sure that he didn't get in the following year. But a few weeks later a chap burst into the Badminton office, grinning from ear to ear, and proudly showed us a whole heap of photos of various members of the royal family buying things from his stall. As he now considered himself to be "by royal appointment" we couldn't really turn him away after that.

'During the late eighties, the present Duke agreed to move the Deer Park fencing so that the trade-stand area – or village, as it is now called – could be expanded. During the early eighties there was definitely a growing trend for more and more people to come on the dressage days to tour the shops and walk the course in peace; those people quite often remained at home on the Saturday to watch the action on television. Fortunately enough enthusiasts also rolled up for cross-country day so the Saturday numbers did not fall – but numbers were definitely rising for the first two days. An oft-told tale, but one worth repeating, is of the two couples meeting outside a trade-stand and asking what all these horses were doing at a Sunday market?

'The beer tent rapidly became a popular meeting point for the "Yuppie set", many of whom never set foot outside of it all

day. For them, Badminton was not a horse trials, it was an all-day party – which must have been particularly encouraging for our sponsors at the time, Whitbread Breweries. Now there is an enormous TV screen on which they can see everything.

'As sponsors, Whitbreads were very helpful, generous and undemanding, although there was a sticky patch when they brought in some whizz kid to handle their PR – then the sparks flew! I particularly remember a cover he had designed for the programmes: it was simply awful, and it took a man as brave and honest as Frank to put his foot down and say he was not having it. Time was running out by then, and they produced a watercolour painting of Badminton House as an alternative which, from some angles, looked like a big brown coffee

strain – although it was an improvement on the original! In fact divine intervention saw the event cancelled in 1987, and so the "brown smudge" enjoyed only limited circulation – though Frank had to suffer it the following year. Ironically this was his last year as director!

'They were exciting times for us. The biggest rise in interest in the event came during the seventies: Great Britain was competing successfully in international eventing, and the interest of, and close proximity to, the royal family helped enormously, and even more so when Princess Anne arrived as a competitor. Under Frank's direction, Badminton became a major event, which truly earned its place in the sporting and social calendar. By the time we both retired, Badminton was probably due a change in regime; things keep progressing, often when humans don't. For instance, nowadays there are computers and faxes in the office! I obviously missed the involvement for a while, but it is also a huge relief to visit Badminton now simply to enjoy it without the worry. It is good to see the improvements and developments each year.'

Today, it is easy to see how Major Dyson's quiet charm and modesty would have lent itself to the smooth and peaceful administration of the Badminton Horse Trials. He remains a popular and welcome visitor.

# 1972

# Tightest margin for victory

**Richard Meade** and **Laurieston** – 1.25 time penalties in the showjumping cost him the Badminton title; he finished second to Captain Mark Phillips and Great Ovation

Badminton in 1972 was remembered for the hard-fought contest from start to finish between Lt Mark Phillips and Richard Meade. Riding Great Ovation (see 1971), Mark Phillips had taken the lead after the dressage – but just seven penalties behind him sat a determined Richard Meade. Having won the previous year, Mark's expectations this time were somewhat greater than on his last visit when his intention had been 'just to get round' – but things began to go wrong when he forgot to start his stopwatch as he set off on the steeplechase. He had to rely on his own sense of

pace, but incurred 8.8 time penalties; across country he was clear, but again, he clocked up 38.8 time penalties.

Richard Meade and Laurieston also incurred a couple of time faults on the steeplechase, but they were fractionally faster round the cross-country course and so at the end of speed and endurance day had taken a small lead of 0.6 penalties. Going in reverse order on the final day, Mark and Great Ovation piled on the pressure by jumping clear, and Richard knew that he also had to produce a clear round to win. He remembers Laurieston as '...a fiery little horse who had to be kept well under control in order to produce a clear showjumping round. However, I overdid the "keeping control" and lost time. Having jumped a clear round I thought the title was ours, but then the look on everyone's face told me that something was wrong. In fact we had incurred 1.25 time faults and had therefore lost the title by a margin of 0.6 penalties. I remember turning to Laurieston's owner, Major Derek Allhusen, and saying that I hoped by the end of the year it wouldn't matter anyway.'

Richard's thoughts were justified, because later that year riding Laurieston at Munich, he became – and remains – the only British three-day event rider to win an individual Olympic gold medal.

Mark Phillips was only too happy that Richard had made this error; as he says: 'If Richard had won I would have felt that I had handed the competition to him on a plate – all for the sake of forgetting to start my stopwatch!'

However, a number of the more seasoned spectators were only too well aware that Richard was in danger of exceeding the time in the final phase – one was caught 'riding a finish' in an effort to indicate to Richard that he needed to speed up over the last few jumps!

Sadly there was no consolation to be found in Richard's second ride, Mrs Wilkin's Wayfarer II, who had two showjumps down to drop from fourth to seventh (see Richard Meade, 1982).

## Complications on the course

In 1972 there were not as many clear rounds as the year before, but there were fewer eliminations and retirements. A preview of the course had prompted much talk as to the distance Frank Weldon had put in the Sunken Road combination: it measured 18ft, leaving some riders unsure as to whether they were meant to try and ride it as a bounce or as a one-stride distance. But that was precisely why Frank had made it an odd distance, because he knew that the bold, scopey horse would bounce across it, whereas the less brave could take a stride – or even two, as some did. The only eliminations here were at the first element, perhaps because those riders hadn't decided positively enough which stride option they were going for.

The Lake caused the most trouble: the log pile in was only 3ft high, but because of its spread, horses had to be prepared to jump out over it into the water, rather than just step over it.

The Stockholm Fence caused further consternation – this was a short, steep slope with a huge tree trunk suspended in front of it: so did you try to ride slowly down the slope to jump the log, or should you let fly off the top and take it all in one? Over the years competitors have demonstrated that it can be jumped perfectly well either way – although few have tried the route taken by Rachel Bayliss in 1973: her horse, Gurgle the Greek, tried to refuse the fence but found himself slipping down the steep slope anyway, so he ducked his head, as did his rider, and they wriggled out underneath the log, and continued unpenalised. This manoeuvre prompted a rule change to ensure that anyone trying the same thing would be penalised!

It was noted that Richard Walker seemed to have taken over Lorna Clarke's mantle as the 'corner expert': the year before, Lorna was the only one to try the corner option at Tom Smith's Walls, and in this year Richard was the only one to do it. He was also the only rider to jump the corner option successfully at the Munich Pen – five others tried, but failed.

It wasn't only the riders who experienced problems in this year: a surge in spectator numbers – 100,000 people on cross-country day – caused deplorable traffic delays; though quite similar were the queues for the loos!

Frank Weldon kept his promise of providing more loos in future years!

**A talented family**  In 1972 Mrs Bridget Parker rode her own Cornish Gold (above) into third place at Badminton. They were selected as reserves for the Munich Olympics, but then were co-opted into the team at very short notice when Debbie West's horse Bacarrat went lame. They won team gold and finished ninth individually – and in 1974 they won team silver at the World Championships. Bridget Parker went on to become a 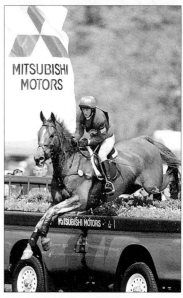 BHTA steward, technical delegate and dressage judge. She also chaired the board of selectors from 1993 to 1996, and remains as a selector for the build-up to the Sydney Olympics in the year 2000.

In 1995, Bridget's daughter Katie rode Cornish Faer (right) into twenty-first place at Badminton. Cornish Faer was by Ben Faerie out of Tregea, a half-sister to Bridget's Olympic horse Cornish Gold. A 'nephew' of Cornish Gold's, Cornish Envoy, was ridden by Katie at Badminton in 1998 and finished twentieth. Later that year they finished sixth at Burghley.

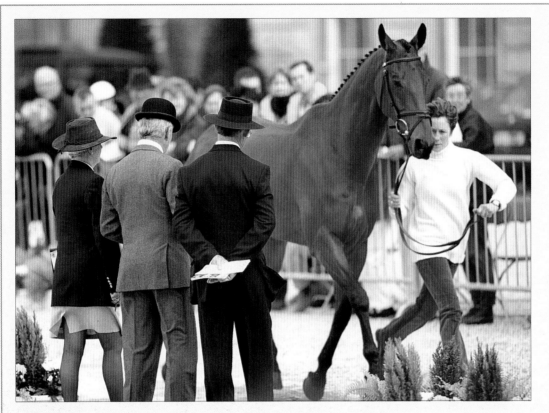

The **Ground Jury** – whose decision is final

Below: The veterinary inspection can be a bit of a fashion parade in some years. Here is the flamboyant **Ralph Hill** with **Johnathan Morgan**, sporting a patriotic sweatshirt in 1996, and the elegant French rider **Marie Courréges** running up **Cool Fool** in 1991

**Judge and jury** Up until this year the 'ruling body' at Badminton during the three-day event was the Ground Jury; this consisted of three people plus a veterinary official, and their decision on any matter was final unless it was taken up by the committee of appeal, which was another panel of three officials. Three dressage judges were separately appointed to judge the dressage phase.

From 1972 onwards the system changed somewhat, and for the first time a technical delegate was appointed; on this occasion he was Major Laurence Rook, Olympic team gold medallist, former Badminton winner, and already on the organising committee – so he was fairly well qualified! The technical delegate is responsible for overseeing and approving every aspect of the competition, from the stabling to the cross-country course, from the practice areas to the final showjumping arena. He has to ensure the competition is run to the standard required by, and to the rules of, the FEI.

Another change was that instead of there being a Ground Jury and a separate panel of dressage judges, their roles were now combined: so the Ground Jury judged the dressage and the showjumping, and generally took control of the event once it started. Today the Ground Jury is made up of a president plus two other members, and they officiate at the horse inspections along with the veterinary delegate.

# The first of six victories

When Lucinda Prior-Palmer took the Badminton title in this year, there were many who thought there was a good chance of seeing her name on the Whitbread Trophy again. But none could have foreseen Lucinda's remarkable and, to date, unbeaten record of six victories at Badminton on six different horses.

## Introducing Be Fair

Lucinda's first Badminton horse, Be Fair, had been bought for her as a Pony Club eventer, when she was fifteen. He had good credentials in that he was the result of an unplanned mating between a young colt who went on to become Sheila Willcox's international horse Fair and Square, and a mare called Happy Reunion.

The cheeky 16.2hh chestnut soon got the measure of his young rider and caused her no end of trouble. But Lucinda persevered, and gradually learnt to handle and ride this talented horse. Their first international success was winning team gold at the 1971 Junior European Championships when Be Fair was eight; and the following year they went to Badminton for the first time.

Lucinda recalls, 'I walked the course with Mark Phillips who just kept saying "You want to kick on here ...I should keep kicking here..." It didn't seem to matter what type of fence we were looking at, the advice seemed to remain the same: just keep kicking! By the time we got to the end of our course-walk I had a streaming nosebleed from the stress of it all!

'When it came to riding it, we were clear until Tom Smith's Walls. I had planned to take the long route here, but as I tried to turn to jump the second wall the reins slipped right through my fingers and we missed it. I had worn leather gloves, and this is a mistake I have never repeated because once they are wet from the horse's sweat they have no grip at all (see Martin Whiteley, 1965!). But even with those twenty penalties for running out at the wall, we still finished fifth.

'Our victory in 1973 almost didn't happen as a result of another error of judgement in terms of equipment. The Coffin at fence no 3 was causing a great many refusals and elimina-

tions (twelve competitors got no further than here). I had set off on the cross-country without a martingale because I didn't think Be Fair needed one – and how wrong I was again, because as I tried to slow him down so that he could see what he had to do, he threw his head in the air and accelerated towards it. He somehow stayed on his feet as he clambered over the

**Be Fair**, the talented horse who gave **Lucinda Prior-Palmer** the first of her record-breaking six Badminton victories

first rail, without ever really seeing it, but landed and turned hard left away from the ditch in the bottom. Quick thinking saved the day – I grabbed the right rein so that he ran along the bottom of the ditch, which gave us time to reorganise ourselves. It was then a case of pulling hard on the left rein and giving him a good kick so that we jumped out of the ditch, up the bank and out over the exit rails. And because we had stayed between the red and the white flags, we weren't penalised! We had two fences in hand as we went into the final phase, but Be Fair jumped clear to win.

'I remember driving home on my own in the lorry and listening to the voice on the radio saying who had won Badminton, and I couldn't begin to take in that it was Be Fair.'

This was the start of Lucinda's domination of the event, and of all her six victories here with different horses, as well as numerous

*The novel technique used by **Rachel Bayliss** and **Gurgle the Greek** to tackle the Stockholm Fence in 1973 led to a change in the rules. Now competitors must pass between the flags and over the obstacle*

later that year at the Kiev European Championships, and in 1975 won team silver and the individual title at the Luhmuhlen European Championships. He deserved to end his career with success at the 1976 Montreal Olympics, but his fairy-tale was not going to have a happy ending because he slipped the tendon from his hock as he completed what had been a superb cross-country round at the Olympics. He recovered sufficiently to enjoy hunting for the rest of his life.

## Chance ride takes second place

Richard Meade was offered the ride on Bar Hammond's Eagle Rock just five days before Badminton. It was very much a case of *déjà vu*, as Richard explains: 'My parents had bred Eagle Rock, but had sold him as a four-year-old because they thought he would be too small for me. As it turned out, he grew to nearly 16hh and gave me the best ride I had ever had at Badminton! He was one-quarter Connemara, and combined the very best of pony and Thoroughbred blood. We were about forty-fifth after the dressage – they used a new test that year which proved very unpopular and was dropped the following year – but he was such a fast horse that he moved up to second place. I had only been given the ride because Bar had not been well, and so unfortunately I didn't get another chance to enjoy him across country! But Bar continued to have great fun, and a good many seasons in the sport with him.'

In third place, with a clear cross-country round but one showjump down, was Virginia Thompson and Cornish Duke. Behind them, having recorded a double clear, was Merlin Meakin and Lynette. Merlin had been Merely-a-Monarch's groom when he won Badminton in 1962, and had looked after him in his retirement.

successes on the national and international circuit, Be Fair has remained in her mind as her very best horse – not necessarily in terms of his sheer ability, but because he allowed for, and forgave, her inexperience as a rider.

Be Fair went on to win a team bronze medal

# A royal reward

The striking grey gelding, Columbus, owned and bred by HM the Queen, took the Badminton title in 1974. And had things gone the way Her Majesty had planned, it would have been her daughter Princess Anne in the saddle, and not her son-in-law. As it was, Columbus had proved too strong for the Princess Royal and so Mark had taken him on.

Columbus was by Colonist II out of Trim Ann. He stood 17hh and was nine years old when he triumphed at Badminton. Mark had had a chance to get to know him at Badminton the previous year, though things had not started well:

'Princess Anne had competed Columbus successfully in one-day events, but at Burghley she had found him too strong on the steeplechase and had retired. So he had a reputation for being a bit of a tearaway. In 1973 I made the mistake of over-bitting him, with the result that he didn't really feel able to go forwards into his fences, and this misjudgement caused us to have a fall at both Luckington Lane and at the Lake. By 1974, however, I felt we had all our ducks in a row – I really thought, as we drove to Badminton, that Columbus was going to win it. He was the best horse I have ever ridden. You could do anything with him – get him in deep to a fence, ask him to stand off, whatever distance was there he could do it for you. He was not the easiest in the dressage and needed to be worked in for quite a long time, but across country he was everything you could wish for. He really was a great horse.'

It is just as well that Columbus earned the reward his ability deserved, as his competitive career was to be short-lived: at the World Championships later that year he was leading the field after the cross-country, but Mark had felt him falter towards the end of the course and he pulled up lame. He had slipped the tendon off his hock. An operation failed to cure the problem, but he evidently did not feel any pain from this injury so he enjoyed himself out hunting for a few seasons. He then slipped the tendon off the other hock – but instead of it ending his career, this actually enabled him to work level again behind.

Amazingly Mark rode him one more time at Badminton in 1979 and finished third.

'We had had no preparation at all, as it was the last thing we expected to be able to do with him,' remembers Mark. 'He had been team chasing and doing all sorts of fun things – such as riding round the Aintree Grand National course alongside Richard Pitman – and so we only had a few weeks left in which to do something about his dressage, and that was too late really. I really regretted that afterwards, because with a little more work

**Captain Mark Phillips** records a third victory, this time riding HM the Queen's **Columbus**

this year; everyone had been delighted to see that the Coffin had been moved to the Vicarage Ditch and so did not appear until fence no 21. The previous year's winners, Be Fair and Lucinda Green, had a stop at the wall into the Quarry, and then fell at the Crooked S.

Probably the most poignant 'hard done by' story was that pertaining to the American rider Bruce Davidson riding Irish Cap. Bruce had based himself at Wylye since January in order to prepare meticulously for Badminton, and he rode Phase D very precisely 'by his watch' so that he finished just inside the time – only to find that the scorers had given him 13.6 time faults. The organisers admitted that there had been a ten-second discrepancy between the optimum time the competitors had been given at the briefing, and the time given to the official timekeepers, but they refused to make any adjustments to the score as they argued that all competitors had ridden under the same impression. But in truth it did

**Debbie West** on the pint-sized **Baccarat** – 'a liver chestnut bullet'

Right: **Janet Hodgson** on **Larkspur,** who were second in the 1974 competition, at the Keeper's Rails

Top right: **Bruce Davidson** and **Irish Cap** at the Zig-Zag Rails

his dressage could have been a lot better and he might just have won it again.

'I hunted him in his retirement; he was a very good hunter and would jump absolutely anything, which was a bit unnerving for any-one trying to follow him!'

## Trials and tribulations

Princess Anne had led the Badminton 1974 dressage with a very impressive display on Doublet, but a fall on the steeplechase led to them retiring. However, a clear round inside the time on Goodwill allowed her to take fourth place.

The Sunken Road and the Crooked S fences were the first real questions on the course in

affect those competitors who rode strictly to their time and distance checks.

Second place went to Janet Hodgson and her own Larkspur. They had been tenth at Badminton in 1972 and won Burghley that autumn. The following year they won team bronze at the 1973 Kiev European Championships, and later, team silver at the 1975 Europeans. They finished sixth at Badminton in 1976. This consistently successful gelding was born in 1962 and stood 17.1hh.

Bruce Davidson and Irish Cap showjumped clear to finish third, but without the time faults they would have won the title. Many years later Bruce Davidson was able to take his revenge (see 1995) though it meant that Irish Cap did not receive the recognition that was his due.

It is too late to know Frank Weldon's private thoughts on this mistake. As someone who had lost a Badminton title himself due to a timing error, he had always prided himself on ensuring that this did not happen again.

**Qualifications** In 1974, for those wanting to compete at Badminton, the following criteria had to be met:

* Owners and riders had to be members of the British Horse Society, and horses had to be registered with the society.
* Horses had to be Grade I or Grade II (Advanced or Intermediate), and had to have won at least four points at Intermediate or higher horse trials.
* Horses had to have completed at least one, and riders at least two, three-day events.

In 1975 the Badminton competition was cancelled after the dressage due to saturated ground.

# 1976
# Triumph superseded by tragedy

Wideawake had joined Lucinda's yard in 1973. The 16hh bay gelding had been born in 1966 and was by Hereward the Wake out of Serenade. He was owned by Mrs Vicki Phillips, whos daughter had hunted him and evented him at Novice level until Mrs Phillips decided to give the ride to Lucinda. Things did not start well, as Lucinda candidly admits:

Badminton's director, **Hugh Thomas**, rode **Playamar** into second place in 1976

Opposite: **Wideawake** on his way to achieving his greatest victory in 1976. Everyone was devastated when he collapsed and died within minutes of winning Badminton

As a triumphant Lucinda Prior-Palmer completed a clear showjumping round on Wideawake to take her second Badminton title, she wrapped her arms around her horse's neck to hug and thank him for his efforts. This was a horse which she had struggled to get on terms with, and they had finally proved that they could work as a partnership. At the final presentation Lucinda and Wideawake had collected their trophy and were awaiting their lap of honour. As the others left the arena so that the final spotlight could fall on them alone, Wideawake suddenly reared, staggered, and fell to the ground. He died within minutes.

'Wakey really did not like me very much when our partnership began; he once even squashed me against the partition of the lorry with great purpose to the extent that I had to shout for help, and he seemed to take great delight in being as annoying and unhelpful as possible. He would back you into the corner of his stable and leave you there, he would wait until the mucking-out bin was full and then tip it all over the clean floor, and when you tried to put his boots on he would wave his leg around until it connected with your knee or your toe. And worse was to come when I actually tried to ride him.

'He was such an extraordinary horse, very

**Clarissa Strachan** on **Merry Sovereign**

The cause of Wideawake's death was never discovered, but he died knowing he was a star. For his rider it continued to be a wretched year, the principal disaster being that Be Fair suffered an Achilles' tendon injury after completing the cross-country at the Montreal Olympics later that year.

## The ups and downs of eventing

A good many other riders were also experiencing the ups and downs of the sport of eventing. The Badminton course had come in for some criticism because of the number of drop fences which in this year coincided with hard ground: there were five between fences no 20 and 26 – the Normandy Bank, the Ski Jump, the Sunken Road and the Quarry; and although these fences themselves did not cause the most trouble, it is the cumulative effect of such a course that can lead to difficulties elsewhere. Fence no 4, the Chevrons, consisted of three angled rails which could be tackled in a number of ways, each of which involved a different stride pattern. These caused some problems, as did the next fence, the Zig-Zag Rails over the ditch. Aly Pattinson, who had won Burghley the previous year on Mr Alex Colquhoun's Carawich, had a crashing fall at the Star Fence. She bravely completed the course, and showjumped clear the next day, but could not recover from the 207 time faults collected on the cross-country.

Hugh Thomas rode his ten-year-old Playamar into second place, and this was an encouraging result for him. They had previously won the individual bronze medal at the 1974 World Championships, and as a result of this Badminton placing were selected for the Montreal Olympics in the autumn of 1976. This was the 'up': the down side was that, having gone well across country, Playamar was found to have sprained a tendon and could not showjump the next day. As Be Fair had also sustained an injury, the British team was eliminated. However, Badminton had not seen the end of Hugh Thomas, because he took over from Colonel Frank Weldon as director of Badminton in 1989.

sensitive without being highly strung. Once he galloped loose up the drive; a van was coming down the road and the two collided, sending Wakey flying over the bonnet and onto the other side of the road. He escaped with a few scrapes and bruises, but his fear of traffic – the only fear he knew – remained with him always.

'When we jumped, the more I tried to help him, the more likely he was to hit the fence, and it took me a long time to realise that I simply had to leave him alone. I had only ever known one way of riding across country and that was to kick on, and pick up my stick when in doubt. Wakey would not tolerate the whip, or even a kick from your heels; he just wanted to be left completely alone. I began to get the hang of this by the time we went to the Boekelo three-day event in 1975, which he won. His win at Badminton proved that we had finally become a partnership – or rather that I had finally learnt how to ride him as he needed to be ridden.'

# Gorgeous George confounds his doubting rider

George was a perfect three-day eventer to look at; he stood 16.2hh and was beautifully proportioned with excellent limbs. He was owned and bred by Mrs Elaine Straker out of their mare Winnifrith, who was by Sheila's Cottage, the winner of the 1948 Grand National. George was by the Thoroughbred stallion St Georg, and had been born in 1966. However, when George was offered to Lucinda to ride at Badminton in 1977, his record was anything but that of the perfect eventer. He had had five falls that Lucinda knew of at events in the past four years, and her initial reaction was to say thanks, but no thanks! But as Lucinda recalls:

'At the time my father was dying of cancer and we were all moping around that winter dreading the inevitable conclusion of his illness. When the offer of the ride on George came, I think my parents thought it would be a good distraction for me. In fact he arrived at our yard only a few weeks before Badminton, and then went lame, so I hardly had a chance to get to know him. He had been ridden previously by Mrs Straker's sons, Nick and Matt, but they couldn't get leave from the army to ride him on this occasion; Captain Mark Phillips had also ridden him in the past, and I was encouraged when he said he thought he was a good horse – but my own impression was that we would do very well indeed to stay upright over Badminton's big fences. However, despite some pretty uninspiring practice sessions at home, George went out and won the Brigstock one-day event, our only run before Badminton. No one was more surprised than me, and Badminton began to look survivable after all.

'I had been drawn first to go at Badminton on my other ride, Mr Charles Cyzer's Killaire. After the dressage George was fourth overall, whilst Killaire was ten penalties behind him in tenth place. For the first time ever, Frank Weldon had built a bounce fence into the Lake. We were all perfectly familiar with bounce fences on the flat, but plenty of us had doubts about whether a horse could successfully bounce when he then had to drop into water. Going first on Killaire I approached the Lake, and for the first time in my life, rode at a fence

which I was not convinced was jumpable. Luckily Killaire was operating on a different wavelength, and tackled the question by popping a tiny stride between the rails. He completed a clear round.

'As I set off on George on the roads and tracks it began to rain. I had been feeling fairly confident until we started the steeplechase, but then George locked his jaw and hung heavily to the left. If we met the fence well he jumped it

**George** dispelled **Lucinda**'s fears with a faultless cross-country round to claim a fourth victory for his rider

well, but if our stride wasn't spot on he just ploughed through it. At the open ditch he took off from on top of the guard rail, dragging it through the fence with him; on our second circuit it was lying across the face of the fence! As the rain poured down, and George seemed intent on ploughing us both into the ground, I closed my eyes – I couldn't see that we had any hope of surviving the cross-country at all. But despite my own doubts, George's owner, Mrs Straker, had never lost faith in her horse. She wanted me to take the bounce into the Lake, when my own feeling was that, if we got that far I would prefer to take the alternative. However, all the rest of my support team were making an effort – they hadn't given up; even my father, despite his illness, put himself in charge of leading George around in the ten-minute box, and it was their optimism and belief that finally shook me out of my own depths of despondency.

'As we set off from the start box, Elaine's last words to me were, "He'll look after you. He is brilliant!" How right she was: he gave me a faultless ride finishing inside the time, to take the lead. We had three showjumps in hand

going into the final phase, but again, George jumped a perfect round. It was St George's Day, and George did his bit for us and for England by winning Britain's finest three-day event, with Killaire finishing in third place.

'I rode George at Burghley that autumn in the European Championships, and he won team and individual gold – but it was not a happy occasion. George felt as if he had really given his all to succeed at Burghley and he had begun to feel like an old horse. I told Mrs Straker that I could ask no more of George, and that I thought he should be retired. It was sad when I saw him come out the following year to compete again, but luckily it was a short-lived comeback, and soon afterwards he was retired to a life of teamchasing and hunting.'

Lucinda's beloved father had lived to see her third Badminton victory, but sadly not her win at Burghley.

In second place, and the only other combination to have finished the cross-country with-

Right: **Diana Thorne** and **The Kingmaker**

Below: **Aly Pattinson** on **Carawich** who finished fifth

spooky horse. He was highly strung and would take exception to the flowers, or the judges' boxes, and so on. It was all great fun though – something which is perhaps lacking to the same degree in todays competition. When I go to Badminton these days I still feel slightly aggrieved at having to pay to get in – I got rather too used to having a competitor's pass to get in with. And it is such a shame that the public are no longer allowed into the stables. We coped with all of that and we were just as serious about doing well in the event as today's riders!' The Kingmaker died at the age of nineteen. Diana married the National Hunt trainer Nicky Henderson.

out time faults, was Miss Diana Thorne and The Kingmaker. Owned by Diana and her mother, The Kingmaker was an eleven-year-old grey gelding by Warwick. He had finished second at Burghley in 1973 and won Haras du Pin in 1975. After taking second place at Badminton in 1977, they were fourth in the European Championships at Burghley. The following year they finished seventeenth at Badminton and eighth at Burghley, after which the big grey was retired to the hunting field, where Diana's father used him as his Field Master's horse. As Diana recalls 'This was the second time I had been beaten by someone who was riding a "borrowed horse". We were second at Burghley in 1973 behind Captain Mark Phillips on a last minute ride, Maid Marion. And at Badminton in 1977 we were beaten by Lucinda Prior-Palmer who had taken over the ride on George from Matthew Straker. We were usually handicapped in the dressage as The Kingmaker was a very capable but very

**Scoring systems** Since 1971, eventing competitions have been scored on a penalty point basis, meaning that the lowest score at the end of the day wins. Moreover, each of the three phases of the competition is scored in such a way that it has a fair influence on the overall result: for instance, because the main part of the competition is the speed and endurance test, this should exert the most influence. Those who truly appreciate the sport would not be happy to see a horse that had performed a superb dressage test, but which then had a stop on the cross-country, go on to win the event. So a ratio is used to try to ensure that each phase exerts the required influence on the overall result. The relative influence ratio was dressage, three; speed and endurance, twelve; showjumping, one. So the speed and endurance test should have four times more influence on the result than the dressage, and twelve times more than the showjumping.

In the dressage, a new scoring system in 1977 meant that each movement in the dressage test was marked out of ten rather than out of six, so the maximum good marks available increased from 144 to 240 (in 1998 the test used had more movements, and therefore the maximum good marks rose to 250). The average of the three scores given by each judge is subtracted from the maximum possible mark, and is then subjected to a multiplying factor of 0.6 ($\frac{3}{5}$) to give the final penalty score.

In the showjumping, another change in the FEI rules meant that the penalties awarded for a knock-down or a foot in the water were reduced from ten to five penalties; this was done to prevent the showjumping having too great an influence on the final result. Today the penalty system remains the same: five penalties for a knock-down, ten for a first disobedience (refusal or runout) and twenty for a second disobedience. The third disobedience results in elimination. A fall of the horse or rider incurs thirty penalties.

# Jane's fighting spirit

Jane Holderness-Roddam, who as Miss Bullen had won Badminton in 1968 with Our Nobby, claimed another victory in this year with her 1976 Burghley winner Warrior.

Warrior was a 16.1hh bay gelding by Warwick, who also sired Diana Henderson's The Kingmaker (second in 1977 and seventeenth in 1978), and he was bought for Jane to ride by Mrs Suzy Howard; she had bought him from John Shedden when he had been ridden by Sheilah Michaels, who had competed him successfully at Novice and Intermediate level. Jane remembers going to see him and thinking he would look better as one of Prince Phillip's team of four bay carriage horses:

'He was very heavy through the shoulders and his hocks creaked, but I thought I might as well ride him while I was there. Once on board, however, he gave you a very different feel, and he was a real jumping machine. He was built very much "downhill", which was

The smiling face of Badminton winner **Jane Holderness-Roddam**

**Jane** and **Warrior** take a bold leap off the Normandy Bank

going to make his dressage difficult, but I knew I had my sister Jennie [Loriston-Clarke] to help me with that. John then held up a huge cherry-roller gag and told me I wouldn't get anywhere with him across country unless I rode him in it. I was fairly horrified, as in those days most of our bitting was pretty simple – and again, I thought to myself that Jennie would soon have him so that he wouldn't have to wear that. But John was quite right, and I was never able to ride him in anything but the gag across country.'

'Our first three-day event was Bramham, and I was first to go in our section. When we walked the course we were obviously meant to take a smaller route through the Normandy Bank, but when I got there I saw that they

hadn't changed the flags from the more advanced class. I thought I had better ride through the flags, and so tried the harder way. Warrior was always a very careful horse and liked to see where he was going, and so when we got to the big drop fence off it, he hit the top of it whilst he was still trying to check out the landing. I was tipped over his ears and he followed over behind me – his front feet came down on either side of my head and pinned my hairnet to the ground, so I have pretty vivid memories of that fall! However, I knew I had to complete to qualify for Burghley, and so climbed back on quickly, particularly as I had spotted Lady Hugh Russell storming towards us in her mini-moke shouting "Don't carry on!"

'We duly qualified for Burghley in 1976,

on. He somehow jumped eight more fences, but at the Serpentine, when you had to change direction three times, he had simply had enough and we were eliminated. The whole experience totally demoralised him as he had never met anything before that he couldn't tackle. Even when he was home and had recovered from the stress of it all, he still didn't look or feel himself at all. We took him to a local hunter trial so that he could just go round for fun, but to start with he really didn't feel keen at all: I had to press him to keep him going, and it was only by about half way round that he started to feel as if he was enjoying it. We had brought a rosette from home which we pinned on his bridle, so that he knew how clever he was, and made a big fuss of him — and in fact he won his own, because he finished second.

'We went to Badminton the following year, 1979, although in hindsight I really wish we hadn't taken him — I think all the Lexington horses needed far longer to recover than any of us appreciated at the time. He went clear across country but strained a tendon and couldn't jump on the final day. He was third at Burghley in 1980 — but he was never the horse that he had been before Lexington. After Burghley he retired from major competitions and Suzy Howard gave him to me to enjoy in his retirement. He continued competing in one-day event classes until he was twenty-three (they used to have veteran sections for horses rather than riders!), when he was put down. He also starred in the film *International Velvet* as "Magic Lantern"; all the actors adored him, and would visit him in the stables to give him biscuits.'

Jane remains a successful and popular competitor; she also does a great deal to organise the training of event riders. She chaired the senior selection committee in the run-up to the 1992 Barcelona Olympics.

## Jane Starkey and Topper Too

Jane had made her debut at Badminton in 1974, along with Ginny Holgate (Dubonnet) and Diana Thorne (The Kingmaker). 'Those were the days, when you stayed in hotels!' recalls

which he won. The following year he was fourth at Badminton, and he won team gold at the Burghley European Championships.

'He won Badminton in 1978 with an obedient and accurate dressage performance, a fast cross-country round and a clear round in the showjumping; on the strength of this he was picked to go to the Lexington World Championships, which was a disaster because of the heat. Warrior had felt fine until about two-thirds of the way round, then at the fence before the big Normandy Bank into the water he started to stagger. As he landed on the bank he simply collapsed, and we both just fell off the other side into the water. Then I had the awful feeling of knowing that I was riding for my country and that I had to carry

Opposite: **Lucinda Prior-Palmer** and **Village Gossip** took second place: 'Gossip went everywhere at his own pace, which was very, very fast — although he would never admit that it was because he lacked scope! Like Wideawake, he hated interference from his rider, which in his case extended to his dressage as well. I had got the hang of him completely by the time he was fifteen.'

# The 1970s

'Topper Too was placed at the 1978 Lexington World Championships and was eighth at Badminton the following year. He went to Badminton for the last time as a fifteen-year-old in 1982, and won Tetbury horse trials that autumn. On that note he was retired. He had always had extraordinarily odd-looking back ankles which had sometimes given him trouble. They finally went twang when he was about twenty, and he was put down'

Jane. 'We stayed at the Hare and Hounds in Westonbirt. After that we were demoted to caravans – most of us travelled our horses in trailers, so there was no question of staying in the comfortable living quarters of a horsebox like we do now. Both Acrobat and Topper Too had qualified for Badminton that year, but I thought I might be pushing my luck if I tried to get round on two seven-year-olds; so I went on Acrobat, and finished twenty-eighth.

'Topper Too was my belated twenty-first birthday present, bought with some money my grandmother had given me. He looked more like a smart hunter than an eventer, but he proved to be a very consistent competition horse; he was entered for Badminton eight years running and completed five times. Our best result was in 1978 when we were third – he led the dressage by something indecent like eight penalties, which just doesn't happen these days. I had been having some help from David Hunt, and suddenly everything just seemed to fall into place – if I was ever going to win Badminton, that was the year I should have done it. But I diddled around the cross-country at my usual pace and picked up twenty-eight time faults. Frank Weldon had built a big technical track to help prepare us for the Lexington World Championships later that year. Topper was quite good at that sort of thing – he was genuine and honest, but just not very fast.

'The first year Frank built the Footbridge at Badminton I remember walking the course and deciding it was simply unjumpable, so I only walked the alternative route. But when I got to the ten-minute box Mum said she thought I'd better have a word with Dick Stilwell (the trainer). He told me that the alternative route was riding really badly, and that I would be better to jump the Footbridge. I told him I hadn't walked it, and so he quickly described which post I had to line up with what in order to get a good line over it. The video I have of my ride shows me cantering along and looking at each post, obviously saying to myself: "No, that can't be it, that's not it – hang on, this must be it"; and with that, turning Topper into the fence and just kicking like mad. After all my worrying, it felt as if he just stepped over it!'

**The course designer's art** By 1978 Colonel Frank Weldon, Badminton's director and course designer, had been at the helm for thirteen years. His reputation was by this time renowned the world over, and British riders were reaping the benefits of learning how to answer the challenges he threw down to them. The first Duke of Beaufort's purpose in creating the Badminton three-day event had been to help a British team to succeed at the 1952 Helsinki Olympics, and Frank Weldon continued this theme by designing courses that would best prepare riders for the testing fences they would face at international championships such as the World, the European and the Olympics. Success breeds success, and in 1978 Badminton attracted its biggest ever crowd: 150,000 people on cross-country day.

Frank Weldon knew the importance of appreciating the paying public, and he went out of his way to ensure that they could understand and gain the full benefit from what they had paid to come and see. During the late seventies, the Badminton Horse Trials programmes carried a piece about course-building written by him; it was a fascinating insight into the pyschology behind the design of the Badminton course.

When planning the course each year, Frank took into account firstly, how he felt our British riders had performed at the previous year's international championship, and secondly what they were likely to face in any forthcoming ones. The Badminton Three-Day Event is invariably used as a trial by the team selectors, and Frank's intention was always to design a course which would encourage riders to display the sort of qualities the selectors would be looking for in potential team members.

In the previous year, 1977, the emphasis of the course had been on speed, because Frank had felt that at recent major international events some of our riders could have been more adventurous in their efforts. Later in that year the Burghley European Championships had taken place, and the Germans and the Russians had been expected to be our strongest opponents; we were unlikely to be able to beat them in the dressage, and so we would have to make up any deficit with fast, clear cross-country rounds. Frank had therefore designed Badminton that year to encourage riders to produce just that, and the selectors could then see which riders could best achieve that aim. The end result, for whatever reason, was that Britain won team gold, and Lucinda Prior-Palmer won the individual gold medal.

When building the 1978 course, Frank had in mind the forthcoming World Championships at Lexington. Here our greatest rivals would be Germany and the Americans; again, we would be unlikely to match their supremacy in the dressage, and so fast, clear cross-country rounds were again the objective; also, the Lexington course was likely to be more technical than the course for the 1977 Europeans. Frank's aim was therefore to help prepare riders for what they might have to face in America – although at the trickier obstacles, he also had to build an alternative to suit the younger, up-and-coming horses and riders, so that they were not overfaced. However, those wanting a World Championship team place would have to show that they could tackle the technical fences successfully, and post a fast time.

The following year, 1979, there were two conflicting requirements demanded of the Badminton course: first, a team had to be chosen for the Luhmuhlen European Championships. The course there would almost certainly not be as demanding as Lexington had been, but because of our lesser ability in the dressage, the competition would probably be decided by speed across country, and so potential team members would have to be prepared, and able, to tackle big fences at speed. But looking even further ahead, to the 1980 Moscow Olympics, the course also needed to offer a good but fair challenge to those younger horses and riders who might be at their peak in the year after, ready for the Olympics. So at the more technical fences Frank built even more alternatives than usual so that every rider could decide on a route that best suited his own, and his horse's, temperament and ability.

**The course in 1978** The first few fences on any course should be designed to warm the horse up after his ten-minute halt, and to allow horse and rider to get into a rhythm. But most importantly at a three-day event, the first fence should in no way resemble a steeplechase fence, as this could confuse the horse as to what he was about to tackle. As Frank famously said of fence no 1, the Fallen Tree, in 1978: 'This would be an ideal obstacle to school a four-year-old over on a Monday morning, and not even the stupidest horse could mistake it for another steeplechase fence, or be in any doubt that the cross-country had begun.' Similarly fence no 2, the Woodpile, was designed to have a kind, inviting profile to it. (This fence has an interesting history: at its heart lay an old tree trunk, which was one of the oldest obstacles on the course. It had been felled about twenty-five years before in the Pleasure Gardens, but it was found to be hollow and filled with concrete, and was therefore unsaleable. For many years it had made a good fence in its own right, but it had begun to weather and had to be added to – and so the Woodpile was conceived.)

The technical questions started to come at fence no 4, the Cat's Cradle (above): this involved a jump over some rails to another set of rails on a one-stride distance, and then a bounce distance. At home, set up with showjumps, this would be a simple schooling grid, but here the solid nature of the obstacle and the 'crossed poles' in the middle, combined with the need to tackle it at cross-country speed, would make an uncomfortable question for some. The other option was to jump the double of corners.

The Stockholm Fence, at no 14 (below), was identical in concept to the notorious fence at the 1956 Olympic Games, but with two important modifications which made it a far more acceptable obstacle: by using a very large tree trunk instead of a spindly rail, the fence became instantly more inviting and removed the risk of a horse getting trapped on it, as Countryman did at the Olympics. Secondly, the banks were reinforced and constructed of gravel so there was no risk of the horse slipping on take-off.

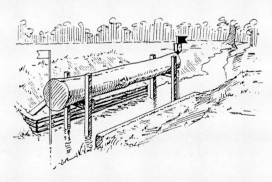

The Normandy Bank (fence no 20) (below) was an optical illusion which the rider had to ignore: on the approach it looked as if there was enough room on the top to take a stride before jumping the rail off; the uninitiated might there-

fore be tempted to approach slowly to allow time for this. This approach would be wrong, however, and the answer was to bounce off the bank and over the rails: therefore the more 'dash' the rider approached with – provided he kept his rein contact – the easier was the task for his horse.

The fences in Huntsman's Close were all interrelated, meaning that the way the rider tackled one would affect the way he tackled the rest. Huntsman's Grave (below) was a

sheer-sided wide ditch, a type of fence common on the Continent; this sort can, however, badly injure the horse's hindlegs if it misjudges the width, hence the special padding which was added to this version. An open ditch is normally tackled at speed, but taking this one too fast would make it harder to take the quickest route at the Post and Rails (below). Then the quickest line to the next fence, the

Arrowhead (above), involved jumping a hazard, an unmarked permanent fence – and it was worth bearing in mind that although a horse would not be penalised for stopping at it, if he fell he was still within the penalty zone and would incur penalties. So the rider had to tackle this whole sequence of fences almost as if it were one combination fence.

**The course in 1979** In the following year, 1979, Huntsman's Close was jumped from the opposite direction, although it still obviously remained an interrelated problem. The most direct line to the Arrowhead (below) and on to the next obstacle involved jumping both the 'hazard' fence on the

approach, and a higher set of rails to the right of the Arrowhead. Those who then felt they had to gallop at the next, Huntsman's Leap (above), in order to clear the depression on the landing side, had then committed themselves to taking the longest route to the left of the Post and Rails (top right). The more confident rider could choose between two

'medium' routes, whilst the expert would 'pop' the hedge and be sufficiently controlled to turn sharp right to the Post and Rails, thereby saving the most time of all.

The Sunken Footpath (no ll) (below) also appeared in 1979; this was modelled on the coffin-type fence. An experienced combination would make nothing of it, but the inexperienced horse or rider tended to find that if they had a stop

at this type of fence, they were often eliminated there. So the first rails were curved, so the rider could, if he wanted, reduce the worst effect of the downward slope and keep his horse's eye off the ditch in the bottom by jumping the rails at one side. And if the worst came to the worst, he could run along the bottom of the ditch and avoid jumping it altogether!

Jumping into water is the ultimate test of the horse's trust in his rider. To help the horse, the rider has to decide on the correct speed on the approach, and the speed to take through the water. Because of the negative effect of the drag of the water on the horse's legs, the rider should aim to approach and cross the water as slowly as is practically possible. The more difficult bounce into the water offered the shortest, and therefore by far the quickest, line as there was so much less water to cross than when taking the alternative.

The above are just a few examples of the thinking that goes into the course designer's 'setting' of the questions, and give a good idea of the degree of thinking the rider must do to answer the questions correctly!

**The sponsors' fences**   The course designer not only has to build fences to challenge the riders and entertain the public, but if he has any idea of public relations, he will also design fences which please his sponsor. Whitbread Breweries sponsored Badminton from 1961 to 1991, and they gave Frank Weldon plenty of scope to use his imagination. The

Whitbread Bar appeared in 1967 as the penultimate fence, and in 1969 began its long reign as the final fence. A roof was added in 1974, although this caused the 10th Duke of Beaufort some concern because he was not convinced that the rider would not be decapitated; however, the Beaufort huntsman, Brian Gupwell, was happy to test the system and jumped through on his hunter, proving that it was perfectly safe. At the time, 'roofed' fences were a relatively new idea, but today it is not uncommon for horses and riders to jump through far smaller 'holes'; for instance the 'owl-hole' fence has become a popular concept at many competitions.

In 1978 the Whitbread Drays were placed in front of the Lake; this was a fantastic advertisement for the sponsor

and provided a very impressive-looking, but relatively simple, fence for the riders. The Whitbread Barrels were an equally appropriate first fence in 1979: nothing is more readily associated with beer than a beer barrel, and the barrels themselves offered an inviting and kind profile to the horse and rider. However, it would be with a wry smile that some competitors viewed the advertisement that Whitbread placed on the back of the programme for several years: it featured a drawing of the final fence, the Whitbread Bar, with the words 'You'll never have a refusal at the Whitbread Bar'. Unfortunately the answer for some riders has been 'Oh, yes you will!'

In 1992 Mitsubishi Motors sponsored Badminton for the first time, and Hugh Thomas, who had succeeded Frank Weldon in 1989, again had plenty of scope to use his imagination. Thus the Mitsubishi Pickups were a quick and easy replacement for the Whitbread Drays, but a lot more thought had gone into the Three Diamonds; the design of this fence represented the Mitsubishi emblem and

was fairly technical, offering riders at least four ways of tackling it. The Whitbread Bar was replaced by the Mitsubishi Garden. Then in 1995 the Mitsubishi M appeared, which again offered two technical routes through it. The Shogun Seat replaced the Whitbread Barrels as the opener for riders – and although both of these fences look inviting and easy, Badminton has had its share of first-fence faulters.

# 1979

## 'It's the seconds that count'

**HRH Princess Anne** and **Goodwill** parade before the final showjumping phase, when they finished sixth

Twenty years on, when you talk to Sue Benson (née Hatherley) about her second place at Badminton, the disappointment and frustration at missing the top spot is still apparent. Many people dream of 'just getting to Badminton' – just to get round and complete the event is an enormous achievement. But to someone who is fiercely competitive, particularly when mounted on a really class horse, coming second is almost harder to bear than coming nowhere.

### So near – and yet so far

Here, in her own words, Sue relives the Badminton that was so nearly hers:

'There had only been three clear rounds by the time I set off on the cross-country – Jane Starkey and Topper Too, Clissy Strachan and Merry Sovereign, and HRH Princess Anne with Goodwill. Monacle and I set off in determined fashion; we had had our problems in the past and he was still strong, but I had learnt from experience that bitting him strongly and fighting him just created a battle that I would always lose. I now had him in a rubber snaffle and adopted the principle that if I didn't pull, then he couldn't pull, and kept my interference to an absolute minimum.

'The ride Monacle gave me was the sort that every rider dreams of: he galloped effortlessly, focusing on every fence as it came; he never wavered from the line I asked for, and over the

true galloping fences he simply soared with feet to spare. As I checked my watch my heart soared with him, because we were going to finish inside the optimum time. However, just as I was savouring the glory of taking the lead in this phase, Lucinda Prior-Palmer and Killaire were setting out on the cross-country. She had a ten-penalty advantage over me due to their better dressage performance – but surely she would not be able to finish inside the time. Lucinda herself would be the first to admit that Killaire could not gallop – he had to cut every corner to make up for his lack of pace. I didn't want to lis-ten to, or watch her progress; I didn't want my performance to be overshadowed, my hard-won lead to be taken away.

'Lucinda asked everything of Killaire, and to his credit he gave everything he had to give. I led for twelve precious minutes, because although Lucinda had time faults (6.8) she was still able to steal ahead of me by 3.2 penalties.

'There was still hope – there must always be hope. If I could jump a clear round tomorrow, and if she had a fence down, then I could still win.

'The night before the final phase was a

**Sue Benson** and **Monacle** enjoying an effortless and fast clear round

# The 1970s

Opposite: **Lucinda** with Charles Cyzer and **Killaire**. Killaire was selected for the European Championships in Luhmuhlen later that year, and produced another inspired performance which put him in second place at the end of cross-country day, and Britain as a team in the lead. But within a few hours it became obvious that he had sustained some sort of injury to his off-foreleg, and could not showjump on the final day. Nevertheless, he was back to take second place at Badminton in 1980 as a thirteen-year-old. Killaire was retired to Charlie Cyzer's yard where he led the two-year-olds up to the gallops. He was put down in 1995.

**Sue Benson** and **Monacle**

turmoil of emotions. The magical ride Monacle had given me was being replayed in my mind over and over again: I could still feel the thrill of his effortless gallop, his exuberant jumping. But then I worried – will he be tired, has he injured anything, did I ask too much of him, will he pass the horse inspection in the morning? And even if he does, how will he feel in the final phase? Could I hope for our normal clear round, or would today's efforts have taken their toll? More than anything I prayed for us to be all right.

On showjumping day, the tension was rising: 'Monacle passed the vet, now we just had the final phase to come. Pat Burgess helped us warm up for this crucial contest. As I waited to go into the packed arena, third-placed Jimmy Wofford from America and Carawich were jumping. He had two fences down: the crowd groaned in sympathy. He dropped to fourth, and Captain Mark Phillips and Columbus, who had jumped one of only two clear rounds so far, moved up to third. It had given me a little more space – although I needed to jump clear to put the pressure on Lucinda, it meant that if I did have a fence down, at least I would keep second place.

'As I waited for the bell the pressure mounted and I tried not to feel panicked. The commentator introduced us: "Sue Hatherley riding Neil Lawson-Baker and syndicate's Monacle II" —and I was reminded that all my syndicate owners were watching, waiting and, like me, praying for a clear round. I concentrated on establishing a relaxed rhythm, then the bell broke the oppressive silence – but suddenly I could have been anywhere, even jumping quietly at home; it was just me and my horse concentrating on doing our best. But the cheers and clapping brought me back to Badminton: and we'd just jumped a clear round! I couldn't help myself, but I kept praying that Lucinda would make a mistake. I was only minutes away from the title I had always dreamed of holding.

'Lucinda rode into the arena. As she passed me I wished her luck, but if I was really honest I didn't mean it. I didn't want anything awful to happen to her, but she had already savoured this victory three times before. Was it too much to ask for luck to be on my side this time? The shouts and cheers then told me the last thing I wanted to hear: Killaire had jumped a clear round, and Lucinda had won her fourth Badminton title.

'Somehow I managed to do all that was expected of me: I congratulated Lucinda, and smiled the smile of the noble runner-up – but then I had to move away, to stand alone with my emotions. Much is said about being generous in defeat, but I could only act it out, I couldn't truly feel it. I now know it is possible to feel entirely alone, even while being surrounded by thousands of people, and observed on television by thousands more. I really wasn't sure how I was going to keep up the pretence for long enough – there was still the prize-giving, and then the laps of honour to get through. When it came to the bit that mattered most, the cross-country, we had performed the best and yet that wasn't good enough. Yet as my mind raced with my mixed emotions, it took just a few simple words to put everything back in perspective: standing beside me was Neil Lawson-Baker, the head of Monacle's syndicate: "Just remember," he said, "it's the seconds that count." His words allowed me to enjoy the moment, and to value its true worth.

'To be second at Badminton was a tremendous achievement. Monacle and I were not best suited to each other. He was one of the few horses I never came to love – we tolerated each other because together we could do what we each loved most. He had almost been sold abroad when I couldn't afford him myself, but Neil's determination in pulling together a syndicate to buy him meant that he had stayed with me. Later that same year we won the team silver medal at the Luhmuhlen European Championships.'

## A fourth victory for Lucinda

Killaire was owned by Charles Cyzer and was another of Lucinda's challenging rides. His preferred way of going was to scuttle along with his head and neck low to the ground, and because he lacked speed he was always having to operate in top gear. Lucinda never doubted his honesty, but she did not believe he would be able to win a major three-day event. However, at this year's Badminton, having already been third in 1977, he gave every ounce of effort and speed that he could muster to claim a victory for himself.

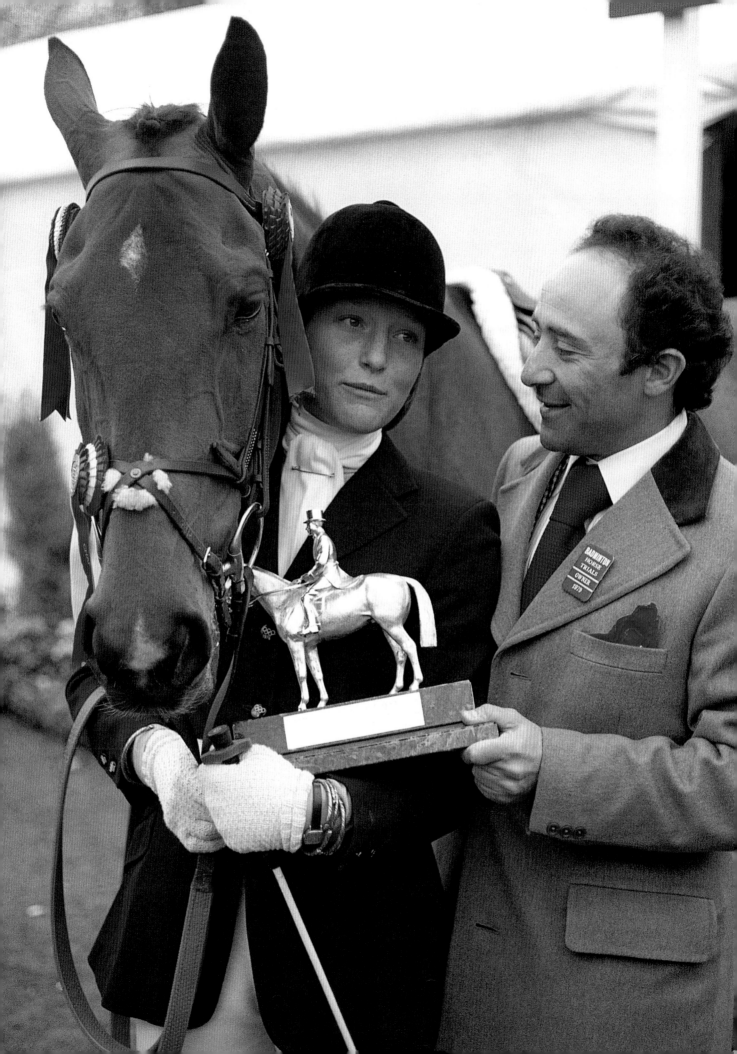

# The 1980s

# 1980
# The underling from down under

A still relatively unknown **Mark Todd** won Badminton on **Southern Comfort** at his first attempt in 1980

Pages 144–5: **Lucinda Green** and **Beagle Bay** make an impressive leap into the Lake in 1984

Mark Todd had announced to his mother at a very young age that he was going to ride for New Zealand at the Olympics, but when he arrived in England to compete at the Badminton Horse Trials in 1980, his experience to date did not persuade the nation to back him as a likely winner, let alone an Olympic candidate. He had been selected to ride for New Zealand at the 1978 Lexington World Championships, but Top Hunter, a normally thoroughly honest horse, was eliminated on the cross-country; afterwards it was found that he had injured both front tendons. Mark could not afford to take his horse back to New Zealand, and so he was sold. His buyer, a Swiss dealer called Jurg Zindel,

had a yard in England and offered Mark a job.

Having walked the Badminton course in 1979, Mark was confident that it was jumpable if he could find the right horse. On a trip back to New Zealand for Christmas, Mark bought Southern Comfort, or Monty. He was already a grade B showjumper and had jumped two Advanced tracks in New Zealand. Mark got on well with the big bay horse and brought him to England just six weeks before Badminton. A few cross-country lessons with Lady Hugh Russell at Wylye left him confident that they were ready for the challenge. The money in this year was on a win for Mark Phillips, Mike Tucker, Richard Meade or Lucinda Green; the little known New Zealander, Mark Todd, was left in peace to work things out his own way! Fellow New Zealander Andrew Nicholson groomed for him on this momentous occasion.

The cross-country course in this year had not been altered much, and so perhaps it was a case of familiarity breeds contempt, because it caused more than the usual amount of havoc. Mark had been lying about fortieth after the dressage, but a fast, clear cross-country performance pulled him up to third place. He showjumped clear, and then sat and watched whilst Lucinda and Killaire faulted at the water, and then the overnight leaders, Helen Butler and Merganser, had four fences down. Mark Todd had won Badminton at his first attempt. Having only seen television pictures of the Queen presenting the prizes to the Badminton winner, Mark knew that the girls normally curtsied; he quickly decided that that probably wasn't required from him, and managed a bow.

Southern Comfort went lame later that season and so was unable to go to the alternative

Above: **Mark Phillips** and **Lincoln** were expected to do well this year but a mishap on the cross-country meant they had to wait until the following year (1981) for victory. They were fifth in 1980

Left: **Goran Breisner**, riding his own and Lars Sederholm's **Ultimus**, earned Sweden a third place; this combination also took fourth place the following year. 'Yogi' Breisner still works closely with Lars Sederholm of the Waterstock Training Centre. Today they are both much in demand to improve the jumping skills of event horses in particular, and also racehorses.

# The 1980s

'The Slide', which posed a similar problem to the Derby Bank at Hickstead, caused no trouble at all when used in previous years, but the rails were a little higher than usual in 1980: here **Nils Haagenson** and **Monaco** suffer the consequences

Olympics at Fontainebleau. He came right again, but by then Mark's money was running out and reluctantly he decided he would have to sell him. He was sold to Torrance Fleischmann and went on to become leading horse of the year in America. As many of us know, Mark went on to do a good many greater things (see 1984, 1994, and 1996).

## Chaos on the course

Perhaps it was Frank Weldon's encouraging comments to the effect that on 1980's course little had been changed that lulled so many riders into a false sense of security; he even went as far as to say that if a rider chose to take all the alternatives it would probably be one of the simplest Badminton courses designed – but just to get round slowly is not the aim of most riders.

Back in 1967 Badminton had featured its first 'bounce fence' in Huntsman's Close, and although its inception was a shock at the time, bounce fences soon featured on courses at all levels. The double bounce at the Chevrons, ten years later, was a natural progression, and so, one could argue, was the treble bounce featured in 1980 at the Badminton Dog Kennels (fence no 4). The alternative either side was to take a corner and a narrow parallel, with the obvious risk of a run-out. The double of banks at the second Luckington Lane crossing caught out any rider who lost his position and therefore his ability to maintain the horse's balance and impulsion. The Quarry offered three routes, none of which was any more inviting than the other – it was down to the rider to choose the option which best suited his horse.

Also, the steeplechase changed route in this year, so that instead of galloping twice round an oval track, the course now described a figure-of-eight; this was to help introduce riders to the tighter, twistier steeplechase courses often featured at Continental three-day events.

Of the sixty-three cross-country starters on Phase D, thirty horses were either eliminated or retired; and although the top four had all produced clear cross-country rounds, the fifth-, sixth- and seventh-placed horses all had cross-country jumping penalties.

# 1981

## Fourth and final victory for Mark Phillips

Riding the Range Rover Team's Lincoln, Captain Mark Phillips recorded his fourth win at Badminton. A 16.3hh black gelding, Lincoln was already qualified to compete at Advanced level when he was bought for Mark, but he had not actually tackled an Advanced track. The partnership took a long time to gel, as Mark recalls:

'I did not find Lincoln easy, as he tended to charge at his fences and then suddenly back himself off to jump them. I spent eighteen months trying to teach him to keep an even rhythm on the approach to a fence, but the more I tried to do that, the more often he would stop – so in that respect I totally failed with him. In the end I thought, "Stuff it, I'll let him charge at everything and just hope for the best!" And his system seemed to work, as he was second at Batsford and then second at

**Outside assistance** Miss Sandy Brookes, one of two sisters competing at Badminton this year, had to fight off the unwanted assistance of a well-meaning spectator during her cross-country round. No outside assistance is allowed, under penalty of elimination, unless the rider falls or dismounts, or needs his whip or hat handing to him. After nearly falling from her horse Welton Lightfoot, Miss Brookes had quite a job to disentangle her reins, and despite her protestations, one of the nearby spectators insisted on trying to help her. The fence judge recorded that the rider had done all in her power to ward off the unsolicited help, and so she was not eliminated! All horse trials programmes explain the rule that outside assistance is not allowed – but spectators rarely expect to have to read the rules!

Boekelo. At his first Badminton, in 1980, we had a stupid stop at the Zig Zag Rails when I found we were galloping straight into the sun and I couldn't see a thing. So it was more a case of me stopping him, than him refusing to jump. Then at the Quarry I had to take a hard check to avoid a dog on the track, and that was enough interference for Lincoln to choose to stop. But even so, the course caused so much trouble that he still finished fifth.

'The following year we were lying nineteenth after the dressage so I didn't think we had much chance of overhauling the leaders. But the ground conditions were wet and heavy and the time was proving difficult to get. I saw that Charlie Micklem and the thirteen-year-old Village Gossip had got round in a quick time, and I thought, "Damn it, if Village Gossip can do it, then so can we!" So I set off with a very

positive attitude – everything to gain and nothing to lose. We recorded the fastest time of the day and that pulled us up to take the lead. Miss Sandy Pfleuger riding Free Scot was just behind us in second. We had a showjump down, but so did my now wife, Sandy, so she stayed in second place – which did not endear me to her at the time!

'In the past Lincoln had suffered an injury in the field when he had put his foot through the perimeter fence, and eventually he got some arthritis in the joint and had to be retired. He and Columbus lived together at Gatcombe for years, and then in the late eighties, when they had both got a bit creaky, and after one last good summer, they were put down together.'

It is interesting to note that when Mark won Badminton with Columbus in 1974 the first prize was £1,000; in 1981 it was £3,000.

Opposite: **Sandy Pfleuger** (now Mrs Mark Phillips) took second place on **Free Scot**

Above: **Richard Meade** and **Kilcashel** took third place. This nine-year-old bay gelding by Fray Bentos was owned by Richard's sponsors, George Wimpey Ltd

# 1982

# Badminton — the pressures and the pitfalls

In 1982 Rachel Bayliss and her much admired Mystic Minstrel took third place; but Rachel had always had mixed feelings about competing at Badminton:

'Badminton was always an awe-inspiring challenge. I am sure many riders arrive there feeling confident, but I always felt totally over-awed, something that never happened to me at Burghley or any other major championship. Badminton has a pressure all of its own because everyone expects so much of it, and of you. I always made more mistakes at Badminton than anywhere else, and I'm sure it was simply down to the pressure I felt there. I had been to watch Badminton as a child and the fences had looked unjumpable, and that feeling always stayed with me – arriving at Badminton was a bit like arriving on the moon!

'Having said all that, I am so glad that I was riding there during Frank Weldon's reign, because he had no equal in his ability to build a natural fence in the lie of the land that tested the rider more than the horse: if you got the horse there correctly, he could jump it easily. His direct routes often looked impossible, but you were impelled to use them because the alternatives weren't viable as a first choice if you went there intending to get placed.

'Up until 1988 Badminton was held in April rather than in May, so the weather was usually colder and bleaker, and it also gave you less time to prepare. All this seemed to add to the daunting atmosphere for me – though I would never have missed out on going. I was lucky in that I could always do the dressage – and enjoyed it, too! – but that meant I was often leading after the first day, and then of course we were made to feel even more pressured! I was lucky enough to have three international event horses which were just the tops, but I don't think I ever rode them as well at Badminton as elsewhere.

'In 1982 I had two rides at Badminton. The first was the eight-year-old Cuthbert the Celt. He had gone clear until the last fence, and then he ducked under the roof of the Whitbread Bar and fell. He turned the bar over so there were bottles everywhere!

'Mystic Minstrel, who was eleven, had led the dressage and we were going very well on the cross-country. On the last quarter of the course I could see that we were up on the time, and I was so terrified that something would go wrong again that I slowed down a little. Apparently my support team were shouting frantically, "Keep going – that's costing you about £1,000 per second!"

'That year the ground was perfect, the weather was perfect and everything fell into place. Taking third was good enough for me!

'The following year we again led the dressage, and as a special treat someone invited me into the members' tent for lunch. I ate a salmon sandwich and suffered a dreadful attack of food poisoning; I couldn't eat another thing after that, and felt dreadful the whole time. Minstrel pecked on landing over Tom Smith's Walls and I was so weak that I just fell off, whilst still within the penalty zone. However, later that year we became individual European

A Badminton victory in 1982 was a fitting reward for **Speculator**, a horse who had promised so much for so long

Champions at Frauenfeld, which was some consolation. I then concentrated on dressage with Minstrel, taking him to Grand Prix level and competing internationally. When he retired from top level events I lent him to a pupil of mine. He died aged twenty-one.

'Before Minstrel I had Gurgle the Greek. He didn't like Badminton – I frightened him by taking him there as a seven-year-old in 1976, and he never forgot it. We became famous for going under the Stockholm fence unpenalised, but then he was eliminated three fences from home at another fence with a ditch. He hated the ditches at Badminton, and yet he would jump similar things anywhere else – he proved this by winning the individual silver medal at the Luhmuhlen European Championships in 1979. Gurgle enjoyed competing at one-day events until he was fully retired. He was pampered at home until he had to be put down aged twenty-five.

'In the late 1970s I had help from John Shedden, winner of the first Badminton Three-Day Event. He gave me the advice and direction that I had lacked; his guidance gave me the confidence to perform better. However, I have done my bit at Badminton now; I went seven times on three fantastic horses and I had some good rides, but I had some bad experiences, too. Generally it has not been a lucky place for me – in particular when Cuthbert the Celt fell at the Stockholm fence in 1984 and had to be put down after breaking his foreleg. I have helped other people who compete there such as Tim Randle and Helen Bell and they have all been lucky there, but it is not for me.'

## Speculator wins for gold medallist

Richard Meade had attended the very first Badminton Horse Trials as a child; he was second there in 1963 with Barberry when it was a one-day event, second in 1968 with Turnstone, won it with The Poacher in 1970, took second with Laurieston in 1972, and was third with Eagle Rock in 1973. Along the way he won team gold at the Mexico and Munich Olympics, and a bagful of team and individual World and European Championship medals; moreover he remains the only British three-day event rider to have won an individual Olympic gold medal (in Munich 1972). Riding the appropriately named Speculator, Richard won his second and final Badminton title in 1982. He has some wonderful memories of Badminton in 1949:

'I remember standing by the Luckington Lane crossing in 1949 and watching the horses and riders jumping their way around Tom Smith's farm. In terms of the number of spectators and the informality, it was on a par with a Pony Club event. We sat on straw bales to watch the dressage, and if you got there early enough and put your coat on a bale, that was your seat reserved for the day! I was nine years old at the time and thought the whole thing was brilliant. I adored hunting, and the prospect of jumping across this wonderful park was just glorious; it truly inspired me. Since then I have had many wonderful rides around Badminton, and the one with Speculator was no exception.

'Speculator was bred in Rutland out of a hunter mare, Golden Rose, by the HIS premium stallion Specific. He went into training,

and as a four-year-old stood 16.3hh with huge feet which dished badly. His trainer Mrs Sturrock described him as very unathletic but as brave as a lion; she was amazed when she heard he had even completed Badminton! As a nine-year-old he was evented by Mary Gordon Watson. She rode him at Badminton despite having broken a bone in her hand. He was a very strong horse, and with this injury Mary could not hold him; he overjumped and fell with her at the Lake. The following year he again proved too strong for Mary, falling twice as a result of taking off too far away from his fences.

'At about this time I had a call saying that George Wimpey Ltd wanted to sponsor some British Olympic initiatives, and this included buying me two horses. I had Speculator on a three-day trial. We went cross-country schooling at Chepstow and that's where I discovered what Mary had had to cope with: over galloping fences he was fantastic, but at anything technical, when you tried to slow him down so that he could work out what to do, he would just bound forwards and barge his way through. I was immediately filled with admiration for Mary who had ridden him successfully at Advanced level for the last two years.

'Despite my doubts Pat Burgess, my jumping trainer, was convinced that he was the horse for me, and with considerable reservations I was persuaded by her to let George Wimpey Ltd buy him for me. After a fall and a good few lucky escapes at one-day events, Pat and I devised a system that suited him: he needed to be set up for a fence much sooner than most horses, then he felt free and unhindered in front of the fence so he wasn't tempted to rush. At our first Badminton together in 1980 he thundered round effortlessly to be one of only six clear rounds; but in the course of it he sprained a tendon which had to be operated on, and so he had the rest of the year off.

'This was the year when most riders had underestimated the difficulty of the course, largely because Frank Weldon had written in his preview that little had been changed from previous years. I always made a point of not reading anything about a course before I had

# The 1980s

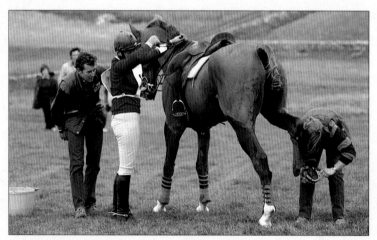

walked it, and I would avoid listening to other people's thoughts about it until I had seen it for myself; in that way you are viewing the course in the same way as the horse will – with no prior knowledge at all. I actually thought the course looked extremely difficult – though when I heard those around me saying how straightforward it was, I began to wonder if perhaps I was getting too old for this game!

'In 1981 some help from Ferdi Eilberg really paid dividends with Speculator's dressage at Badminton. He gave me a wonderful ride in all three phases, though he was penalised for a slip-up on the flat within the penalty zone at the Crooked S.

'In 1982 he was fourteen, and it was his fifth Badminton. In the dressage he was only bettered by the unbeatable Rachel Bayliss and Mystic Minstrel; just two points behind us was Bruce Davidson and JJ Babu. While I was on the roads and tracks I heard that Bruce Davidson had gone clear inside the time, but that Rachel Bayliss had picked up time faults.

'Spec rose to the occasion as never before, and by winning Badminton finally proved just what a good horse he was. I remember turning to Bruce Davidson [see 1995] who finished second and saying what an exciting competition it had proved to be, not least because he had pushed me all the way. His reply was simply, "That was the intention"!

'I had hoped that in 1983 Spec could have successfully defended his title, but because of a slight suspensory strain he was retired that year instead.'

Looking back on his long and successful competitive career, Richard counts himself very lucky that he was always able to have complete confidence in the horses he rode: 'It is always a case of trying to find the key to the horse's character and then building a partnership. It is about meeting them half way – never trying to impose on them, but working towards gaining their confidence and co-operation. To succeed, the horse has got to want to go across country, and when training him you have to do everything to make that experience as pleasant as possible for him. Sometimes that means using an awful lot of leg, at other times it means sitting very quietly!'

# A testing cross-country

Frank Weldon, who was seventy this year, summed up the challenge he had set at Badminton by saying, 'Riders must make up their own minds which option is best suited to their own or their horse's capability ... but if they are over-ambitious they will have only themselves to blame.' What he meant by this was that by providing several different options at the more technical fences, he was giving riders the chance to pick what suited them best; thus the least experienced could take the longer options, but those wanting to show off their dash and skill would have plenty of opportunity to do so. With the European Championships coming up later in the year, and even more importantly, the Los Angeles Olympics the year after, there were plenty of riders intending to demonstrate their abilities – but many would leave the event with Frank's words of warning ringing loudly in their ears!

In special evidence this year was the effort that the Badminton Horse Trials always makes to put something back not only into eventing, but into the rural way of life: thus several fences were designed and named with the unashamed intention of focusing public attention on the fund-raising efforts of particular groups or bodies. For instance the British Field Sports Society, needing funds to cover the costs of fighting the threat to hunting, had their own fence at no 18. Fence 7 pro-

**Regal Realm:** 'He had an incredible jump, but did everything with his head in the air – he was so ewe-necked that when he galloped along his ears were in your mouth! He combined great enthusiasm with tremendous sensitivity, which made him difficult in the dressage. He won team and individual gold medals at the 1982 World Championships, team and individual silver at the 1983 European Championships, and team silver at the 1984 Los Angeles Olympics. He went back to Australia to retire in the sun, and died when he was twenty-one.'

1983 brought a fifth victory for **Lucinda Green** riding **Regal Realm**

moted the British International Equestrian Fund, and their efforts to raise money to cover the expense of sending British horses out to the Los Angeles Olympics; whilst the Aintree Chair and Beechers drew attention to the Grand National Appeal. With over 200,000 people in attendance this year, the above initiative must have been invaluable.

After the dressage Rachel Bayliss and Mystic Minstrel were the easy leaders, followed

by Ginny Holgate on Priceless and Lorna Clarke (née Sutherland) on Danville. However, as things turned out, only nineteen horses jumped clear on cross-country day. Afterwards, Frank Weldon made it quite clear how disappointed he was at the number of mistakes made at what he considered to be the 'none too difficult' obstacles. This included some experienced riders, for example:

Mark Phillips and Classic Lines tried to take the bounce at the Pig Sties, but fell when Classic Lines tried to squeeze in a stride. This mistake certainly put a number of others off trying this route, although Yogi Breisner and Ultimus made it look easy. Sadly Ultimus had given the others a head start in the dressage.

Dressage leader Rachel Bayliss fell at the Park Wall, whilst Marjorie Comerford and Charlotte Steel both fell at Tom Smith's Walls.

David Green was unseated from Marangi Bay in spectacular fashion at the Bull Pens: they strayed off their line going through the combination, and Mairangi Bay hit one element hard. David was thrown up in the air, and came back down in the saddle on his tummy, facing his horse's tail with his legs one side of his horse's neck; he actually managed to stay on his horse as it jumped the last element, and only then did the force of gravity prevail!

Diana Clapham and Windjammer tripped up the step out of the Lake and stopped at the Upturned Punt.

Nils Haagensen and Waterloo, gold medallist at the 1980 Fontainebleau alternative Olympics, had a stop at fence no 3. They continued to the Quarry where Waterloo jumped over the wall and straight down into the bottom, unseating Nils in the process.

Ginny Holgate and Nightcap also had trouble here, when Nightcap followed Waterloo's example and leapt to the bottom of the Quarry. His young rider managed to stay on board, but his leap up the steps to the rail and drop was too big and bold, with the result that his front feet slipped between the rail and the bank, so he couldn't take off. Over the rest of the course Ginny produced a lovely round from him.

Mike Tucker, who finally took second place

with General Bugle, had a very sticky moment with Dalwhinnie when his hind legs slipped back into the ditch at the Footbridge; however, both stayed upright to continue clear.

Kingsbridge Kip must have infuriated his rider Laura Tierney when he repeated his trick of the previous year with a stop at the final fence!

The Quarry was responsible for most of the penalties incurred. The New Moon, a very upright, crescent-shaped set of rails at the bottom of a steep incline, which had been described by several riders as horrific, jumped well for most. Also, although Frank Weldon's course this year caught out more riders than he had intended it to, the riders did extract their own small revenge: at the Footbridge, they discovered a short-cut that took only a fraction longer than the intended quick route, and was very much quicker than the long route the designer had in mind!

In the final phase on the third day, the top three horses after the cross-country each had a showjump down but kept their positions; this resulted in a fifth victory for Lucinda Green (née Prior-Palmer) riding Regal Realm; a best Badminton performance for local farmer Mike Tucker and General Bugle; whilst Ireland had their best placing for a long time when Jessica Harrington and Amoy took third. Lorna Clarke showjumped clear with Danville to retain her fourth place.

Opposite: A sticky moment for **Lucinda Green** and **Beagle Bay,** her second ride in 1983

**Lucinda** and **David Green** who had vastly different experiences at Badminton in 1983. Lucinda continued her habit of winning, David had a spectacular fall

**Mike Tucker** and **Dalwhinnie,** with whom he finished seventh, preparing for the steeplechase phase

If only... Mike Tucker after finishing second on General Bugle behind Lucinda Green and Regal Realm: 'If we hadn't gone the wrong way in the dressage, or had one showjump down, we would have won.'

**Mike Tucker: from competitor to commentator** The voice of Mike Tucker is now a well established part of Badminton: along with Lorna Clarke and Lucinda Green, Mike is the BBC's Badminton commentator. But during the sixties, seventies and early eighties Mike was a regular competitor at what, for this Tetbury farmer, was a local event. He first rode at Badminton in 1964 when he finished sixth on The Viking, in spite of suffering what could have been one of the more embarrassing moments in his career: in the final showjumping phase, there was a sharp turn to be made right in front of the

Left: **Mike Tucker**, as spectator in the 1950s. He is flanked by William and Roger Alexander. William Alexander is married to Carol who works in the Box Office

Opposite: On his way to recording his best result at Badminton: **Mike Tucker** and the home-bred **General Bugle** finished second

royal box, and as Mike's horse turned, the saddle slipped round under its belly. Remarkably, Mike managed to stay on, re-right the saddle and complete the course, though with three fences down; and in his own defence he explained that 'in those days we didn't have things like overgirths or breastplates. I was very lucky to stay on board, as the saddle was right back on my horse's loins as we left the arena – and yes, the incident did create a great deal of mirth locally!'

Mike's proudest moment came in 1983 when he finished second on his favourite horse, the home-bred General Bugle, and seventh on Dalwhinnie. Mike recalls that it was a very special moment when he paraded his two horses in the main arena: 'I was never usually a two-horse rider, and so to have two to ride at Badminton was wonderful. Badminton's host then was the late Duke of Beaufort, and he knew both myself and Bugle well from the hunting field. It made the occasion even more memorable that he was busy telling the Queen as much about Bugle as I could have done myself!'

As a retired competitor and now an international course designer, Mike has plenty of experience to draw on when commentating on the great event. But as he explains, the whole procedure is almost as technical and complicated as riding round the course itself:

'From a filming point of view, the course is split into two,

with about eight cameras in each section. The shots from one section of the course are relayed to us through what we call the Luckington scanner, and the shots from the other side of the course come through on the main scanner. The main producer is in charge of what shots we actually use, and so it is he who effectively "tells the story". The system which we as commentators feel suits us best is for me first of all to introduce the rider, and then at the end to "bring them home", whilst Lucinda and Lorna do the "expert bit" in between. What is difficult is that we can't actually see the live action, but only what is shown on the scanners, besides which we are sat in the BBC compound which is well away from all the action and excitement — so any enthusiasm that comes across in the commentary is entirely self-generated! We are, of course, wearing headsets so we can hear what the producer is saying — but unfortunately it means we can also hear him speaking to all the camera crew, to his assistant, to cross-country control and anyone else. So all the time that you are trying to keep up with whichever screen you are meant to be commenting on, you have several different conversations going on in your ear which you can't ignore because sometimes the producer is speaking to you! So it is very easy to lose your concentration — though it does get easier with practice.

'As well as all this, our "mics" have a three-way switch: off/on and "lazy", which allows us to speak to the producer. Until you get used to it it is quite easy to start your commentary and find you are switched off or on "lazy", in which case only your colleagues will be enjoying your oratory!

'As with most things, the hardest situation for us is when something goes wrong, such as the year Mandy Stibbe had a bad fall and the course was held for about forty minutes while they attended to her. We quickly ran out of any "prefilmed" action, and then it was a case of just trying to think of anything relevant to say to keep things going — and then you run out of air time just as the action is restarting. At the best of times, live commentary is much more of an adrenalin-pumping activity than recorded commentaries, because obviously as soon as the words leave your mouth they are heard by your audience — there is no second chance, no editing!

'Another difficult year for us was when Toddy [Mark Todd] was the first to go and took the lead after the dressage, and

then led from start to finish [in 1994 with Horton Point]. It was very hard to drum up any excitement about the outcome of the competition because it was such a foregone conclusion. How easy or difficult our job is depends very much on how the story unfolds on the day; the more exciting and dramatic the story, the easier is our task. But then it is all a part of our job to make whatever you can of the material you have got.'

With a wife and until recently a daughter both competing, Mike has also had the task of commentating on members of his own family as they progress around various courses: 'That situation is always fine until something goes wrong.

Fortunately for me nothing has gone wrong when I have been doing television commentary, but it has when I have been doing the public address. You have to make yourself take a detached, professional approach as far as is humanly possible. With regard to Badminton, one of the hardest tasks for me was commentating when my wife Angela rode round on my old horse, General Bugle. I had only recently given up competing him myself and so I knew the horse inside out and could anticipate where things might be about to go right or wrong. And it meant there were two souls on the course at the very same time who meant a great deal to me.'

# 1984

# A record-breaking sixth title

The part-Welsh pony **Beagle Bay** took **Lucinda** to her sixth victory

Opposite: 'The little horse with a big heart': **Charisma** finished second at Badminton in 1984 and went on to win individual gold medals at the next two Olympics (Los Angeles in 1984 and Seoul in 1988)

In 1980, Lucinda Prior-Palmer wrote a book called *Four Square*. It was a tribute to her four Badminton winners: Be Fair, Wideawake, George and Killaire, each of whom feature in earlier chapters. When Lucinda won her fourth Badminton with Killaire in 1979 she described it as 'drawing the fourth and final side, and thereby closing an unbelievable square'. She considered herself extraordinarily privileged to have enjoyed such harmony and communication with four very different horses during the greatest three days of their lives. Imagine, then, how it must have felt to win twice more after that! Six wins on six different horses: only Captain Mark Phillips comes anywhere close, with four wins on three horses.

A handsome fourteen-year-old grey gelding gave Lucinda her record-breaking victory: Beagle Bay, who had won Burghley in 1981. However, he was never a very sound horse, and often disappointed at major three-day

events when he had to be withdrawn before the showjumping. Lucinda describes him as 'half pony, as he was part Welsh. He had that ponyish streak in him which meant if you were not 100 per cent "with" him he would stop or run out just for the hell of it. I thought he was too much of a pony to be top class, but he proved me wrong. He had a huge girth which we used to laugh about and call his "fat pony tummy", but it must have housed a huge pair of lungs as he had tremendous stamina. He led the dressage in this year, and our only sticky moment across country was when he skidded right across the top of the Frauenfeld Platform; this was a bridge-like platform which could either be jumped over or "banked" [it made a reappearance in 1998]. We had a fence in hand on the final day, but Beagle Bay jumped clear anyway to finish on his dressage score.

'After this victory my Badmintons were not particularly happy. I flew over Willy B's head when he hurled himself over the Ski Jump [1988] – Ginny Leng had the same problem with Murphy Himself; both horses ejected their riders at the speed of light, although they kept on their own feet quite easily.

'Then there was Minns Lincoln; he was the only horse I got as far as Badminton with, only to find he didn't have the heart for it. I had never believed there was such a thing as a horse that would win at three-star level but could not cope with a four-star event. He proved that there was, and he positively shook with fear over the Badminton and Burghley ditches.

'Seven is my lucky number, and I have thought about having one more go – but I know life rarely works like that. Anyway, these days I think I would need a horse that would pick me up in its arms and carry *me* round!'

## Charisma

Since his win at Badminton in 1980, New Zealander Mark Todd had not given up on his intention to be successful at the Olympics; he had ridden at the alternative Olympics at Fontainebleau in 1980, but not on the best of horses, and had been eliminated on the cross-country. But in 1983 he was offered the ride on a little New Zealand horse called Charisma.

Charisma was already at Intermediate level and was a Grade B showjumper when Mark took over the ride on him, but at 15.3hh he wasn't exactly made to measure for a 6ft 6in Mark Todd! When he brought Charisma over to England in the spring of 1984 most people were surprised that the horse was being aimed at Badminton – but Mark already knew he was something special, as they had been unbeaten in five runs they had had in New Zealand the year before, which included a three-day event.

At Badminton in 1984 the little horse was sixth after the dressage, and sailed round the cross-country to pull up to second place. They produced one of the most impressive showjumping rounds the next day, though a clear round from Lucinda meant they couldn't improve on their position. From here Charisma, aged ten, went on to win the individual gold medal at the Los Angeles Olympics.

Mark did not think for one moment that he would be able to take Charisma to the next Olympics: 'I just assumed he would have retired by then, but he just got better and better. He was second again at Badminton in 1985, and second at Burghley in 1987 – "Podge", as Charisma was known, obviously didn't like to win three-day events in England! I was very tempted to enter Badminton in 1988, the Seoul Olympic year, but having decided to try for the Olympics if Podge felt fit and happy to do it, we didn't want to overdo things.

'He did one Advanced event that season – where he felt so well he exploded in the dressage, had five showjumps down and ran away with me on the cross-country! He was given a serious amount of work before his only other run prior to the Olympics – this was at Gatcombe, which he won. He then went to Seoul where he led the dressage, recorded the fastest cross-country round, and had just one fence down in the showjumping to win his second individual Olympic gold medal.'

Charisma was then retired and spent a few years in New Zealand. However, Mark has bought his own place and made his home in England, together with his wife Carolyn, and children James and Lauren, and now Charisma has come home too.

# 1985

# When things go wrong...

A great deal of the excitement of the three-day event lies in its unpredictability. The extra phases and the official horse inspections means that, compared to a one-day event, there is a whole lot more scope for things to go wrong!

Having survived a winter's training and a couple of months of preparatory competitions, horses arrive seemingly fit and well to compete at the Badminton three-day event. Most come on the Tuesday or Wednesday and settle happily into their stabling, and the first horse inspection is held on the Wednesday evening. But horses can, and do, fail this inspection, and they are then not allowed to take any further part in the event. It can be something as straightforward as treading on a stone whilst waiting to be trotted up, or the horse may simply knock into himself, and infuriatingly this type of lameness will probably have disappeared by later that evening – but later is too late, because the horse has to be passed fit at the official inspection.

The dressage phase can spring some surprise results, too. It is always judged by three people, each sat at a different place at the end of the arena, which means they each see the horse and rider at a slightly different angle. In this year, 1985, the international Ground Jury consisted of Vicomte de la Gravière (France), Mrs J. Hall (UK) and Mr Tony Buhler (Switzerland) – the latter had long-standing connections with Badminton, having been a member of the winning Swiss team, along with his brother, at Badminton in 1951.

At the end of the dressage phase in 1985, two of the three judges had Mark Todd and Charisma as their best test, but the third judge had him as seventh; the average of the scores put him in second place. America's Torrance Watkins-Fleischmann with Finvarra had not been the first choice of any of the judges, yet they took the lead. Two of the judges had Ginny Holgate in seventh place whilst the other put her first, and she ended up fourth. However, far worse than simply not earning the approval of all three judges is if the horse leaves the arena during his test, because he is then instantly disqualified – and it can be

**Ginny's reign begins** A truly great rider rises above the rest by being consistently successful. There are plenty of 'flash-in-the-pan' champions, and many 'single' prizes have been won by riders who have never hit the top again – but the mark of the truly great horseman is that he or she keeps coming back and winning. Ginny Holgate gave a good indication of what she was capable of when she took the Badminton title in 1985 with Priceless, and finished third with Nightcap – but this was only the beginning! (See 1989 and 1993.)

# The 1980s

**Charisma's** best was yet to come

An uncomfortable landing for **Mandy Stibbe** (née Jeakins) after **Woden** says 'No thank you'

harder than it looks to keep a fighting fit event horse within the confines of a 60 x 20m arena. In this particular year no one suffered this fate, but in 1995 Polly Clark, making her Badminton debut on Poggio, was unable to prevent him stepping outside the arena boards when he shied half-way through his test. There is no second chance: disqualification is immediate.

For those that complete the first phase without mishap, the potential for problems only gets greater on cross-country day! In this particular year nearly half the competitors were riding at Badminton for the first time, and only forty-two out of the seventy-six starters completed the cross-country – but it wasn't always the debutants who had problems. To mention just a couple: David Green incurred

sixty penalties for a fall when his horse Walkabout went 'walkabout' in Huntsman's Close and knocked him off against a tree. Some years later David had another discussion with a tree – and having given a memorable display of acrobatics when Mairangi Bay hit an element of the Bull Pens in 1983, he would probably be the first to say that Badminton was not his luckiest event!

Then Duncan Douglas and Spider had only got as far as fence no 3 when his stirrup iron broke. With great presence of mind Duncan calmly lengthened his stirrup leather and stuck his foot in that before continuing on his way. In 1995 Mark Todd was less fortunate: while

riding Bertie Blunt his stirrup leather broke as he landed in the Vicarage Pond at fence no 13. With two-thirds of the course still to ride, Mark hitched his leg up between fences so he could rest his knee on the pommel of the saddle in order to keep his weight off Bertie's back, and in this manner they completed a fast clear round.

With the speed and endurance test behind them, competitors now have to survive the final horse inspection and the showjumping phase, and fortunes invariably alter between the end of the cross-country and the end of the showjumping: there are a great many things that can go wrong in this particular space of time. In 1985 Mark Todd went into the lead at the end of cross-country day, with Torrance Watkins-Fleischmann in second place, and Ginny Holgate lying in third place with Priceless and in fourth with Nightcap.

Both Ginny's horses jumped clear, and next into the ring came Torrance. She was clear until the treble, and then unbelievably she and Finvarra completely missed their stride and crashed through the first element, to a shout of surprise from the crowd. With his rider sitting right up his neck, Finvarra carried on gamely through the whole combination but, needless to say, it was impossible for him to leave everything standing. Mark Todd had to jump a clear round with Charisma to keep his lead, but the final element of the treble fell. For Mark there would be other Badminton victories, but for Charisma there was never a Badminton title – just another Olympic gold medal three years later!

In fact the showjumping can hold far worse catastrophes than that of just slipping a place or two, and being more, or less, experienced seems to offer no guarantee against taking the wrong course. In 1970, the hugely experienced Bertie Hill was lying in second place when he came into the showjumping arena and jumped the stile in the wrong direction, and of course was eliminated immediately. Then more recently in 1998, Charlotte Ridley and Mistatiger were lying in fourteenth place when Charlotte turned and jumped the wrong fence. No words can really describe quite how a rider feels at such a moment.

**Ginny** and **Priceless**, Badminton winners in 1985

Everybody loves a winner – **Ginny** is besieged by autograph hunters

# 1986

# Why be good at dressage?

**Rachel Hunt** and **Piglet II**, who improved from forty-seventh after the dressage to second place, jumping the Whitbread Drays fence and receiving the Whitbread Spurs from HRH Princess Anne

For many years it was a popularly held concept amongst event riders that the dressage was just something to be endured in order to be allowed to do the cross-country. In fact dressage per se can be a perfectly enjoyable discipline, but the problem for the event rider is that it does not always coincide with what a very fit, good cross-country horse would prefer to be doing. An event horse must, first and foremost, be a master of the cross-country phase, and to be a master of it, he must also enjoy it; so when he arrives at a competition, he knows that soon he will be asked to do the bit he loves best, the cross-country – and it is often extremely difficult to keep such a horse's enthusiasm contained within the confines of a dressage arena.

Some horses find the requirements of the dressage test harder than others, depending on their temperament and physical attributes, and some riders enjoy the discipline of dressage training more than others. But as standards have risen throughout the sport of eventing, if you want to win nowadays, you must be a master of all three phases. Even at the lowest levels of the sport, the Pre-Novice one-day event, the competition is usually won by a horse that was in the first five after the dressage and produced a double clear inside the time; it is very rare indeed these days to make much headway on a bad dressage score. However, in 1986 the conditions conspired to make the dressage less influential than usual – which was especially good news for Rachel Hunt and Piglet II.

The weather was dreadful and the ground became really deep. Several riders incurred time penalties on the steeplechase, and more time penalties than usual on the cross-country. Although the eventual first three, Ian Stark and Sir Wattie, Rachel Hunt and Piglet II, and Rodney Powell and Pomeroy, had all recorded clear cross-country rounds, the fourth-, fifth- and sixth-placed riders had each incurred twenty cross-country penalties, which shows how much trouble the cross-country caused.

Rachel had been sitting glumly in forty-seventh place after the dressage, a position which normally would relegate the rider to 'just being there for the ride and the experience'; you might hope to move up a few places

if you recorded a fast cross-country round, but you couldn't begin to hope to be in the top twenty. And at Badminton there is a big difference between being placed twentieth, and being placed twenty-first, because normally it is only the top twenty horses which showjump in the afternoon in front of a capacity crowd and the television cameras! But Rachel was not one to give up – which was just as well, as it turned out. As number 18, she and Piglet went quite early in the day, which was probably too early to appreciate just what a fast, clear cross-country round could do for them. But that is

exactly what they produced, and what it did was to move them up to second place behind Ian Stark and Sir Wattie.

Sadly for the top twenty riders this year there was no capacity crowd to celebrate their performance on the final day: the car parks were completely unusable, and as the ground conditions continued to deteriorate, the decision was

Left: A bruised but unbowed **Karen Straker**, after a fall from **Running Bear**. Karen first rode at Badminton in 1982 when she was just eighteen. Her greatest successes came later on Get Smart who completed Badminton six times and was never out of the money.

They were also sixth at the 1992 Barcelona Olympics, won team silver at the 1988 Seoul Olympics and the 1990 World Games and team gold and individual bronze at the 1991 European and the 1994 World Championships

made to carry straight on down the whole order in the showjumping. Despite the weather, the stands weren't as empty as everyone had feared because a good many supporters parked in the village and walked in.

When Rachel and Piglet II came in to showjump, the heavens opened; the rain was coming down so thick and fast that Rachel could barely make out where she was going. Luckily she saw the funny side of this and was laughing as she made her way round – no risk of cracking under pressure there! With only one fence down, they kept second place. Their performance would have been custom-made

Left: **Sir Wattie**, the winning horse in 1986, with his groom in the picturesque setting of the Badminton stableyard. Badminton regular Duncan Douglas chooses an alternative form of transport to do the Badminton circuit!

Above: **Rodney Powell** and **Pomeroy** soar off the Normandy Bank

Jumping for fun: **Polly Schwerdt** and the diminutive **Dylan II** in 1984. Their partnership had begun during Polly's Pony Club days, when Dylan was sent to her from Ireland by some people who couldn't sell him. She planned to do a bit with him and sell him on – but he stayed longer than expected!

for the Glentrool Trophy which is now presented each year by Mrs Lorna Clarke (nee Sutherland) for the rider making the most improvement on their dressage score; to move up from forty-seventh to second place is unlikely to be equalled very quickly!

## The diminutive Dylan

Making his final appearance at Badminton this year was the dashing little black horse Dylan – and he made sure it was a dramatic finale to his eventing career. It was Dylan's fifth consecutive Badminton and he was by now a sprightly eighteen-year-old. His owner and rider, Polly Schwerdt (now MacDonald) recalls there being quite a lot of interest in their performance, as Dylan was about to become the first horse to complete five consecutive Badmintons. However, his round was far from straightforward:

'We set off out of the start box and had jumped the first fence. You then run down into a bit of a dip on your way to the second, and as we made our way down into it, I remember being aware of the fact that a car was making its way towards the cross-country course. As we came galloping out of the dip, the car drove across the course and Dylan hit the back of it. I had tried to pull him up when I realised the car hadn't seen us coming, but Dylan had his sights set on the second fence and he wasn't stopping. I jumped off and checked him all over and led him round to see that he was OK – and then I was in a real dilemma as to what to do. All the crowd were shouting at me to go back and ask to be restarted, part of me thought I should retire – and part of me didn't want to let him end his Badminton challenge on such a bad note. So once I was certain that he was unharmed, I jumped back on and set off again.

'At the next fence he stopped, which was

In 1987 the
Badminton Horse
Trials were
cancelled because
of atrocious
weather.

something he had never done before, and I just thought, "Right, Polly, either you wake up and tell him it's OK and that you want him to get on with it, or you give up now." We didn't want to give up, so I said, "Come on, Dylan, you know what's what here!" – and away he went without another hitch. But he finished way down the order, because when he had collided with the car the judges hadn't thought to stop their watches and so we had a whole load of time faults.

'At the end of cross-country day I was under all sorts of pressure: I knew Dylan must be OK, otherwise he wouldn't have carried on round the cross-country in such good style, but there was always the worry that there might be some bruising or stiffness which would worsen overnight. So I wanted to be absolutely sure in my own mind that he was completely fit and well, otherwise I fully intended to withdraw from the showjumping.

Some sections of the media were being very provocative and were trying to persuade me to jump him come what may; they were obviously hoping to write about how cruel the sport was if I had gone ahead and done that, and he had looked sorry for himself. Others were telling me I shouldn't showjump, no matter how well he seemed, because then there would be no risk of a newspaper "story". However, I knew Dylan inside out, and I just knew that I would know myself whether he was OK or not. And then he went out and showjumped clear, and that was brilliant because it wiped any doubt out of anyone's mind as to his fitness.'

'Dylan was a very special horse – he had to stand on his tiptoes to make 15hh, but he had a huge heart. I wasn't old enough to event when I first got him so we went showjumping, and he went to Grade A in his first season; then of course people started offering enormous sums of money for him. But the people who owned him were incredibly kind, and said that as I got him with him so well, they would like me to have him.

'We first went to Badminton in 1982; I was incredibly naive, but also very fortunate to have gone there on a horse like Dylan. He was a real jumping machine, and a show-off, too, so he loved every minute as there were so many people to watch him! My father was watching on the closed-circuit TV in the ten-minute box as we set off on the cross-country, and someone next to him piped up, "What's this, the Pony Club trying to get round?" – and apparently Lucinda Green replied, "You just watch, the Pony Club *will* get round!"'

Dylan was retired after his fifth Badminton. Polly felt that probably he would have gone on and on, but she wanted to avoid getting to the point where he couldn't do what she asked of him. He was given to the Sturgis family when Polly emigrated to New Zealand, and competed at Pony Club level and went hunting.

He had to be put down in 1996; Mark Todd was staying with the Sturgis family at the time, and they found Dylan in his stable looking very disorientated. They rang for the vet and then rang Polly, and knowing that he was in such good hands, she accepted that his time had come.

# 1988

## Ian takes first and second

**Ian Stark** and **Sir Wattie** recorded the second of their Badminton wins. This was just one victory in a huge run of success achieved by this combination

Right: It was this incident in 1988 that led to **Ginny** swapping **Murphy** for Ian Stark's Griffin; a decision she 'regretted from the moment he was loaded on to the lorry'

place on Glenburnie. He remains the only rider ever to have achieved this at Badminton, and is justifiably proud of the entry this earned him in the *Guinness Book of Records*!

Ian Stark was born in 1954 into a totally non-horsey family. His sister had been having riding lessons and one morning he went instead of her, and was hooked from then on. Having started work as a DHSS clerk, for a while Ian's riding activities had to remain a hobby, and most of his competitive experience was in showjumping, simply because he was offered more opportunities to showjump than anything else. But having done a few hunter trials, Ian knew that what he really wanted to do was more cross-country – and the only way to do that competitively was to go eventing. Ian gave up his job to make competitive riding his career.

'My initial approach was to ignore the dressage in the hope that it would go away, but it quickly became obvious that I was going to have to get my act together in this area. When I did my first Intermediate event I invested in a dressage saddle because I thought at least I ought to look the part, but I can still recall the agony of bumping and banging around on a

In 1988 Badminton moved its date to early May, and has kept to it ever since; it was hoped that this would help guarantee better weather, or at least drier conditions underfoot. With the trade-stand area becoming a huge event in its own right – there were over 200 stands by now – it was becoming impossible to set up this area in the wet conditions that so often prevailed in April.

This was also to be Colonel Frank Weldon's last year as Badminton director, and so it was fitting that the event should see a record-breaking result: Ian Stark took first on Sir Wattie (who had also won in 1986) and second

rock-hard new saddle! We were last in the section by about ten penalties, and even the judge couldn't believe we were really that bad – her comment was, "It's just not your day!". My wife Jenny's mother first tried to teach me the finer art of dressage, and later I had help from Barbara Slane Flemming.'

Ian first rode at Badminton in 1984: 'Just being at Badminton is daunting, and suddenly I found myself there with two eight-year-olds, Oxford Blue and Sir Wattie; this was probably pushing my luck, but I didn't know if I would ever have another horse good enough to go, so I wasn't going to miss the chance. Although Oxford Blue ended up with the higher placing (third), it was Sir Wattie (sixth) who was the real star. I wasn't very experienced, and had followed the advice of everyone which seemed to be "just keep kicking". I did just that, though in retrospect I'm sure I kicked poor Wattie into some pretty tight situations – but he baled me out every time. By the time I went round later in the day on Blue, I had a better idca of what I should be doing and gave him a much better ride. The selectors were really keen on Blue, which surprised me because in my heart I knew Wattie was the better horse.'

Ian and Oxford Blue won team silver at the Los Angeles Olympics in 1984, individual bronze and team gold at the 1985 Burghley Europeans, and team gold at the Gawler World Championships in 1986. Blue then retired from eventing, but ran in a few hunter chases as an eleven-year-old with Ian on board. He then became Lady Vestey's hunter. He was finally put down when he was about eighteen.

'I had first ridden Sir Wattie as a very naughty five-year-old. The Edinburgh Woollen Mill kindly offered to lease him for me from his breeders Jean Maxwell-Scott and Suzy Luczycwyhowska (the niece of Colonel Gordon Cox-Cox). Wattie was a real trier, although for some reason he never liked bullfinch fences; he got to Burghley in 1984 and tried to put a stride in the bounce of bullfinches and banged his tendon. Jenny brought him back into work in the winter of 1985 and hunted him all season with the Duke of Buccleuch's.

'When he got to Badminton again in 1986 the ground conditions were the worst that anyone had seen since 1975 when the event was cancelled; but of course after his hunting, Wattie thought all the mud was perfectly normal. On the last day the ground was so bad that the car parks couldn't be used at all, and as no one was expecting any spectators, the decision was made to run the showjumping straight through; normally the lower placed horses jump in the morning, and the top twenty jump in the afternoon, after the parade

**Julie Cooper** and **Priory Gold** were eliminated for three refusals at the final fence, the Whitbread Bar. In fact without realising it, Julie had already been eliminated for not taking all the elements of the alternative at fence no 4, the Beefeater Double, the most influential fence on the course. The quickest route was over a left-hand corner followed by a right-hand corner; forty-seven riders tried this, but only thirty-three managed it successfully. The rest took one of several alternative routes through the maze of posts and rails. In all, this fence caused one elimination (Priory Gold), one fall and twelve refusals of all the competitors. As it happened, a good many loyal spectators parked on the roadsides and walked in.

'Because of the dreadful weather, the atmosphere and the crowds were somewhat muted in 1986, and I always felt that Wattie missed out on much of the fuss and adulation that he was due. That is why I was especially thrilled when he was able to retain his title at the next running of the Badminton Championship in 1988. That year I was riding Wattie and Glenburnie: Glenburnie had been bred at Thirlestane Castle by the Maitland-Carews and he should really have been a Gold Cup horse – I'm sure that if I hadn't got my hands on him first, he would have been! The Edinburgh Woollen Mill leased him for the duration of his competitive life.

'Glenburnie and Sir Wattie were very different horses to ride, which made it especially difficult when riding them both at a major competition. This was Glenburnie's first Badminton – he was an out-and-out galloper, and needed a lot of setting up in front of his fences, which cost time and energy. Wattie was certainly not the fastest thing on four legs, but he was so quick and neat that you could save time by cutting corners and by not having to check him so much in front of his fences.

'The thing I remember most about Badminton 1988 was that so many people wanted to interview me and talk to me on the final morning, that when I got down to the showjumping arena it was too late to walk the course! Everyone else was telling me where to go, and how many strides there were between fences. When I went in on Glenburnie I was terrified that I would take the wrong course. Glenburnie had one fence down but still held his second place, so when I went in on Wattie I had already won the competition, whatever happened! But as I said, I desperately wanted Wattie to have his due share of the attention, and to win in front of a packed house. Wattie gave 100 per cent as he always did, and won his second Badminton title.

'The following year Sir Wattie won team gold and individual silver at the Luhmuhlen European Championships, and then crowned his career with team and individual silver at the Seoul Olympics in 1988. He was retired after the Olympics – Jenny hunted him for a while, and then he went to Henrietta Knight to be her trainer's hack. He is twenty-three now, and has pride of place in her yard. He is still ridden out occasionally, but spends most of his time keeping the young racehorses in order.'

## Ian and his competition horses

Knowing Ian's record now, it seems strange to hear him say that when he first arrived at Badminton in 1984 he didn't know whether he would ever have another horse good enough to take there. But Ian has remained an enduring presence at the top of the eventing ladder, and many would envy him the selection of horses he has had to ride.

The two 'grey boys', Glenburnie and Murphy Himself, were famous for their hard pulling, and for their exuberant jumping, and both tested Ian's abilities to the limits: 'When I first started riding Oxford Blue and Sir Wattie I had a snaffle bridle for each of them, and that was about the extent of my tack. By the time Murphy and Glenburnie had retired I think I had the biggest bit/contraption box on the circuit – now everyone else borrows from it! Oxford Blue and Sir Wattie may have lacked the superstar talent and scope of those that followed, but they were both out-and-out triers and very trainable. Murphy and Glen were just so exuberant and scopey but also very strong and difficult to ride. It is only now, with Arakai and Stanwick Ghost, that I have horses with the same scope and class but which are also easier to ride.

'Badminton has many good, and some bad memories for me: falling in the Ha Ha with Glenburnie in 1992 is a very bad memory for me – it was an awful accident for such a brave horse – and Murphy not actually winning in 1991 was sad, although in my own mind it was a victory. That year he gave me the best ride across country that I have ever had anywhere from any horse, and it broke my heart that he didn't win, because if any horse deserved it, he did. He dropped to second place after knocking down the triple bar (the easiest showjump on the course), but in my mind he won that

Two of the most popular horses the eventing circuit has known: **Murphy Himself** (left) and **Glenburnie** (right)

Opposite: **Glenburnie** misjudges the Ha Ha in 1992. Ian wanted him to jump over the gap, but it all went wrong and Glenburnie crashed into the bank on the far side. He escaped with only bruises

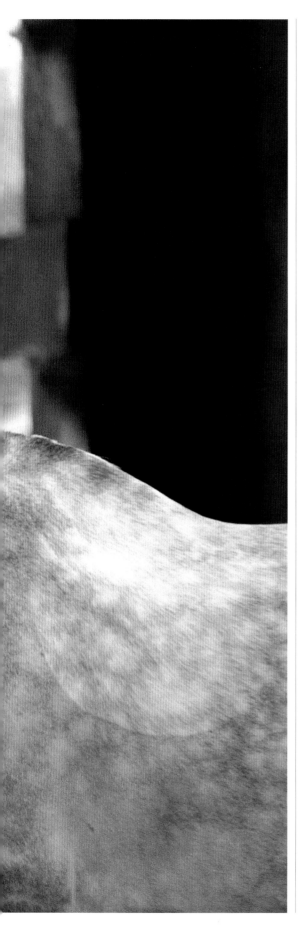

year – and I'm sure he thought he had, too.' [Murphy won team and individual silver medals at the 1991 Stockholm World Equestrian Games. He went to the 1992 Barcelona Olympics where he failed the final horse inspection after an extravagant and clear cross-country performance.]

'In 1996 and 1997 Stanwick Ghost led after the cross-country but lost the title in the showjumping. In fact when we bought him we knew the showjumping would be his problem because he tends to jump very high but dangles his legs. The first year, 1996, I knew it would be expecting too much for him to jump clear, and two fences down dropped him to

Left: The handsome, but headstrong, **Murphy Himself** with **Ian Stark** at the veterinary inspection

**Stanwick Ghost** with **Ian** and his owner **Lady Hartington**. In both 1996 and 1997 the adorable grey lost his chance of the title in the showjumping arena

sixth. But in 1997 we had put so much work into his showjumping with Lars Sederholm that I was sure he would jump clear, and it was very disappointing when he didn't. It was only afterwards when watching the video that we saw that he wasn't hitting the fences in front as he normally did, but was knocking the back rail down with his hind legs. When he went to Newmarket for his usual check-up – he has melanomas on his throat which are checked each year – they scanned his legs as a precaution, and it was found that he had damaged both his front tendons. He has therefore had a year off, but hopefully will be back in contention for Badminton's fiftieth anniversary – mind you, Jenny has said she will leave me if we find ourselves leading after the cross-country at Badminton again!'

# 1989
# Hugh Thomas takes over

A victorious team: **Ginny Leng**, **Master Craftsman** and groom Elaine Pickworthy

Opposite: **Mary King** and **King Boris**. Mary will forever feel that this should have been 'their Badminton'

Colonel Frank Weldon, Badminton's course designer since 1965, had become a legend in his own lifetime, and event riders the world over knew that to negotiate one of his Badminton tracks successfully, great courage and ability was needed. Imagine then what was required to take over from the legend himself. The honour fell to Hugh Thomas, who was eminently well qualified having just designed the course for the 1988 Seoul Olympics. But that was a once in a lifetime task – for Hugh, this new undertaking was particularly daunting because Badminton had to be faced year after year.

Because of his Olympic commitments it wasn't until the autumn of 1988 that Hugh could really focus his attention on the Badminton course: 'Colonel Frank's words were, "You do what you like, but here's part of the course if you want to use it. Other than that you will have to think up something else." His was a wonderful example of not interfering with his successor, whilst being extremely supportive. His attitude was, "You know where I live, ring me if you need anything." He was immensely

helpful, both then and over the next three or four years. I always took him around the course while I was working on it; whatever he personally felt about it I don't know, but he told everyone else it was excellent!

'In my first year I did not set out to change anything at all. I thought it was all jolly good anyway, and I wanted to get a feel for what it was like actually running the event, rather than visiting it.'

## The tail-swishing Boris is denied victory

In second place this year was the ever-popular combination of Mary Thomson (now King) and King Boris. Every rider has an 'if only' story and Mary is no exception: she says, completely without irony, that this is the Badminton that Boris should have won, and it is quite hard not to agree.

In the previous year, Mary Thomson and King Boris's Badminton challenge had come to an end with a crashing fall at the Normandy Bank. As Mary recalls: 'Boris was getting tired by then and was leaning heavily on the bit. I had wanted to shorten his stride in front of the Normandy Bank, but with him so much on his forehand it was impossible. I should have kicked him forwards to the fence, but instead I carried on holding him all the way in. He jumped up onto the bank with so little impulsion that it was impossible for him to bounce off over the rail as he was meant to. He tried to help us out of the muddle by putting in a little stride, but this brought him far too close to the rail. He somersaulted over it in what looked an absolutely horrific fall, though luckily escaped without injury. I was knocked out cold!

'When we came back to Badminton in 1989 Boris was by then ten, and we were far more of a partnership. I was particularly enjoying our dressage training, and that showed in his way of going. I always look on Badminton 1989 as the one Boris should have won: two of the dressage judges had put Boris in first place, but the third judge, who had never seen him compete before, put him thirty-first – this particular judge had regarded Boris's habitual tail-swishing and flattened ears as a resistance, but

# The 1980s

this is how Boris always performed, be it in the dressage, showjumping or across country. The judge did apologise after the event as he had not appreciated that this was simply Boris' normal way of going – in fact at future events he tended to mark us more generously than the other judges. But the margin between winning and losing is so tight that had he marked Boris more kindly in the dressage that year, Boris would have won Badminton. He ended up fourth after the dressage once his marks were averaged out, but jumped clear in both the cross-country and the showjumping.

'The following year he was third at Badminton, and then he won the 1990 British Open Championships at Gatcombe. At Badminton in 1991 he led after the dressage, and I was convinced that he would now achieve his long-overdue win. But he had to stretch to clear the second element of the bounce into the

lake and just caught his girth on it, which made him land very steeply in the water; he stayed on his feet, but I was tipped off! He completed the course clear, but we then found he had damaged a suspensory ligament, and this ended his three-day eventing career. I competed him at one-day events after that, and finally retired him from eventing when he was sixteen. He completed eighty-five events during his career, and was placed in seventy-five of them.'

**Mark Todd** and **The Irishman** at the veterinary inspection. Mark demonstrated his capabilities as a horseman by taking over the ride at a few days' notice. The Irishman's usual rider, Rodney Powell, had broken his collar bone at an event the weekend before. So with just one cross-country schooling session as an introduction to each other, they set off for Badminton. The Irishman jumped clear and inside the time, which took them into the lead. One showjump down proved costly, though, dropping them to third place. Both had their share of glory later

# The 1980s

**Hugh Thomas** (left) and **Malcolm Wallace** (centre)

## How the course is planned

Speaking in 1998, having survived his first 'decade' as Badminton's director, Hugh explains how the course is planned and what particularly inspires him: 'As an example, at the end of Badminton 1998 I would probably have half-a-dozen ill-formed ideas in my head for 1999. By September I would hope to have the route finalised, and half to two-thirds of the fences planned. We used to start working on the course in earnest in November, but our course builders, Willis Bros, are now working abroad so much – they are building the course for the Sydney Olympics – that we start in September.

ing the fences I want to use again, and simply leave gaps where I want to try something new. I am very lucky in that I am based at Badminton and can see the course progressing at all stages.'

## The inspiration for course design

'The inspiration for the course design comes from three main sources: I look first at what we have, and how it jumped. By watching videos of various Badmintons I can see how every fence has ridden and where it might be improved, either because it was too easy, or too difficult, or because horses did something unexpected there.

The Colt Walls Corner was one of Hugh Thomas' new designs for 1998. **Andrew Nicholson** and **Cartoon** clear it easily

Opposite: Angled fences, corners and ditches test the horses' accuracy and scope: **Wiiliam Fox-Pitt** and **Steadfast** at the Vicarage Vee in 1989

We try to get all the groundwork out of the way, such as removing old fences, repairing the ground, earth moving, rivetting banks and ditches. At this stage there is not much to see in terms of obstacles, but everything is ready to start serious building work in January. The final detail of some of the fences may not be decided until we are actually building them. We do use a lot of existing fences and that will always be the case. I usually start my course plan by list-

'Other people's fences at other events can be very inspirational. It does not normally mean simply transplanting their fence onto your course, because its position on the course and the terrain will be different; but it gives you an idea to play with. Very often you end up creating a completely different question, but the basic idea has come from someone else.

'Certain inspiration comes while sitting in the bath, having a shower, or just generally

# The 1980s

doodling! The most difficult fences to design are often the relatively straightforward ones to jump. You can plonk a set of post and rails down anywhere if you want to be boring, but coming up with ideas to make a straightforward fence look imposing and impressive gets quite difficult. From time to time people send me ideas for obstacles and they are invariably complicated combination fences. I spent a lot of time just driving and walking around the park in a haphazard way, because this can give you a feel for a different piece of ground, or make you suddenly see where a fence would be better sited.

'I am not the sort of course designer who goes in for particularly elaborate or fancy decoration – a few flowers or shrubs to make the whole thing look attractive, but I'm not one for building houses for riders to jump through. I am a fan of relative simplicity.

'Other people contribute ideas; for instance the technical delegate appointed each year obviously studies the course carefully – they usually first see it at about 75 per cent complete and they often make suggestions, as do other people who see the course. I showed Sue Benson round one year, and we had got as far as the Quarry; I was explaining what my idea was and pointed out that the difficulty was designing it so that you could still get back to jump the wall out. She just said, "Why jump the wall?" The honest answer was simply because we always had. That opened my eyes to a revamp of the Quarry. It sometimes needs a fresh pair of eyes to point out the obvious!'

## The level of difficulty

'The course at Badminton used to be designed so that it became progressively more difficult the nearer you got to the Olympics. Nowadays my objective is to keep the course at a similar level of difficulty each year. The Olympics and the World Championships are usually four-star competitions, whilst the Europeans tend to be nearer three-star level. But I don't think Badminton should be made easier in a "European" year, for example; whilst Badminton is used by many countries as a selection trial for other major championships, it is now a competition in its own right and most riders see it as the unofficial individual world championship title to aim for each year. It is generally recognised that if a horse and rider can tackle Badminton sucessfully, then they can cope with whatever else the world may set for them. So Badminton has achieved a status of its own which needs to be maintained and enhanced. In addition to everything else that has been built up around the event, Badminton has to offer a serious cross-country

The upright bounce into the Lake in 1991 required accurate, clean jumping. **Andrew Bennie** and **Lismore** part company

track which does not take too much notice of what else is going on.'

Hugh is the first to admit that the course does not always work quite the way he intended it to. An example within the last few years was the way in which the 1997 course rode much easier than he had planned it to:

'These things happen because course design is a subjective art, and course designers are fallible; we don't always get it right!'

## Setting stride distances

One of the most intriguing aspects of course design, particularly in these days of more technical courses, is quite how the designer decides what distance to set in a cross-country combination:

'When going across country, horses do have significantly different lengths of stride,' explains Hugh, 'much more so than in showjumping. Mostly you have to deal with the middle range. Having said that, if you look at the two extremes, a smaller, short-striding horse, provided he is an athletic type of horse, is probably more able to cope with a distance that does not suit him perfectly than the big, very long-striding horse. But all horses now have to be noticeably more athletic than they did twenty or thirty years ago. You can no longer just gallop flat out on a 17hh horse and let it take off where it feels like it.

'When setting distances for higher level competitions, I would tend to push the distance out a bit rather than shorten it. This is partly to encourage a particular style of riding along the lines of "Let's get on in there and attack it!" rather than the feeling of "Help, please don't jump in too big here!". Having said that, the exceptionally long-striding horse has got to be trained at home to handle the tighter distances, otherwise he is not a top-class event horse of the nineties.'

## The Little Badminton Drop offers a distance to suit all

A good example of the course designer's art in setting a 'distance to suit all' was admirably illustrated at the Little Badminton Drop used

in 1998. This was a drop of over 6ft to an arrowhead brush fence. The difficulty for the rider was in wondering how far out his horse would land off the drop, as this affected whether he would successfully tackle the arrowhead. As it turned out, some horses 'bounced' it, and others put in a stride. This fence was also a test of the horse's attitude — can he come to a big drop like this and react sensibly? He is not a safe cross-country horse if he gets to a big drop like this and launches himself off it into space. The fence was designed to be difficult for the horse that does this, in that he will find it hard to jump the arrowhead if he has landed in a heap off the drop. As a safety precaution, the arrowhead fence had a solid top on it so that a horse could bank it safely if he got everything wrong.

Hugh recalls that, 'Quite a lot of time was spent deciding on what the distance should be between the drop and the arrowhead. Wherever you have any form of up or down, or broken ground like this, the distance is found by simply standing on the ground and getting a feel for where the horse will jump from, and where he will land.

'Then you put the fence in what you consider to be the most suitable position. Then you go back and get the tape measure if you want to know what the distance is!'

**Laurent Gallice** of France with **Faritamer** at the Little Badminton Drop. It tested the ability of horse and rider to land in balance after the drop so that they were able to then tackle the arrowhead on either a bounce or one stride distance

# The 1980s

Below: Part of the course designer's task is to provide alternative routes for the less experienced, or for when the unexpected

happens. Here **Simon de Yonge** takes **Salland K** through the alternative at the Coffin. The direct route would have been over the rails on the right and straight over the ditch to the exit rails

Right: **Lorna Clarke** and the athletic **Fearliath Mor** exit the Lake in 1989

Opposite: 'Not quite what I had in mind ...' **Karen O'Connor** and **Biko** both escaped unhurt in 1997 after Biko jumped too big onto the island in the Lake and ran into the face of the fence

Pages 188–9: **Lynne Bevan** on **Horton Point** takes a quick time-check on the steeplechase in 1993

## Reducing the risks to the horse

'The thing that has changed most dramatically, even in the time that I have been at Badminton, is the huge emphasis on doing everything possible to reduce the risk of the horse being injured. Frank Weldon was famous for saying that he didn't mind scaring the riders because they chose to be there, but the horse had no say in the matter and so did not deserve to be

hurt. This philosophy of reducing the risk to the horse is even more paramount today, and the way in which we build fences to reduce the risk of a fall has improved beyond all recognition. It is a joint responsibility between the course designer, the technical delegate and the course builder: you always have to look at a fence and think, "What will happen if the rider gets it wrong?"'

## Providing a spectacle

'I always have to be aware here that I am trying to do several things at once with the course. I have to test the horses and riders, but I also have to provide a spectacle for the public, and something that comes over well on the television. I have worked a lot with televised events, and personally I don't consider that it makes my task any harder; it is just something else to be considered. I learned several very good lessons in Seoul when I had the chance to walk round the proposed course with a television producer before we had even built a fence; sometimes it was just a case of placing a fence

five yards away from where I had planned it, to avoid its being stuck behind a tree and so out of view of the TV camera.'

## Setting the optimum time

Another responsibilty of the course designer is to set the optimum time for his course. This is done by measuring the tightest line it is realistically possible to ride, and by taking all the direct routes. If too many riders finish 'inside the time' and therefore do not incur time penalties, the cross-country phase then starts to have less influence on the overall result. Hugh used to agonise to some degree about the number of riders achieving the time in some years, but he accepts the situation more readily now:

'I have come to be relaxed about the fact that if I build a flowing, galloping track which rewards bold, attacking riding, and if we have good going, it is an inescapable fact that there will be quite a number of horses inside the time. The numbers achieving the time have crept up steadily, and I did go through a stage a few years ago of thinking that I had got to slow these horses down somehow – it is a slightly better competition if only a few achieve the time, and I could easily design a course which would slow everyone down. But that would destroy the type of course I want to build and the style of riding I want to encourage, and it would not be nearly as attractive to watch, nor to ride.'

## The horse's welfare is paramount

In an age when the sport of eventing is becoming increasingly 'professional' and commercialised, it is more important than ever that certain principles remain above the froth of fashion. Provided that the welfare of the horse continues to rise above all else, and that Hugh Thomas can continue to stand by his desire to build courses which reward the bold, attacking combination, then the future of the Badminton Horse Trials – and with it the future of the whole sport of eventing – looks promising.

As always, the proof of the pudding is in the eating, and one statistic stood out above all others at the 1998 Badminton: not one single horse fell whilst negotiating the cross-country fences.

# The 1990s

# 1990

# ...and the poles kept falling

Claire Bowley was afforded the chance of a 'practice run' in the dressage phase the year before she took on the real thing, because in 1989 she acted as the 'guinea pig' rider for the Ground Jury: each year a non-competing rider goes through the test before the first competitor comes in, to give the judges a feel for what they will be seeing and how their marking compares. Having been awarded a Range Rover Young Rider scholarship, Claire was based with Captain Mark Phillips; she went on to take the title at the National Young Rider Championship at Bramham that same spring.

Arriving at Badminton actually to compete the following year, was the realisation of a long-held ambition. Riding Fair Share, the horse she had partnered through Juniors and Young Riders, she was fourth after the dressage – and then the following day they produced one of the most impressive cross-country performances ever given by a Badminton debutant, blazing their way round to take the lead. 'He was such a special horse,' says Claire. 'I completely and utterly trusted him, and my only concern was whether or not the heat would affect him. I don't think you realise at your first Badminton quite what you are taking on – you walk the course without really absorbing the reality of what you are about to do; and later, you leave the start box with a completely blank page, and make of it what you can. The following year I was far more nervous!'

After such a performance it is a shame that Claire and Fair Share are now remembered more for what happened next, rather than for what they had already achieved. As cross-country leader, Claire was the last competitor to enter the packed showjumping arena, with just a single mark putting her ahead of Nicky McIrvine and Middle Road. But it was not to be a fairy-tale ending: to the groans of those watching, they had five showjumps down and also incurred time penalties. The crowd agonised with her as she dropped to twelfth place. As Claire recalls: 'I didn't do anything, that was the problem. I was completely overwhelmed by the situation, and I just sat there and let it happen. It was a huge learning curve, and at the time it was enormously disappointing. But looking back on it, I don't believe that it took anything away from the occasion. It was just so tremendous, and such a privilege, to be a part of Badminton – so many riders never realise that ambition, or are lucky enough to have a fantastic cross-country ride like I did.'

Fair Share went to Badminton four times. He was twelfth in 1991, and ninth in 1992, and his first three performances were good enough to win Claire the award for the best cross-country performance for a rider under twenty-five years of age. In 1992 they 'laid the ghost' when they recorded a clear round in the showjumping as well. In 1993, when Fair Share was fifteen, he injured himself on the steeplechase and had to retire. He is still with Claire and enjoys hacking out and the occasional dressage competition.

Claire is now Mrs Johnston; she married a vet, and their baby daughter was born in 1998. Claire says her riding is purely a hobby now – but even so, it is difficult not to dream about Badminton: 'It seems to be the only place where all the competitors unite as one big team, and everyone is "rooting" for everyone else. In the ten-minute box, despite their own ups or downs, and the fact that they really ought to be trying to beat you, they still seem to genuinely want you to do well. It is an atmosphere I have never experienced anywhere else, not even at Burghley which is very much our "local event". And that is why what happened to me personally takes nothing at all away from the Badminton experience as a whole.'

## Middle Road

On the drive home from a preparatory one-day event at Bicton just before Badminton in 1990, Nicky McIrvine (now Coe) bought a car sticker which read 'Be the Best'.

'We stuck it on the lorry for the drive down to Badminton, because I just had a feeling that things were going to go right this year,' recalls Nicky. 'I even turned to my groom and said, "You do realise we are going to win Badminton, don't you?" She was far too loyal to disagree, though plenty of people did doubt our ability to do well. A few years previously I had found the showjumping phase really difficult, having

lost confidence in how I should be tackling it; but I had overcome that, and my horses had been jumping really well since then.

'I bought Middle Road as a four-year-old; in fact I tried him out for the first time in some fields on the Badminton estate! He was quite naughty as a five- and six-year-old, and used to run off with me and then run out at his fences. But I persevered, and learned how to ride him. However, he was also accident-prone, which meant it took a long time to get him to the stage where I could prove how good he was. We had been to Badminton in 1986 and he had gone brilliantly, apart from tripping up at the jetty. Then in 1987 it was cancelled. We went back again in 1989, when we had a run-out at the Vicarage Vee, that was really my fault, so when we got there in 1990 I was

**Blyth Tait** took second place on **Messiah**. A successful showjumper in his home country, Blyth had only recently turned his attention to eventing in England. Riding this eleven-year-old New Zealand Thoroughbred, he took the individual World Champion's title at Stockholm later in 1990

Opposite: **Claire Bowley** and **Fair Share** during their costly showjumping round. 'It took nothing away from our Badminton experience as a whole...'

191

'He came out the following spring and had three really good runs, but a leg infection meant that he missed Badminton that year. As he was by then fifteen, I decided to retire him to a less strenuous life. Soon afterwards, however, both his hind fetlock joints collapsed. We were able to keep him comfortable for a while, but at the end of the summer that he was seventeen it was obvious that we were fighting a losing battle, and he was put down.

'In the August after our Badminton win I married Sebastian Coe [the Olympic athlete and, at the time of writing, an MP] and before long I found myself constantly torn between our young children and my young horses. I still own a few horses; these included New Flavour who went so well for Leslie Law at Badminton to finish fourth in 1996, but who tragically died from a blood clot in 1998. But for the time being at least I shall confine myself to being an owner.'

Third after the dressage, **Nicky McIrvine** and **Middle Road** won the title with a clear showjumping round

Right: **Eddy Stibbe**, a popular and generous Badminton regular, seen here on **Bristol Autumn Fantasy** at the Lake

Stepping out in style at the final vet check – **Greg Watson** with **Tekainga Fred**

absolutely determined to go out and show everyone that we were up to it!

'Middle Road was third after the dressage phase, and moved up to second after a fast cross-country performance. My only disappointment was the fact that the video camera at the Lake broke, so I haven't got a record of him going over the difficult white post and rails, which he did brilliantly! In the final phase I was confident that he would jump clear. I knew Claire [Bowley] pretty well, and I also knew that Fair Share wasn't the best showjumper – there was only one point between us, and I just felt that things were going to go our way. Whilst it must have been awful for Claire, the sport is all about being consistently successful in all three phases, and that is what Middle Road achieved in that year.

'After the excitement of winning had died down a bit, our next aim was the final trial, where we hoped to be picked for the Stockholm World Equestrian Games. However, although Middle Road went well, the selectors said they did not think he was quite right. I was pretty devastated by their decision, though in hindsight I am convinced that they had already decided that, at fourteen, he was too old.

**An undone chinstrap is the undoing of Vaughn** Another New Zealand rider, Vaughn Jefferis, was enjoying a fabulous cross-country round on his horse Enterprise. But early on the course the chinstrap of his riding hat came undone (see right). He continued regardless, although the rules state quite clearly that the rider must keep his chinstrap fastened all the while he is mounted otherwise he will be eliminated. Poor Vaughn had nearly completed the course – he was at fence no 25 – before he was stopped and given the bad news that he was eliminated for breach of the rules.

# 1991

# Olympic contender lost to America

Leading up to the 1991 event there was a great deal of discussion as to whose name would appear on the famous Whitbread Trophy, since this would be the last occasion that the event would run under Whitbread's thirty-one years of sponsorship. In the respected opinion of Captain Mark Phillips – team trainer to the Spanish and *Horse & Hound* columnist – the smart money should fall to Blyth Tait or Virginia Leng. The Captain was looking forward to the duel which he considered should develop between these two 'on-form' world-class riders, although his own feeling was that Ginny Leng and Master Craftsman would come out on top. As it turned out, both of these horses were withdrawn, 'Crafty' suffering a knocked foreleg, whilst a tense and naughty Messiah was pulled out after a dressage performance that put him in thirty-sixth place; this left the competition much more open than usual.

## Victory for The Irishman II

In the final result, victory went to Rodney Powell and The Irishman II, although by Rodney's own admission this was probably not what the selectors were hoping for – and even for him, victory was bitter-sweet: whilst nothing could detract from his delight, he knew that he would not be reaping the long-term benefits which would usually come with such a triumph. Most riders would know that a win at Badminton should virtually guarantee them a team place for any forthcoming championships, and the timing of Rodney's win should have left him hopeful of a place at the 1991 European Championships in Punchestown that autumn, and looking further ahead, possible selection for the 1992 Barcelona Olympics. But because of an unhappy episode at the 1990 World Equestrian Games, Rodney had become thoroughly disillusioned with the selectors and the whole concept of team membership, and had made up his mind that he would never again ride for the British team even if he was asked. In the light of this decision, he knew he really could not justify keeping The Irishman: in spite of their win, he knew that he would feel obliged to sell the horse.

Badminton has generally been a happy hunting ground for Rodney Powell. Whilst based at the Talland School of Equitation in Gloucestershire, he rode at Badminton for the first time in 1984 when he was twenty-one. His horse was Pomeroy, and their performance won them the Silver Spurs for the highest-placed competitor under twenty-five years of age.

The Irishman, or 'Dobbin' as he was known at home, was first ridden by Rodney's partner, Alex Franklin; she bought him as a four-year-old after someone offered to put up the money for a horse for her to produce. 'He didn't do very much as a five-year-old because he had been kicked in the field and fractured his forearm. But once he came back into training he was the sort of horse who just wanted to get on and enjoy his work. He wasn't soppy – he didn't like kisses and cuddles – and was very much his own man. Right from the beginning across country he felt that he just knew what to do – he never felt "green". During his second season as a six-year-old I was injured in a car crash, and so Rodney was allowed to ride him at one event for me; after that Rodney sulked until I agreed to sell him!'

The Irishman was well known for his peculiar action on the flat – he 'dished' very badly, and the first time Alex trotted him up in front of his prospective buyer, all Rodney could do was roll about laughing. However, it was something that dressage judges and ground juries just had to get used to. With Rodney as his new owner and rider, The Irishman quickly upgraded. They finished fifth at Badminton in 1987 and thirteenth in 1988; then in 1989 Rodney was sidelined by injury and had to sit and watch Mark Todd ride his horse into second place. Reunited in 1990 they finished sixth, and were selected for the British team to ride at the World Equestrian Games in Stockholm that autumn.

Rodney is the first to admit that, as far as the selectors were concerned at the time, he might not have been the perfect model: 'I didn't get up early enough in the mornings, I didn't shave often enough, and my hair wasn't short enough – although it is now!' In the team briefing, Rodney was told to take the long route at a fence called the Redoubt. Karen

Straker had also had instructions, in her case to jump the right-hand route at the water, instead of the left-hand route she had wanted to take. Rodney recalls:

'While I was out on the roads and tracks I heard that Karen had had a stop at the water, going the route she had been told to ride. All the way round I had been wrestling with the idea of following my gut feeling and taking the direct route at the Redoubt, and on hearing what had happened to Karen I suppose I felt that I would be justified in doing things my way. So I did, but unfortunately we had a run-out at the last element, and in hindsight I realised that the selectors were right and that I should have done as instructed – and I did admit that at the time. But that was only the start of our problems.

'When we finished the course The Irishman was pretty stressed out because of the heat. Now, obviously I really didn't like seeing him in that condition, but I am not very good at dealing with things like that, and so I left him with Alex who I knew would be of more use to him than me; she has always looked after him for me, and I knew he was better off with her. I went to see if I could help the rest of the team. Anyway, by the end of the evening I had been effectively cold-shouldered by the rest of the camp – I was told I had behaved disgracefully, and that the rest of the team were not to speak to me!

'The upshot was that Alex and I had to cope with the final horse inspection and warm up for the showjumping on our own. Of course, when Dobbin finished in sixth place and helped secure a team silver medal, with Ian Stark the only member of the British team ahead of us, well, suddenly it was all right to talk to us again.

'The whole episode left me thoroughly disillusioned, and I determined not to ride for a team again. However, without the help and recognition that comes from being in the senior team, I knew that the future would be pretty tough. So after Badminton my best option was to sell The Irishman and to use the money to help set myself up with my own home and yard. My attitude today would be more mature than it was then, and I have

**Rodney Powell** and **The Irishman II** at the vets' inspection

Opposite: **Rodney Powell** receives from a young Prince William the Hunter Improvement Society (HIS) trophy for the most successful horse sired by an HIS stallion (Good Apple), and the Silver Jubilee Plate for the most successful rider on his own horse

missed that horse ever since he left. I miss him for his toughness and soundness, and for the genuine trier that he was.'

The Irishman II was sold to the American rider Bruce Davidson as a potential ride at the 1992 Barcelona Olympics; ironically he went lame and was unable to compete. He was ridden for a while in Junior teams by Bruce's son, and at the end of his long competitive career was retired to a palatial home in Pennsylvania – a home befitting a Badminton winner.

## The rest of the field

It goes without saying that winning at Badminton depends on the skill and experience of both rider and horse, but it also very often needs an element of luck – that little bit of good luck which keeps things going the way of a top contender, and maybe that little bit of bad luck sent the way of his or her closest rivals to compromise their chances. Badminton 1991 certainly had both.

The popular leader at the end of the dressage phase was Mary Thomson (now King) and King Boris, five points ahead of Helen Bell and

**Frenchman on a go-slow**  At Badminton in 1991 the French rider Pascal Leroy (pictured left) managed to 'hold up the traffic' on the cross-country phase, thus following the traditional road-blocking habits of his fellow countrymen. After a spectacular fall with Logical Song into the Lake, he continued so slowly that he significantly inhibited the following competitor, Claire Bowley and Fair Share. Presumably unaware of her presence behind him, he not only held up her speed, but also forced her to take a longer alternative at one fence to avoid colliding with him. Claire appealed to the Ground Jury, who reduced her time penalties to 2.8; this lifted her into fourth place, though unfortunately three showjumps down on the final day dropped her and Fair Share right down to twelfth. Pascal Leroy finally completed the cross-country with 123 time faults.

Troubleshooter; Rodney and The Irishman were lying sixth. However, cross-country day was to bring a complete turnaround in the fortunes of many competitors. As always, the course was big but fair; Hugh Thomas's aim had been gradually to reduce the number of punishing drop fences early on in the course, and to this end he had altered the exit from the Quarry, replacing the usual steps and drop with a full-height log pile at the top of a steep incline. The first combination was the five-element Beaufort Staircase: a narrow curved wooden wall, then three steps down and a short stride to another curved wall. The Lake was as influential as ever: in over a double of unforgivingly upright Garden Rails, the exit a step up and a bounce over a garden seat. Another new fence was Henry's Corner: built on the site of the old Footbridge, the direct route involved jumping a ditch and the point of a V all in one; the alternative was to run along the footbridge itself and to jump off it over a hunting gate, then turn sharp right to jump a corner.

The pathfinders in 1991 were Anne-Marie Evans and Tombo, and their round did little to ease the nerves of their fellow competitors. Anne-Marie was tipped off when Tombo hit the final element of the Beaufort Staircase, but continued nevertheless, only to have the same thing happen when he hit the Garden Rails into the Lake. Their retirement meant that William Fox-Pitt and the aptly named Steadfast became the first to complete with a steady clear. Dressage leader Mary Thomson lost all hopes of victory when King Boris hit the Garden Rails and tipped her into the Lake – a very significant bit of bad luck. However, she enjoyed a thrilling round on the young King William, even though he had the misfortune to slip up on the flat in Huntsman's Close, early in the course, a fall which incurred 60 penalties as it was within the penalty zone – another bit of bad luck, because William had been in the running for a place, too.

Rodney Powell and The Irishman put in the fastest round of the day. Ironically they incurred 1.6 penalties on the steeplechase because Rodney misjudged their pace, but they made up for it by being the only partnership to finish inside the time on the cross-country. The powerful Murphy Himself, suitably anchored in a new cherry roller American gag bit, gave Ian Stark the ride of his life. They were a picture of controlled power, yet Murphy's exuberance was still able to shine through, such as when he bounced the Luckington Lane crossing and the last element of the Beaufort Staircase.

For Ginny Leng it was a wretched Badminton. Crafty was sidelined because of injury, and she then had to sit and watch Murphy, formerly her horse, put in a marvellous performance. Griffin, the horse she had accepted from Ian in exchange for Murphy, gave her a nightmare ride, ending with their retirement at Luckington Lane. Sadly the swap now looked desperately one-sided.

On showjumping day it looked as though Ian Stark would claim another Badminton victory, although with less than a showjump in hand over Rodney Powell and The Irishman, the margin for error was very narrow indeed. Helen Bell and Troubleshooter had capitalised on their good dressage score with a fast, clear cross-country round; they had just one fence down, but this was good enough to hold their third place. Rodney and The Irishman jumped clear, which meant that Ian and Murphy had to do the same. Murphy had managed to contain his wilder instincts throughout the dressage and cross-country phases, but he could not quite keep his cool in the showjumping and hit the ninth of the twelve fences – his only mistake, but one big enough to hand the title to Rodney Powell and The Irishman II.

## Troubleshooter saved by the Bell

Badminton 1991 resulted in a best-ever placing for this partnership when they finished third; but they were very nearly unable even to start the competition. Recalls Helen:

'Troubleshooter has always been a very tough, sound horse, but when I got him out of his stable about forty-five minutes before the first horse inspection, he was lame! We just could not believe it – there was no sign of any heat or swelling, and so I just hoped he was perhaps stiff from standing in. I rode him

round, and as he became lit up by the general excitement as everyone gathered for the horse inspection it seemed to wear off. I kept him on the move, and he trotted up sound for the inspection panel. But we could not risk just leaving it at that, so we called for the farrier to come and take that shoe off just to see if there was any sign of trouble. And there it was: he had a corn.

'His dressage was on Friday afternoon, and we kept him in his stable from Wednesday evening until Friday lunchtime, and poulticed his foot all that time. Then he had his shoe put back on at midday, and I worked him from then until four o'clock – four full hours! Remarkably he performed the test of his life to finish second, just behind Mary and King

**Helen Bell**, with **Troubleshooter** on the cross-country phase they nearly missed

Boris. He was fantastic across country and finished with just 8.8 time penalties, which dropped us to third. I was desperately nervous about the showjumping as we had had a refusal in the final phase at Badminton the year before, but it went well, and we had just one fence down which allowed us to hold on to third place.'

When Helen first set eyes on Troubleshooter he was doing his very best not to impress anyone. Helen had been laughing at him as he tore round the dressage arena at a Novice event in Ireland and managed to record the worst score of the day. But she did notice when he jumped that he had a really powerful engine. 'His owner was amazed when we asked if he might be for sale!' says Helen, 'but as soon as I sat on him I fell in love with him – it was just like riding an overgrown pony! In fact he failed two vettings, but we still went ahead and bought him. He upgraded quickly, but then needed to be hobdayed. However, once he was on a full intake of air again, we found we had braking problems!' Helen attributes the marked improvement in their performance to the help they have had from her trainer, Rachel Bayliss.

Troubleshooter's greatest problem across country was that he hated being pulled off his line, which meant that Helen had to tackle all the direct routes whether she liked it or not! He was the only horse to jump successfully over a new fence at Badminton in 1992, the Ha Ha. Helen remembers galloping through the trees on the approach and suddenly realising that they were travelling over virgin soil, with not a single hoofprint to be seen! But Troubleshooter sprang over this, in effect, open ditch easily – and Ian Stark, who had been watching, obviously thought that if Helen could manage it, then he certainly could. He therefore set sail on Glenburnie, but the big grey misinterpreted what he had to do here, and jumped down into the bottom of the ditch instead of straight over the top; and because of the speed with which he had approached, he came up hard against the back wall of the Ha Ha, resulting in a really horrible fall. This must have been one of the very few mistakes the horse ever made across country.

At the time of writing Troubleshooter is still competing successfully at Advanced one-day event level.

## Murphy Himself

The big-jumping, hard-pulling, handsome grey horse won fans all over the world for his exuberant cross-country performances. Born in 1979, the 16.2hh gelding by Royal Renown had the perfect introduction to eventing when he was bought by Ginny Elliott. Despite the hours of work put in by the famous Ivyleaze team to teach Murphy to contain and control his phenomenal power, Ginny bravely admitted he was just too strong for her. The partnership won three international three-day events before the turning point came at their first Badminton together in 1988. Murphy shot Ginny into orbit when he launched himself off the top of the Ski Jump and raced off riderless across the park. Ginny came to an agreement with Ian Stark which involved Ian having Murphy and Ginny taking Griffin, one of Ian's advanced horses, in exchange. Even without the benefit of hindsight, Ginny regretted the decision as soon as Murphy was loaded into Ian's lorry. Her disappointment was compounded when Griffin failed to live up to expectations and was later sold.

Ian and Murphy eventually represented Great Britain at the 1992 Barcelona Olympics. It was to have been Murphy's last performance and everyone was hoping for great things. After a clear but exuberant cross-country round Murphy failed the final veterinary inspection – not a fitting epitaph for such a great equine athlete.

Ian and Murphy enjoyed some hunting that winter with the Duke of Buccleuch's hounds, then their huntsman, Trevor Adams, tried him out as his hunt horse for a few days. Murphy loved the hounds, and the job, and even stopped pulling as he now had a guaranteed position at the front of the field. He was turned out for a rest the following summer and should have gone on to enjoy a full hunting season with Trevor. But a year and a month after the fateful Barcelona Olympics, Murphy was found in his field with a broken leg and had to be put down.

**Murphy Himself** and **Ian Stark** enjoyed many successes but Ian could never be 100 per cent sure that the great grey would manage to listen to him for the whole of any cross-country phase! They were fifth at Badminton in 1989, fourteenth in 1990, and won the individual silver medal at the Stockholm World Equestrian Games 1990, also achieving their best Badminton result that year when finishing second

# 1992

## Badminton's greatest tragedy

Three of the sport's most enduringly popular and impressive horses, King William, Master Craftsman and Chief, put on a magnificent display to fill the top places at what, sadly, will always be remembered as the most tragic of Badmintons: for there were also three equine fatalities on cross-country day. Wet and windy weather turned this year's course into a tougher test than it had at first looked, although that in itself had little to do with the tragedies. Overall, more horses actually completed the course than in the previous year when the going was as good as usual – but Badminton director Hugh Thomas did not allow that to compromise the

need, and his own inclinations, to learn from what had happened, and to do everything possible to avoid that sort of accident occurring again. None of what follows makes pleasant reading, but it shows the resolve held by all those involved in the sport to face up to their responsibilities. The details of each incident are still clear in Hugh Thomas' mind:

## A course builder's learning curve

'The first fatality was Mark Todd's Face the Music; he was attempting the direct route at fence number 16, the Wiltshire Corner. Undoubtedly the horse slipped on take-off and jumped slightly to one side, but what made this a catastrophe was that in doing so he put a leg between the two rails, and that is how his leg was broken. At the time the Ground Jury decided to remove this fence from the competition, although it had been jumped the previous year, as Henry's Corner. But whenever I now build an arrowhead-type fence with the "arms" going away from the horse and rider, I either make the sides solid, or just use a top rail, so there is nothing that the horse could stick just a leg through.

'Karen Lende (now O'Connor) and Mr Maxwell fell at the Vicarage Vee. Her horse had cleared the corner, but he landed half on

The consistent and generous **Chief** took third place with his owner and rider, New Zealand's **Vicky Latta**

Opposite: **Mary Thomson** with **King William** at his best – a never-to-be repeated performance at Badminton

Above: **Lucinda Murray** making a splash with **Arctic Goose**

Right: **Claire Bowley** with **Fair Share** put on an entertaining display in the dressage! When this sort of thing happens the rider has to keep cool – each movement in a test is marked individually so if they can regain their composure and complete the text without further incident then all is not lost

Top right: A second place in 1992 meant that **Master Craftsman** and **Ginny Leng** had completed a one-two-three at this event with a first in 1989 and a third in 1988

the bank and half in the ditch the other side, and as a result he badly damaged his spine and had to be put down. Since then I have made it nearly impossible for a horse to land in the same way, and have now designed the fence to make it easier for him to run out to the other side where no harm can befall him; also barriers prevent him making the mistake of jumping too far the other way. If he successfully clears the corner he should now automatically land clear of the ditch. Looking at past videos it is possible to see where other horses have done the same thing and walked away without injury – but if the risk can be removed, then it should be.

'The third fatality, Susanna Macaire's Briarlands Pippin ridden by William Fox-Pitt, remains inexplicable. He somersaulted over the rail into the Lake and fell and broke his back. It is extremely unusual for a horse to suffer any injury if he falls in water – if a horse is going to have a fall, water is usually the safest place to do it. So it remains impossible to say why injury occurred in this case.

'The final, and very important lesson, was to try to avoid the slippery take-offs and landings that we ended up with this year. We put in more groundwork in those areas around the

fences, but of even greater importance was the decision to prevent at all future Badmintons the mass of spectators from trampling the take-off and landing areas. It had been dry during the week of the event and a lot of people had been walking the course, which further compacted the ground. Then it rained, and the rain was unable to drain through that compacted layer – and so it became slippery. The following year when this policy was used for the first time, I was sure that we would have no end of disappointed spectators moaning about the change – but a great many actually commented on how much more of the fence they could now see, as it didn't have people clambering all over it.'

Nothing can lessen the distress of all those involved in the tragedies that year; the eventing world is a close-knit one, and there are few partnerships as close as that between a horse and rider, particularly at this level of the sport; each has to know and trust the other, and the loss of a horse is something that no one can ever put completely out of mind. But whilst revisiting the past obviously adds to the hurt and pain, it is important that everyone is made to see how seriously such accidents are taken.

It would have been easy to dismiss all of the above as 'just one of those things', because wherever and whenever you ask a horse to gallop and jump you run the risk of injury; but this will never compromise the ongoing importance of always keeping the safety and welfare of the horse above all other objectives.

## William wins – but at a price

In hindsight, Mary must look back on her 1992 Badminton win with very mixed feelings. Whilst she still considers it, quite rightly, to have been one of the greatest occasions of her life, at the time nobody realised what an effect the win would have on King William:

'The crowd gave William such a rousing reception when he won Badminton – he has always attracted a huge following wherever he goes, and at Badminton everything just reached a climax. At the time we were so wrapped up in the excitement of winning, and also the prospect of going to the Barcelona Olympics, that it was easy to assume that he was as happy about everything as we were. But on the drive back from Badminton that year he became really unsettled

**The Mitsubishi Motors Sponsorship** Having sponsored the Badminton Horse Trials since 1961, Whitbread had now withdrawn its sponsorship; the Whitbread Trophy was replaced by the Mitsubishi Motors Trophy, and Badminton started a new era. When Whitbreads first sponsored Badminton in 1961 there were twenty-seven riders competing in the Great Badminton Championship, and thirty-two entered the Little Badminton Event; approximately 15,000 people attended, and there were twenty trade-stands. The first prize was £250, and a programme cost 2s 6d.

In 1992 when Mitsubishi took over, eighty-two horses started the competition, attendance was around 150,000, and there were over 250 trade-stands. The first prize was £20,000 and the programme cost £2. The Mitsubishi Motors Trophy was made by sculptress Judy Boyt; it depicts three horses, each representing one of the three disciplines that make up the sport of eventing: dressage, showjumping and cross-country riding. By coincidence one of the silver horses had been modelled on King William, the first winner of the trophy.

When Mitsubishi Motors took over the sponsorship of Badminton in 1992 they were not insensitive to the fact that the idea of a Japanese company being associated with such a British institution was not going to be popular with everyone. But it was precisely this awareness that has allowed both Badminton and Mitsubishi Motors to forge ahead with what has proved to be a highly successful and, hopefully, enduring partnership. In an age when sponsorship on any level is becoming increasingly difficult to find and retain, the key to success is for both parties to have something to offer the other. Over the years it has become quite obvious that the Badminton Horse Trials has much to offer Mitsubishi Motors, and they in turn have plenty to offer the great event. As David Miles, press and public affairs manager, explains:

'The Colt Car Company (which is British) has always been involved in equestrian sponsorship of one sort or another. The company name obviously invites an association with horses, and we have found that equestrian sports tend to attract the type of people who mirror our customer profile; we sponsored the Grand National one year, and we continue to support a series of National Hunt races. It follows that when we heard that Whitbreads was giving up the sponsorship of Badminton, it was of immediate interest to us. Our headquarters are in Cirencester, which makes it a relatively local event; it has live television coverage, attracts large crowds, and is the best event of its kind in the world.

'I had attended Badminton on many occasions as a journalist, and had worked on the same paper as Jim Gilmore, Badminton's press officer; a quick phone call to him got things moving, and after an initial meeting with Hugh Thomas and his team it was apparent that we could all get on well – so before long, the deal was done! Part of the contract involved more than just a financial contribution: we were required to upgrade the media centre, which is now recognised as one of the best in the world – each year we have several visitors who come just to see the centre and to find out how it works so they can develop something similar for their own event. For instance in 1998 a delegation from Sydney came to see what they would need to put in place for the 2000 Olympics.

'Another task we had to see to immediately was the creation of a new trophy. The Mitsubishi Motors Trophy, sculpted by Judy Boyt, is impressive as well as unique.

'Throughout our "taking over" of the Badminton sponsorship, Whitbreads was immensely helpful, giving us all their contacts, and plenty of tactful advice on the good and the bad aspects of what we were taking on. Our biggest priority has always been to ensure that Badminton remained a "British" event – run with British money and retaining its traditional appeal. So despite being an international company, we therefore made every effort to continue to use the same suppliers and craftsmen, since most were local, and our own approach to the event is very much "hands on". This is helped by the fact that we are so local, too, and can afford to put in the time and effort ourselves rather than delegating to others.

'From that initial three-year contract the event has been able to expand its programme of improvements, with the aim of allowing it to keep moving forwards whilst retaining its traditional values. An example of the type of innovation which we were able to introduce is Radio Badminton: this was the country's first radio service to be attached to a sporting event, and although now it is quite common for other sporting events to have their own radio service, Badminton was in fact the first.

'When it comes to measuring the success or otherwise of the sponsorship from our point of view, it all has to come down to selling vehicles. Up until 1994 we, as a company, suffered under the import quota which restricted the number of cars that could be imported from Japan, and we knew that when this came to an end we would need some sort of promotional tool to allow us to expand our market share straightaway. As we had hoped, Badminton has done much to increase public awareness of the Mitsubishi name, and we have had record years since that time; moreover we can measure and value the amount of television and media coverage that the event gives us, as well as the "on-site" sales.

'On a personal level we have enjoyed our association with Badminton, and feel that so far our partnership has met the requirements necessary for long-term success: that we are good for Badminton, and that Badminton is good for us. As long as it is able to attract television coverage and retains its number one position, then we want to be associated with it.'

in the lorry; he was very stressed and showed signs of colic. Our vet was waiting in the yard when we finally got him home, though by then he seemed to have settled back to normal. But William never really performed as well again at a three-day event; the excitement of the occasion certainly affected his dressage performances, apart from the unforgettable test he produced at the 1996 Atlanta Olympics – he took the lead with a test that turned out to be the best ever performed at a four-star event!

'Of even greater significance was the effect on his showjumping performances. Whilst maintaining pretty much the same successful form at one-day events, he remained completely unable to produce the same for the final phase of the three-day event; at Badminton in particular, the deterioration in his dressage and showjumping was most noticeable – it is as if he could never forget the excitement of the day he won there. The team selectors were always in two minds as to whether to take a chance on him as a team horse, but despite his handicap in this final phase – and the criticism of many whenever he was chosen for the team – his consistently impressive cross-country performances have helped Britain win medals.' (Team gold in the European Championships in 1991, team gold at the World Equestrian Games in 1994, and team gold and individual bronze at the European Championships in 1995.)

At the 1996 Atlanta Olympics, William surprised everyone with an uncharacteristic stop on the cross-country, and things sank to their lowest ebb when he then had eight showjumps down. However, he confounded his critics when he came back from Atlanta to win the British Open Championship title at Gatcombe, his second victory there.

Mary now accepts that William's major championship career is over; yet despite the frustrations she must have felt at times over 'what might have been', she is always the first loyally to defend him. And he is a fabulous horse: few horses have ever attracted such crowds of admirers in the way that he has done – and like his rider, they are prepared to forgive him almost anything!

**Mary Thomson** holding the Butler Challenge Bowl which is awarded to the most successful British rider. She was also the first rider to win the new Mitsubishi Motors Trophy

Opposite: **Mark Todd** and **Bertie Blunt** in 1996; and the superb Mitsubishi Motors Trophy

# Welton Houdini... braver than we thought

Above: **Tanya Cleverly** and **Watkins** enjoyed their best-ever Badminton performance to take third place. Unfortunately regular Badminton 'watchers' are more likely to remember their performance the following year when Watkins deposited his rider in the Lake and then went for a swim! (see 1994.)

Opposite: An unusual shot of **Ginny Leng** at the Lake on **Welton Houdini**

For the second time **Blyth Tait** had to settle for second place. However, this was a wonderful note for **Ricochet** to retire on: at fifteen years old, this was his first Badminton and he found the whole occasion somewhat distracting; therefore all credit to horse and rider that they were able to rise above that to take the runner-up spot

Ginny Leng had won Badminton in 1985 with Priceless and in 1989 with Master Craftsman, but she arrived at Badminton in 1993 with no expectations of claiming a third title. Welton Houdini was her ride in that year, and she describes him as being a very insecure person:

'I really was not confident about how "Luke" would cope with Badminton,' admits Ginny. 'He had had a crashing fall the year before, and although he had picked himself up and carried on very bravely, horses do not forget experiences like that. However, I had given him a full season's hunting with the Cottesmore, the Quorn, the Pytchley and the Beaufort, and I'm sure this boosted his confidence tremendously. He is the sort of horse who

by nature is not too sure of himself but is very anxious to please. When we arrived at Badminton, Hugh Thomas said, "You never know Ginny, you might just sneak another win this year!" I had laughed, and told him that if I did, I'd buy him a case of champagne – and I did! Our most anxious moment came at the Lake when Luke jumped in bold and fast and I just had to haul on one rein to make the turn to the exit fence. A few years before I had ruined my chance of succeeding with Nightcap by not turning him quickly enough in the water, so although it didn't look very pretty I was determined to be effective!'

After their Badminton victory, the ten-year-old Welton Houdini looked set to enjoy a long career at the top, as all Ginny's Badminton horses have done previously. They were selected for the European Championships that autumn, but to everyone's surprise, Houdini had a runout on the steeplechase. Despite the uncharitable comments made by many at the time, Ginny was convinced in her own mind that the horse was spooked by the barrage of photographers with flashguns, and quite frankly this explanation is far more believable than the idea that a horse which has already demonstrated its honesty at the highest level should suddenly decide to be that 'ungenerous'. Ginny and Luke finished seventh individually – but for the first time in her long competitive career, Ginny was part of a British team that 'failed to complete' (two other team members retired on the cross-country).

Houdini now lives happily at home with Ginny and her husband Mikey Elliot (Ginny remarried in 1993); he is Ginny's hunter alongside another equine star, Master Craftsman, who has the privilege of being the field master's horse – Mike Elliot is responsible for the Heythrop Hunt field. Crafty's only quirk is that if the field has to stop, he has to be faced in the opposite direction to his beloved hounds, otherwise he sees no reason not to stay up with them!

## Ginny's Badminton record

Ginny has a great many memories of her rides at Badminton. 'I guess my most treasured memories are of winning it the first time with Priceless in 1985, and of actually completing the first time I ever rode there on Dubonnet in 1974.

'When I rode Priceless I suppose I felt a good deal more competent, rather than confident, since by then I had had the experience of riding there a few times – and I remember thinking that if I kept my head we could probably do better than the eighth place we had achieved previously. Priceless was not the most stylish showjumper, but he was very reliable and careful. On the third day we were lying second behind Toddy and Charisma, and after our clear round I was delighted that we had retained our second place. I didn't even watch Toddy's round, we were so busy congratulating ourselves on coming second – I heard the crowd groan when he had a fence down, but it was

only when I saw him ride out of the arena that it dawned on me that he hadn't won: Priceless and I had! It was a far greater shock than when you win something from the front!

'I also finished third on Nightcap that year. He was another very insecure person, totally unlike Priceless who was a bit of a bully, despite the fact that they were both by Ben Faerie. With Nightcap you had to be very positive, and organise and place him at every fence; you couldn't just gallop on down to even the most straightforward fence and leave it to him to sort himself out – he just couldn't do it. In many ways I would have loved him to have recorded a win at Badminton. He had been in the lead one year until we ran past the flag for the exit from the Lake; I had forgotten that the stables were off in that direction, and as we landed in the water Nightcap started to drift towards them.

'Badminton can be such a lottery that if you do win it once, the chance of winning it again is really quite slim. So when Crafty won in 1989 we were absolutely thrilled! I did feel terribly for Toddy; once again he had been in the lead, but one showjump down dropped him below both Mary and I – but that's the way the sport is, and the event isn't won until it's over.

'I rode both Crafty and Luke in 1992, and that year was memorable in many ways. Luke had a fall when he slipped going into the rails at the Fairbanks Drop, but he got up and carried on around the course; the weather was absolutely foul, and by the time I came to get on Crafty I didn't have a dry stitch on me. I said to Mum that if it was still raining when I finished the steeplechase I was not going to continue. But as we came to the end of the steeplechase the sun came out and I thought, "OK, someone is on our side"; and on we went.

'When it came to the showjumping the next day there was a related distance of seven strides to a gate which I was worried about. I decided to see how it rode on Houdini, and then I would know how to do it best with Crafty. I came down to it on eight strides and buried poor Houdini right in the bottom of the gate – but he sprang up and jumped it. I told myself, whatever you do, you must not do that with Crafty. And what happened? – I promptly went straight in and did exactly the same thing!'

# The Bevan family's fairy-tale

The Badminton Horse Trials invariably manages to produce a favourable result each year; even if the winner was not your particular 'favourite', it is generally difficult not to admire whichever partnership comes out on top. But it is probably fair to say that in 1994, anyone with any knowledge of the eventing world at all was willing Horton Point and Mark Todd to win.

Opposite: **Blyth Tait** riding **Ricochet** was second in 1993; and (right) partnered **Delta II** to second place in 1994. Despite being a world champion and individual Olympic gold medallist, a win at Badminton continues to elude Blyth. In 1998 he finished first and second at Burghley so surely it is only a matter of time…

The handsome chestnut gelding, Horton Point, was bought in 1978 when he was only six months old, by Mr Bevan. He bought him along with the three-year-old Horton Venture, and both were to provide his two daughters with great success. Ros competed Horton Venture first, winning amongst other prizes Junior European team gold in 1982. She then started to event Horton Point, whilst younger sister Lynne was fulfilling her ambitions to showjump. Horton Point quickly showed his talent as an event horse, and with Ros he was fourth at Burghley, ninth at Badminton, and shortlisted for the 1988 Seoul Olympics. But the following year things took a downturn when they lost their sponsors, and having always struggled as a family to finance their riding pursuits, Ros felt it was time to call it a day in the eventing world. Lynne was still an ardent showjumper, however, and was given Horton Point to ride; though without a sponsor it was still a struggle to keep going – as a last resort the family, who farm near Abergavenny, even sold their farmhouse and lived in a caravan: anything but sell the horse! A family friend, Bob Rose, then helped tremendously by setting up a syndicate to help cover their costs.

Left: **Tanya Cleverly** could only stand and laugh as, having deposited her in the Lake, **Watkins** showed no sign of wishing to reunite himself with his rider, and decided he might as well go for a swim. However, Tanya was saved the prospect of having to retrieve him herself when Australian 'Snapper' Richards swam after the wandering Watkins himself – which earned him a kiss!

Opposite: Probably the most popular result of all time – a win for **Mark Todd** deputising for Lynne Bevan on **Horton Point**

# The 1990s

'Eventing had never been my first choice,' admits Lynne, 'but when Ros offered me "Sid" I thought it was only fair to pursue what we knew he was good at. I went straight in at the deep end and rode him at Advanced level – though to be honest, the size of the fences did not really worry me as I was used to jumping bigger than that in the showjumping ring. We were picked for the Young Rider Europeans in 1990, and won team gold and individual silver. The following year I rode Sid at my first Badminton and finished sixteenth. That autumn we did the Young Rider Europeans

again and won team and individual bronze. We did one Burghley and two more Badmintons, getting placed each time, and I was fully geared up to ride him at the 1994 Badminton. But we were drawn first to go, and when I knew I remember saying to Ros that I'd have no chance now. She just looked at me and said, "Sid is going to win Badminton!" Then the weekend before Badminton I had a fall at the Bicton one-day event and broke my collar bone. Mark Todd had helped me a great deal a few years previously and he had always liked Sid, so he was an obvious person to ask to take over, particularly as he was already entered on Just An Ace. In fact there was a bit of a fuss as to whether he should be allowed to have two rides, but luckily everyone on the waiting list had been squeezed in, and he was given the go-ahead.

'As a family we all considered Sid to be one of the greatest event horses of all time, though other people doubted him because they thought he lacked speed. From our point of view it was more a case that he was a member of our family and we were always extremely cautious with him, never pushing him too hard; as a result he had completed sixteen three-day events and was still a fit, sound horse. However, we knew Mark would be able to go that little bit faster with him across country than either of us had ever done; besides which it was a case of them both having something to prove – Mark had won at his first attempt in 1980 and had had any number of placings since, but he wanted another win.

'Sid and Mark performed a good dressage test to take second place on the first day at

---

**Mark Holliday Memorial Trophy** In 1994 a trophy was presented for the first time to the groom of the winning horse. The trophy is a memorial to Mark Holliday who was killed whilst riding across country at the Hexham horse trials in June 1993. He was twenty-three years old. Mark came from Cumbria, and had been head groom for Ian

and Jenny Stark, taking immense pleasure in caring for his 'two grey ponies, Murphy Himself and Glenburnie'. He travelled out to the 1992 Barcelona Olympics with them, and his ready smile and constant chat were quickly appreciated, helping to keep everyone's spirits up during the trials and tribulations of those Olympics. In the summer that he died he had been about to set up his own livery and eventing yard.

Mark's parents and his brother John – who is the Ledbury huntsman – were very keen to institute some event or trophy by which Mark would be remembered, and knowing how much he had always loved going to Badminton, and how successful and popular he had been as a groom, they asked if they could give a memorial trophy to the winning groom at Badminton. His mother explains how difficult it was for the first few years: 'We couldn't cope with going to Badminton for cross-country day until three or four years later, but we were always there for the final showjumping phase. And it is so good to hear the rousing cheer that always seems to be raised during the presentation of Mark's trophy.'

His family's continued love and interest in horses has helped them to remember and share in all that Mark lived for.

Badminton, and we knew then that it would be possible for them to win.' Unfortunately Lynne was unable to watch the cross-country performance because she had choked on a painkiller and further damaged her broken collar bone; but her sister Ros kept tearing in and out of the Red Cross tent to tell her how they were progressing. But it was their jockey, Mark Todd, who was carrying the greatest responsibility:

'Not only did I have to get the "family pet" home safe and sound,' says Mark, 'But his family were also expecting him to win! I decided to just keep riding him on a forward stride to his fences, and to trust that he knew his job well enough to cope with that. It was a great feeling when, with the most difficult fences behind us, I asked him for a little more pace towards the end of the course and he was able to respond. For the first time in his life he finished inside the time, which put him in the lead!'

The other top contenders had suffered a variety of misfortunes: the overnight dressage leaders, Marina Loheit and the Sundance Kid, had been going brilliantly across country until falling at the second Luckington Lane crossing. Chaka, who had been third after the dressage, had given William Fox-Pitt a depressing ride which included a stop at the Vicarage Vee and at the Luckington Lane. Behind him after the dressage had been Ian Stark and the adorable grey, Stanwick Ghost, but they had retired on the cross-country after a dramatic fall at the Barcelona Corner. So Horton Point was one of the few early leaders to survive the fray; close behind him was Karen Dixon and Get Smart, and Mary Thomson and King William.

For Horton Point's connections it was a fretful night. Sid had had only one 'hairy moment' on the cross-country when he had launched himself over the Quarry wall and landed right at the bottom of the slope; this, combined with being asked to go faster than usual, had left him a little stiff. Nevertheless he passed the final horse inspection, probably as much due to the Bevans' prayers as their tender loving care – and being the true professional, he obviously knew he had one more task to accomplish. By the time they had to showjump, Karen Dixon and Mary Thomson had knocked down eight fences between them, and Mark had two fences in hand over fellow New Zealanders Blyth Tait and Delta III, and Vaughn Jefferis and Bounce, who had both jumped clear. Horton Point went in and repaid both his 'family' and the rider who had put him in a position to achieve greatness: he jumped clear, and fulfilled everyone's hopes by winning the Mitsubishi Motors Trophy.

Horton Point was retired from eventing on this note, and Lynne returned to her first love, showjumping. He competed with her until he was eighteen, and is now enjoying a quieter life as a dressage horse. For Lynne, fate took another strange twist in 1997 when she offered Mark Todd the ride at Hickstead on Grafton Magna, a horse she had been showjumping for Pam Pocklington. Lynne was acting as groom, but at this particular competition Mark found he was not having much success in the international classes. He suggested that Lynne rode the horse in the Queen Elizabeth Cup – and a delighted Lynne went in and won one of showjumping's most prestigious trophies!

**New Zealand sweeps the board**
New Zealand's top riders took four out of the five top placings **Mark Todd** was fifth on **Just an Ace** (top right). Despite New Zealand's supremacy, Blyth Tait could be forgiven for thinking that Badminton is one event he just isn't going to win, because this was the third time he had taken second place here!

In **Bounce** (top left), **Vaughn Jefferis** seemed to have found a partner who well suited his often irreverent approach to the sport – and to life in general! They went on to win the individual World Championship title later in 1994, then at Badminton in 1996 they took second place, and they won team bronze at the Atlanta Olympics. They were tenth at Badminton in 1997 and fourth in 1998

213

# 1995

# A second honeymoon for Bruce Davidson

For Bruce Davidson, 1974 was a pretty special year: 'I married my wife, Carol, and we both rode at Badminton as part of our honeymoon; I was third on Irish Cap, though unfortunately Carol was eliminated at the Park Rails. I also won my first World Championship title, as well as the team gold medal.'

Today, Bruce must be the most experienced rider still competing at top level. Born in 1949, he trained as a vet before he took up competitive showjumping and eventing. He won team silver at the 1972 Olympics, two World Championship titles (1974 and 1978), he has won the Lexington three-day event six times, also Olympic team gold in Montreal and Los Angeles, individual gold and team silver at the 1995 Pan American Games, and team silver at the Atlanta Olympics in 1996. He was the world's top-ranking three-day event rider in 1993 and 1995. However, it took him twenty-one years to claim the Badminton title! In 1995, riding the ten-year-old Eagle Lion, Bruce became the first American ever to win Badminton. (In fact, it was only two years before another American claimed the title; see 1997.)

The previous year Bruce's little powerhouse

of a horse had finished fourth, and had given a conclusive demonstration of his phenomenal jumping ability; Bruce sums him up well when he says, 'Eagle Lion loves four things: breakfast, lunch, tea and jumping'. However, despite a superb cross-country round, it had looked as if Bruce was going to have to settle for something less than the top spot.

Opposite: **Bruce Davidson** became the first American to claim the Badminton title on **Eagle Lion**

Left: **William Fox-Pitt** and **Chaka**, who led at the end of the speed and endurance phase only for Chaka to fail the final horse inspection. He went on to win the British Open Championship at Gatcombe later in the year

Right: Providing the entertainment as usual, **Mark Todd** completed a clear cross-country round on **Bertie Blunt** despite the handicap of losing a stirrup early on the course

At the end of speed and endurance day, William Fox-Pitt and Chaka were leading the field, with Matt Ryan and Kibah Tic Toc in second place. Bruce could realistically consider that Tic Toc might have a fence down, but Chaka in his present form was looking invincible. Chaka had had a chequered career, on some occasions showing great promise – for instance he won Burghley in 1994 – only for things to go wrong on others. Most significantly, at the 1993 European Championships he had retired on the cross-country, and although it later transpired that he had had a virus, many people at the time were beginning to doubt William's faith in the horse. But William had always accepted that when something had gone wrong, there was usually a reason, and at Badminton in 1995 the horse looked in impressive form, leading the dressage and going fast

and clear across country, and thereby silencing his critics. But the next morning, although he appeared sound when he was ridden out, something must have stiffened up while he was waiting to trot up at the first horse inspection: he was failed, and so was eliminated from the competition. His connections were understandably devastated, albeit thrilled with his performance over the first two days; Chaka did, however, confirm his return to form by winning the British Open Championship title at Gatcombe that autumn.

Top: **Karen O'Connor**, rode the huge **Biko** into third place, the handsome 17.3hh eleven-year-old strolled round the course with deceptive ease

Above: In second place were Olympic gold medallists (1992) **Matt Ryan** and **Kibah Tic Toc**

For Matt Ryan, now in with a chance, there was always some doubt as to his whether he could claim the title on the strength of Tic Toc's showjumping. Matt had ridden Tic Toc at Badminton for the first time in 1992 in order to qualify for the Barcelona Olympics; they had been third after the cross-country phase, but five showjumps down had dropped them to eighth. Their performance did, however, earn them a place in the Australian team, and in Barcelona, Matt found himself in pole position going into the final phase. Under immense pressure he had kept a cool head – he convinced himself that he was jumping at 'just another event' – and had claimed the individual gold medal plus team gold for Australia.

The same approach almost worked at Badminton in 1995. Tic Toc was by now eighteen, although his cross-country performance belied his age – particularly when he bounced out over the last rail of the Sigma Hollow instead of taking a stride! But Matt had already resigned himself to the fact that Bruce would jump clear, and he would not – and in all truth he could not have had a more formidable opponent in this particular phase. Eagle Lion is the sort of horse who always looks as if he will jump clear: in fact William Fox-Pitt summed things up very well when he said, 'All Bruce has to do is say "Jump"! to Eagle Lion and he jumps – the hardest part is remembering to say "Down!" again, otherwise he just goes up higher and higher.' No doubt Bruce would claim that there was a little more to his success than that, but in the final outcome Matt faulted at the gate, and this mistake dropped him to second place. Kibah Tic Toc has since retired.

## Only two tackle the arrowhead at Luckington Lane

Only two riders successfully negotiated the new Luckington Lane arrowhead: this involved jumping off a bank down into the road, and then out over a very narrow arrowhead. The two fences were numbered separately, so a good many riders opted to turn a tight circle between the two and jump the arm of the arrowhead. But France's Marie Christine Duroy and her extravagant Summersong BF flew it in fine style; and unknown to US team trainer Mark Phillips, one of his entourage also had plans to impress: making their Badminton debut, Barry Thomason and Chase the Moon showed that they were just as daring. Marie Christine finished eighth, whilst Barry Thomason suffered three showjumps down to finish twenty-second.

# Bertie briefly beats his jinx

Bertie Blunt started his eventing career with Nick Burton. After a good performance at Badminton in 1993 when they finished ninth, they were invited to ride in the British team at the European Championships at Achselschwang; this was their team debut. However, they had a fall on the cross-country, and not wanting to dent the confidence of his young horse any further, Nick decided to retire. Nick was strongly criticised when he came back to England, as both he and William Fox-Pitt had failed to complete the cross-country, thus eliminating Britain from the competition. When you are representing a team rather than riding as an individual it is always difficult to know what to do when things go wrong; but undoubtedly Nick should be given the credit for putting his horse's welfare above all else.

Sadly at Badminton the following year, a general lack of confidence between the two led to them retiring on the cross-country.

Bertie Blunt was then bought for Mark Todd to ride. As Mark recalls, 'By the time Nick decided to sell Bertie, it was a case of neither trusting the other. However, beyond giving the horse a good slap on the backside the first time I sat on him, he never gave me a problem across country. I actually found him harder to get used to on the flat. He turned out to be a "headshaker" which didn't help our cause, although he normally managed to keep his mind on the job once he was in the arena. I rode him at the Gatcombe British Open Championships a few weeks after we got him in 1994, and he finished third.

'At Burghley, later that autumn, we were lying second after the cross-country – though not for long, because Captain Mark Phillips came to tell me that I had been eliminated for missing a flag on the roads and tracks. I could not believe that I would have done anything quite as daft as that – but if I had made a mistake, the organisers had made an even greater one by allowing us to continue and do the cross-country. This meant I had unnecessarily risked the horse when presumably the ground jury knew already that he was eliminated, and should have stopped us from starting Phase D.

'So when we got to Badminton the following

Some good luck at last for **Bertie Blunt**, 1996 Badminton winner

year, in 1995, I felt we needed to be sure we got everything right. However, I hadn't planned for my stirrup breaking as we jumped into the Vicarage Pond! I completed the rest of the course minus a stirrup, which was agonising for me and probably not too comfortable for Bertie. All was in vain, as it turned out, because we had to withdraw him from the final horse inspection the next morning. We had anticipated his back being sore from me bumping about on it and had worked on that, but in fact he had some bruising in his foot, and it was this which made him unlevel.

'Soon after that I lost the ride on Bertie – we had fallen out with Trevor Banks, one of our

sponsors, and he then decided to sell the horse. However, Bertie was actually owned in partnership with another couple, Rob and Melitta Howell, and when nobody seemed prepared to buy him, early in 1996 the Howells offered him back to me. I rode him at the Lincoln one-day event which they sponsored and he won it! And so we went to Badminton again – with mixed feelings, because although I knew the horse was very good, he still had to prove it! In fact after all our bad luck I would have been relieved just to have got round; so when we actually won, I think I was more pleased for the horse than for anyone else.'

**Sandra Simms** and **Clevedon Merry Lady** successfully take the direct route at the Boathouse. The majority of riders opted for the alternative after several of the early competitors fell here. Over a fence like this some horses drop their hindlegs on to the fence to help slow themselves down, but this can make them land too steeply and then fall

**The Boathouse** which Hugh Thomas built on a jetty for the Lake fence in 1996 ended up riding less well than he had hoped. Several horses and riders fell there early in the day, which inevitably meant that those riding later opted to take the long route. This is a frustrating situation for the course designer, firstly because the whole idea is to encourage the better riders in particular to tackle the direct route, and secondly because you are left not knowing whether it would have jumped better as the day progressed. Riders going later in the day can often learn a great deal about the best way to tackle a fence by witnessing the mistakes and successes of the earlier competitors. But in 1996 the general consensus of opinion seemed to be that the long route at the Lake was preferable.

'We were able to study most of the falls on video after the event,' recalls Hugh, 'but it was unsatisfactory in that there was no real consensus as to the reason for the falls. Some of the horses that fell looked as if they hadn't realised they were landing back in water, yet others had most definitely seen where they were landing. There were three possible causes of the problem here:

1) The distance on top of the jetty: I would now shorten this.

2) I think that quite a lot of horses were looking at the exit bank as they jumped up onto the Boathouse and simply did not notice that they were about to land back in water.

3) The distance on top of the jetty meant that some riders were coming in too fast for this type of fence in an attempt to get a big enough jump that would allow them to bounce off as planned.

'I used the same idea the following year, but without the roof on the Boathouse. I made the distance shorter, and removed the revetting off the exit bank so the horses were less likely to focus on that, and more likely to focus on the water they had to land in. It caused very few problems. I personally do not believe the roof made any difference to how it jumped, but the local planners wanted it taken down after the 1996 event anyway!'

Below: **Mark Todd** coaxes an excellent performance out of **Bertie Blunt**

**David O'Connor** riding **Custom Made** and leading **Lightfoot**. A showjump down dropped him from first to third

But Bertie's run of luck was shortlived. Because he was registered as having British owners, he could not be used to represent New Zealand at the Atlanta Olympics, and Mark ended up with nothing to ride there! They entered Burghley, but Bertie injured his fetlock and was not presented for the final horse inspection. The injury flared up again when he came back into work the following spring, and it effectively ended his three-day eventing career.

## Mixed fortunes for the rest of the field

Blustery weather in May 1996 resulted in some rather excitable dressage performances: for instance King William ended up twenty-sixth, and Rodney Powell's Comic Relief spent far too much time on his hindlegs and ended up with a score of 94; he was later withdrawn. But many were able to rise above the weather – or were lucky enough to do their tests on the second day when conditions were generally calmer. America's David O'Connor took first and fourth places with delightful tests on both Custom Made and Lightfoot. Ian Stark and the attractive grey Stanwick Ghost were second, with Mark Todd and Bertie Blunt in third.

Andrew Nicholson and Cartoon were first to go on the cross-country, closely followed by Mary King and King William; they both took the direct route at the Lake successfully. But soon afterwards, two horses in quick succession fell while attempting the Boathouse: Bahlua and Vulgan Nick; then Blyth Tait and Chesterfield tackled it successfully, but the next horse, Bowfred, also fell here. By now riders were becoming somewhat nervous about tackling this route, and as it quite soon became apparent that you could take the long route here and still finish inside the time, most opted to play safe; as Mark Todd concluded, it seemed to be down to luck whether or not you negotiated the direct route successfully, so he wisely chose caution.

However, Badminton first-timer Vicky Collins and her homebred Welton Molecule showed how it should be done: at thirty-nine years old, Vicky had waited twenty years to fulfil her dream of riding at Badminton, and she made the most of it; they also showjumped clear on the following day to finish sixteenth.

Diamond Pedlar proved his kindness and patience; having almost unseated Lucy Jennings taking the long route into the water, he stood still and put his head up to push her back into the saddle before completing a clear round! Lucy was devastated when Diamond Pedlar was killed in a road accident in 1997.

The tiny little mare, Clevedon Merry Lady, seemed to defy her size and was finding it all very easy – so much so, in fact, that having taken the quick route at the Lake, she tried to bounce through the Deer Park Hollow and unseated Sandra Sims in the process.

David O'Connor produced a fabulous clear on Custom Made, and fellow countryman Ralph Hill also went clear while riding Johnathan Morgan (in a bitless bridle!).

Mary King set off to improve on her eighth place after the dressage with Star Appeal. Unbelievably 'Apple' hit the first fence and Mary was unseated. She retired stiff and sore and was unable to showjump William the next day – though some might consider that to have been a blessing in disguise!

Twenty-one year old Wendy Schaeffer from Australia made an impressive debut on the 15.2hh Sunburst, a horse she has owned since she was eleven. They finished eleventh, and earned themselves a place at the Atlanta Olympics where they won team gold. Tragically Sunburst died the following year: having returned home to Australia, he suffered a fatal injury in his field.

Leslie Law enjoyed a good cross-country round on New Flavour (formerly ridden by Nicky Coe) and showjumped clear the next day to finish best of the British in fourth place.

New Zealand's Vaughn Jefferis and Mark Todd both showjumped clear, to put pressure on the top two contestants, David O'Connor and Ian Stark. Custom Made just rolled a pole which dropped David to third place and, as it turned out, robbed him of the Badminton title. Stanwick Ghost had two showjumps down to drop to sixth place behind Blyth Tait and Chesterfield. And so Mark Todd and Bertie Blunt emerged victorious, with Vaughn and Bounce claiming the runner-up spot.

# 1997

# Badminton – a victim of its own success

**B**adminton has always attracted more entries than it can accept (approximately eighty), but in previous years, injury and voluntary withdrawals have usually meant that only a few – if any – riders actually have to be turned away. Obviously to those few it is always a huge disappointment, but over the years the number refused acceptance has remained at a reasonable level. However, in 1997 Badminton received a record 151 entries, which meant that nearly half those hoping to take part would end up disappointed; to deal with the problem the organisers announced that all 'foreign' riders would be limited to one horse each.

## The 'foreigners' are outraged

This decision was greeted with outrage by a number of those 'foreigners' who did not see why a British rider should still be able to ride two horses while they were restricted to one. For a sport which so often succeeds in showing a relatively united front, it was amazing how quickly it fragmented on this subject. Much of the charm and attraction of eventing is the very fact that the true 'one horse amateur' competes alongside the 'professional' with his string of rides. The amateur rider who, week in, week out, enters a horse trial knowing that he has far less chance of winning anything than does the full-time event rider, rarely complains about this small 'injustice' – but the 'professional' riders were very quick to announce that they considered themselves, as the more prominent 'names', to be more entitled to compete at Badminton than their less famous amateur cousins. Indeed, a good many of the top riders

considered that Badminton should accept just the highest-ranked riders, irrespective of nationality – the 'foreign' riders did not see why they should be restricted to one horse when this meant that a lower-ranked British rider was allowed to compete instead of them.

It was also a pity that Blyth Tait chose to refer to the lower-ranked riders as the 'Miss Clippity-Clops' of the eventing world, because it is the true sporting nature of eventing which allows Miss Clippity-Clop the opportunity to

**William Fox-Pitt** and **Cosmopolitan II** *en route* to a third place

Top left: **David O'Connor** and **Custom Made** at the start of their victorious Badminton journey

# The 1990s

**Ian Stark** and **Lady Vestey** owner of Ian's ride, **Arakai**

**Ballycotton**, owned by Mrs Butterworth, jumped into Badminton history by becoming the only horse to complete the event seven times. Previously ridden here on six occasions by **Andrew Harris**, the sixteen-year-old Ballycotton was then leased to **Sarah Longshaw**. They finished tenth at Burghley in 1996, but missed out on a better placing here after a runout at fence 11

beat the likes of Blyth Tait, especially when she finds herself riding her 'one horse of a lifetime'. And Matt Ryan may have regretted his own words when, having declared that the highest-ranked riders should compete because they were less likely to fall off and were therefore more likely to enhance the sport's reputation, he promptly had a fall at fence 16 and retired!

The entry dilemma stems from the strongly held belief by many that, because Badminton was born out of an attempt to help British riders succeed at the highest level – namely the Olympics – British riders should have priority if the entries have to be restricted. However, others argue that since Badminton is considered to be the ultimate annual prize in the eventing world, it should be contested by the world's top horses, irrespective of what country they represent.

Badminton's director, Hugh Thomas, was the first to recognise that Badminton had grown into an event in its own right: certainly it is used by Britain, and many other nations, as a selection trial, but it is no longer purely a 'preparation' for other major championships. It

is now a major championship in its own right, and every top rider wants to win it. He was somehow able to retain his humour throughout the bitter arguments, and even thanked the press for writing so many stories about how horrid he was being to poor Mark Todd and all his friends. They say there is no such thing as bad publicity, and Badminton certainly earned a few more column inches in the run-up to the event this year.

It was too late to find a solution that would please everyone for 1997; in the end it was left that 'foreign' federations could allow their riders to compete on two horses, but that their overall entry would have to remain with the maximum 'per nation' stated in the schedule. This meant that if, for example, New Zealand decided to let Andrew Nicholson enter two horses, it would be at the expense of another New Zealand rider if they exceeded their quota of entries. It is probably just as well that a 'foreign' rider won – David O'Connor became only the second American to win the title in the history of the Badminton Horse Trials. Had a 'Brit' won, the criticism would no doubt have been

levelled that this was because the 'foreign' riders hadn't been given a fair chance, since they had not been allowed to enter all their qualified horses!

The situation was addressed for the future by increasing the standard of the basic qualification needed to enter Badminton. Now, horses have to have finished in the top 50 per cent of a four-star event, or the top 25 per cent of a three-star competition. There is no limit on foreign entries provided all are qualified. Additionally the British selectors can nominate up to ten horses which they would like to see run at Badminton, even if they have not quite achieved the new qualifications. It is hoped that this should result in the highest quality horses being guaranteed a run at Badminton. As for the 'amateur' one-horse rider, provided their one horse is of sufficiently high calibre, they too are guaranteed a place.

## Perseverance pays off

David O'Connor first saw Custom Made competing in the 1994 Young Rider Championship at Blenheim. He had not performed particularly well there, having a runout on the cross-country and three showjumps down; but David felt there was a great deal to like about him. The horse was bought for him by Joseph Zada, and the new combination won at Lexington. They represented America at the 1995 Open Europeans in Pratoni – although here, things went very wrong: they fell on the cross-country and were then eliminated in the showjumping, something which rarely happens at this level of competition. By the next season, however, they had re-formed a happy partnership, and in hindsight, David could see that the horse had not been happy in the bit in which he had been riding him.

They finished third at Badminton in 1996, and went on to finish fifth at the Atlanta Olympics later that year; by the spring of 1997, this ever-improving partnership was ready to peak. Joint third after the dressage, they added minimal time penalties on the cross-country and showjumping to take the lead. Ian Stark and Stanwick Ghost had been the overnight leaders for the second year running, but a dis-

astrous showjumping round dropped them to thirteenth.

Star Appeal made up for his previous year's first fence blunder at Badminton by going clear, and inside the time; their second place was Mary King's best Badminton result since King William's win in 1992. William Fox-Pitt gave the ten-year-old Cosmopolitan a fluent and successful first Badminton outing to finish third.

**Star Appeal** makes amends for decanting **Mary King** at the first fence last year by taking second place

**Out and About out of luck**   The enthusiastic jumping style of America's Kerry Milligan and the delightful ten-year-old Out and About won them many fans at Badminton. In 1996, their efforts had gone unrewarded when it was ruled that they had

jumped the wrong side of the flag at Tom Smith's Walls; so although they completed the course, they were eliminated. However, they were selected for the Atlanta Olympics where they won the individual bronze medal. A similarly dashing performance at Badminton in 1997 looked as if it would earn them a top twenty placing. But once again luck was not on her side – during a rain-drenched final day's showjumping, Out and About's exuberant style literally jumped his rider out of the saddle: with her saddle already soaked and slippery, poor Kerry slid out of the 'side door' and they dropped to forty-sixth place.

# 1998

## Perfect end to a five-year wait for a British victory

Above: With Word Perfect's owners Adrian and Elaine Cantwell, and Steven Morris of the Colt Car Company

By the end of cross-country day in 1998 Mark Todd was lying in pole position with Broadcast News, and it looked as if a British victory would be out of the question once again. Badminton was last won by a British rider in 1993, when Ginny Leng took the title with Welton Houdini. Mark Todd is recognised as a master of his profession, and in Vicky Latta's Broadcast News, he had a more-than-useful horse; they had won the Open Europeans at Burghley the previous autumn, and few would have bet against him not taking the Badminton title. But Mark didn't have even one fence in hand, and as has been proven so often in the past, a clear showjumping round can never be guaranteed. Christopher Bartle

had already jumped his clear round on Word Perfect; there had been one anxious moment when it looked as if he was going to make the same error of course that had eliminated Charlotte Ridley, but the gasp from the crowd would have jolted even the most absent-minded jockey back onto the right track! So now it was down to Mark – and for the third time in his career, Mark saw the Badminton title disappear with the roll of a pole!

So Christopher Bartle, who spends much of his life teaching others how to ride at his Yorkshire Riding Centre, had the enormous pleasure of being able to show that he can teach by example. At forty-six years old he became the oldest rider to win Badminton (Australia's Laurie Morgan who won in 1961 was four days younger!). Back in 1984 Christopher was concentrating on pure dressage as well as eventing, and his sixth place at the Los Angeles Olympics remains the best result of any British dressage rider. His expertise in this field, and his generosity and aptitude as a trainer, led to him being invited to train the British three-day event team, which last year included himself!

Bruce Davidson's Eagle Lion – a horse that would probably be the first choice of any rider faced with the need to jump a clear round – had already demonstrated his consistency in this phase to take third place. And at what was to be their last Badminton, Vaughn Jefferis and Bounce finished fourth. At the time of writing, Vaughn intends to return home to New Zealand to prepare for the Sydney Olympics, after which he plans to retire from eventing to return to a showjumping career.

## We're only the owners…

Adrian and Elaine Cantwell watched in tense excitement as their horse jumped a clear showjumping round to keep his second place – and then in amazement, as Mark Todd had a fence down, and they realised that they now owned a Badminton winner: Word Perfect II. They left their seats in the grandstand and made their way down to the entrance to the arena, wondering what they might have to do or say when presented with their trophy.

'We were just so excited,' recall the proud owners. 'All we wanted to do was rush in and give Christopher a big hug and the horse a big pat. But we waited, and we waited... and gradually we realised that we weren't going to be called into the arena to receive anything. We had been forgotten!'

Badminton's clockwork organisation which each year pulls together that magical mix of pomp and ceremony, fun and informality, had spluttered badly, and the Mitsubishi Motors Trophy was presented to Word Perfect's rider, Christopher Bartle, rather than to his owners Adrian and Elaine.

Such is the charm of Badminton that both now feel it has to be seen as a disappointing memory rather than as a disaster, and their greatest regret, beyond the lack of a photographic memento, is the feeling that they let their beloved horse down by not being there to give him a congratulatory pat.

'Word Perfect isn't the most cuddly of horses,' admits Elaine. 'In fact he's a bit like a Rottweiler in the stable – but on such a special occasion I think he would have condescended to being fussed over!'

Adrian and Elaine had been owners for only a little over a year when they achieved the dream that many wait a lifetime for. Their introduction to the horse trials scene has been one big party, but they are realistic enough to temper the excitement with the knowledge that the trouble with being at the top means there's only one way to go from there!

The Cantwells got to know Christopher Bartle when he visited Hong Kong to give a riding clinic. Christopher knew that he was getting to the stage where he would have to sell his horse Word Perfect, and was exploring every avenue to find a way of doing this whilst still retaining the ride. On his visit to Hong Kong he took a video of his performance at Blenheim the previous autumn (1996) where they had finished third. A notice was put up in the Jockey Club inviting anyone interested in forming a syndicate to meet for dinner the following evening. Elaine, who had taken up riding again two years before, spotted this and thought it would be great fun to own a leg or two.

'Adrian was due in from Bangkok that night and we were having guests for dinner. A lot of people were interested in the syndicate, and I knew that I had only that night to persuade Adrian that it was a good idea. So we had to abandon our guests for part of the evening while we quickly watched the video, and Adrian was impressed enough to agree to go to the meeting. After the initial niceties at the "syndicate dinner" it got down to the nuts and bolts of who was really interested in putting some money into this venture; those with serious intent were invited to go into another room, and there was us and one other couple.'

As Adrian explains, 'I had worked out pretty quickly that owning part of this horse wasn't going to be a money-making exercise – it would be like buying a ticket to have some fun and entertainment. The other couple were more concerned about the financial return, and I could see that having a group of owners was going to be problematical as everyone's priorities would be different. It was going to have to be all or nothing. We both liked Christopher a lot, and when we made a few discreet enquiries everything came back OK! We based our decision on what Christopher had told us, and on what we had seen on the video; at the time I don't think either of us appreciated that Word Perfect was already qualified for Badminton. By then it was February and Christopher went back to England, and we didn't really expect anything much to happen for a while. But suddenly it was Badminton, and we came over not really knowing what to expect at all.'

**Karen O'Connor** took fifth place on **Prince Panache**. Two weeks before she had a fall at the Lexington three-day event and had suffered two fractured ribs and a badly bruised leg. Claiming it was more comfortable on a horse than off, she bravely arrived at Badminton and was rewarded with a double clear

Beaten by a 'Brit' for a change: **Mark Todd** and **Broadcast News** drop to second place after a showjump down

'I had been brought up in Gloucestershire, and although I wasn't "into" horses at all, I can remember us all as a family sitting down to watch Badminton on the television. It was always an exciting and entertaining afternoon – and now we were actually there! Having been away from England for so long it was wonderful to come back and enjoy such a beautiful piece of the countryside, and to meet so many really lovely people. That year Christopher and Word Perfect finished twenty-fifth, and we had an absolute ball.

'We then had to organise my annual leave around fitting in the Scottish Championships and Burghley, as Christopher had been chosen for the team at the European Championships

Above: **Erica Watson** and **The Last of the Incas** looking set to record another good Badminton performance. The tragic death near the end of the course of this talented mare was made more poignant by the birth only a few weeks later of her embryo-transfer foal (pictured above), out of a surrogate mare

there. He won in Scotland, and despite falling off at Burghley, was part of the gold medal-winning team. The whole thing was beginning to feel like a fairy story!

'For Badminton this year we came over with a whole crowd of our friends, and we hoped that our horse might finish in the top twenty. When he was lying fourth after the dressage the pressure really began to mount; the whole event was far more stressful than last year!'

Elaine remembers her own feelings vividly: 'I can honestly say that I have emotionally ridden around the Badminton cross-country course! Cross-country day seemed to go on for ever. Christopher was the second last to go, and not only did he have his fourth place to defend, but we knew he also had a point to prove after

Burghley. When we arrived at Badminton, all we had wanted was for them to get round well, and to come back in one piece. But as your horse and rider rise up through the places, your hopes and expectations rise too. Now we were thinking, perhaps he can finish in the top ten! And at the end of cross-country day when Christopher was lying second to Mark Todd, we thought we could happily settle for him just keeping that position! When we realised Christopher had won it, our excitement and pleasure for them both knew no bounds! Christopher thoroughly deserved his win, and it is a privilege to be involved with someone who actually lives up to their reputation.'

Adrian and Elaine, and their three children, are coming back to England to live and are looking forward to the pleasure of watching 'their horse and rider' over the next few years. 'Everything has been so perfect that, when Christopher retires, I can't imagine us wanting to be involved with any other horse or rider. Maybe by then one of our children will be trying to emulate him instead!'

## The Last of the Incas

The Badminton three-day event in 1998 recorded the happy result of not a single fall of any horse whilst jumping the cross-country track. However, there was one fatality which saddened everyone: Last of the Incas, ridden by Erica Watson, collapsed and died whilst on the gallop home to fence no 32; she was believed to have suffered an internal haemorrhage. Last of the Incas had been a consistently successful performer, being placed several times at Burghley and at Badminton. In 1997 she won a special prize for the highest placed mare, and this included an embryo transfer. Twice previously she had won a stud nomination for being the best placed mare but, not wanting to retire her, meant that nothing could be done at the time. But in 1997 Dr Twink Allen offered the option of embryo transfer. Her first foal, Dollar, a black colt by the thoroughbred Alawir (by Riverman), was the result of this transfer, was born just a few weeks after Badminton, and provided some comfort to her distraught rider, and owner and breeder Liz Sampson.

# Badminton's 50th anniversary

In practical terms the preparations for the 1999 Badminton Horse Trials varied little from any other year. The course had to be planned and constructed, the trade-stands organised, applications for tickets dealt with, and so on. Hugh Thomas's army of helpers rallied to in their usual way. But a glamorous champagne reception, held in early January at the Cavalry & Guards Club, Piccadilly, marked the start of the fiftieth anniversary celebrations. The top three riders from every Badminton to date were invited, along with a large number of key officials, sponsors and media representatives. The immense goodwill and enthusiasm evident at this occasion will no doubt continue throughout the year, but a more tangible and longer lasting memorial to mark the fiftieth anniversary was the presentation of fifty beech trees to the Duke of Beaufort and the Badminton estate. The trees were presented by Hugh Thomas, director, and have been planted between Huntsman's Close and the Quarry. Known as Horse Trials Clump, this will recreate a group of trees that were part of the original landscape of the park in the eighteenth century.

The 1999 event will feature an anniversary exhibition, as well as a parade and presentation on the Sunday, involving the Badminton champions of previous years. Significantly the members of the 1999 Ground Jury all have a long-standing association with Badminton: its president, Major Eddie Boylan, rode at the very first event in 1949, and won it in 1965. He is accompanied by Richard Meade, who topped his many good placings at Badminton with wins in 1970 and 1982, and Lord Carew, who has competed at the event on numerous occasions.

The Badminton Horse Trials has seen many changes. As an event it has never lacked enthusiastic supporters and participants, but it has taken tremendous strides forwards in terms of course design and general growth. The one thing that has not changed is the place that Badminton holds in the hearts of all those who aspire to compete there. There are other four star international events, but Badminton has played such a strong role in the development of the sport of eventing as a whole that it has more than earned the accolade of being *the* event that every rider dreams of winning. More often than

not the prize these days falls to a 'professional' event rider but part of Badminton's charm is its unpredictability, which means that with good luck and a good horse the amateur rider can also hope to see his or her dream come true.

To the spectator Badminton offers the chance to see the world's top horses and riders competing at the world's most imposing annual three-day event.

It is impossible to predict how the event may develop over the next fifty years – for most of us it is enough to hold the simple hope that future generations may continue to enjoy the privilege of competing at Badminton.

Hugh Thomas, the Director of Badminton Horse Trials since 1989

**New FEI scoring system**   The fiftieth anniversary Badminton Horse Trials will see the new FEI scoring system being used for the first time in Great Britain. The scoring has been changed to help simplify it for the benefit of spectators and to emphasise the influence of the cross-country.

**Dressage:** penalties will be expressed in whole figures

**Cross-country:** each second over the optimum time incurs 1 time penalty and cross-country jumping penalties have been doubled, ie 40 penalties for a first refusal or runout, 120 penalties for a fall

**Showjumping:** no change to scoring

# The Badminton Army

### The Badminton Horse Trials Office

Badminton's nerve centre is found in the old village forge, just a few hundred yards from the main gates into Badminton House. Jane Tuckwell (née Gundry) is the full-time secretary, having begun by helping out her predecessor Victoria Sanford in 1974. Jane had been cornered by Frank Weldon out hunting, and had accepted the post on condition that it did not interfere with her hunting! She took over as secretary in 1985, and her main role

is as *aide-mémoire* to Hugh Thomas. Every task that has to be undertaken is listed in her 'Badminton Bible', and covers anything from writing to contractors and advertisers, ordering and printing stationery, tickets and programmes, arranging advertising, rosettes, badges, local accommodation and trade-stand tentage. On top of this are the actual event entries, the riders' and owners' requests and queries and the Young Event Horse class entries. Jane is assisted by Sue Ansell, and whilst some things seem to get easier to organise each year, both are well aware of Frank Weldon's words of warning: 'Jane, just because it worked for twenty years doesn't mean it will work for twenty-one!'

**The box office** is run by Mrs Carol Alexander; she is assisted by Pam Twissell, and from January onwards by Liz Richens as well. The box office itself doesn't open until January, but Carol works from October through to the end of May. In January nearly 8,000 ticket applications are sent out, and the best tickets sell within the first three weeks! They receive about 100 postal applications a day, and since they also take credit card bookings, the 'phone simply never stops ringing!'

During Badminton itself the office moves into the trade-stand village, and for the few

weeks running up to Badminton, Carol receives a stream of visitors either wanting to pick up tickets or to catch up on how things are going. To relieve some of the pressure and to ensure everything is put into practice safely and correctly, there is also a site manager-cum-safety officer, Harry Verney. His main responsibility is the setting up of the trade-stand village with its vast number of stands and marquees.

**Badminton's army** It takes between 500 and 600 people to keep the organisation at Badminton running smoothly during the week of the horse trials. Some are volunteers, some are employed professionals, but all have to be found from somewhere: programme sellers, car-park attendants, road-crossing stewards, arena parties, score collectors, trade-stand stewards, collecting-ring stewards, fence judges, caterers, nannies, doctors, vets, physiotherapists, and so on. When Colonel Frank Weldon took over as director he was very keen that as many local people as possible should be involved with the event, and that is still very much the case

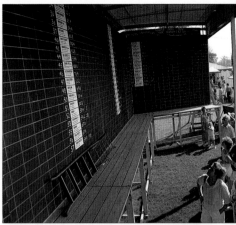

today. Thus the great majority of 'Badminton's army', particularly its volunteers, live within the Beaufort Hunt country.

It is up to Harry Norris to find volunteers to carry out the 250 duties under his jurisdiction, and he puts it even more succinctly: 'The sort of people who help run Badminton are the sort who would have been on the Countryside March,' he says proudly. He and his wife Edwina have helped out at Badminton for fifty years. Harry inherited his 'job' from his father-in-law, Mr W. Pritchard, who used to work on the estate; he died at about the time that Colonel Frank Weldon took over as director, and Harry received a letter from the present Duke asking if he would carry on in his place. In 1992 Harry was presented with a BHS Horse Trials Group award for outstanding service to the sport.

Although the event is so much bigger

Far left: Sue Ansell (left), Jane Tuckwell (centre) and Carol Alexander in the Badminton Horse Trials Office

Centre left: The box office during the event

Bottom left: Edwina and Harry Norris

Left: Tony Norris (left) and Clive Bowsher, runners and scoreboard cleaners. This photograph was taken in 1969

Above: Most spectators take time out to check the scoreboard at some time during their visit – here seen in 1990

Right: (l to r) Mary, Paul and Nigel Woods with Caroline and Derek Price

now, Edwina considers her father had a harder job than Harry: 'Father had to answer to a committee who changed their minds every five minutes,' she recalls. 'At least Harry only has to speak to Hugh Thomas, and he, like Frank Weldon, is a great believer in leaving people to get on with their own job.'

Harry has to find people to sell programmes, take grandstand tickets, steward the start, the finish, the collecting rings and road crossings, write up the scoreboard, do the accounts for the programme sales, and help with the security arrangements.

'Anyone who helps out at Badminton is very proud of their role,' explains Harry, 'and often the hardest thing is telling people when they ought to call it a day and "retire". Their loyalty is absolute and they are determined to be on "duty" each year come what may.'

When speaking to any of those involved, what comes across most is the tremendous pride in the role they have at Badminton, and a determination to involve the next genera-

tion – so Badminton's army is never short of new recruits!

Barbara and Alan Eatwell have been part of Badminton's volunteer army for the last twenty years. 'Recruited' by Harry and Edwina Norris, they demonstrate how the 'numbers' can quickly multiply. As Alan explains: 'We sell the programmes in the South car parks. Once we had learnt the ropes we gathered our own group of volunteers to help on our patch. As soon as our children were old enough they joined in, as did the children of our friends. Now they've started to rope in some of their own friends, and so it goes on. Saturday is our busiest day; we start at about 7.30am, and are really busy until about 2.30pm, when there's time to relax a bit and chat to the many people who stop and picnic in the car parks. It is a great pleasure and a privilege to be asked to help at the Horse Trials, and we all look forward to it every year.'

**The Woods family** Mary Woods first helped out at Badminton twenty-eight years ago, and has saved her official badge from each of those years! For the Woods it is very much a family affair: 'I help on the grandstands for the dressage on Thursday and Friday. On Saturday I sell programmes in the Luckington car park, and on Sunday I am back taking tickets for the grandstand seats. My husband does the collecting ring for the dressage, making sure each competitor goes into the arena on time. On Saturday he helps me and my brother in the Luckington car park, and on Sunday he helps me on the grandstands.

'Our sons have always attended Badminton with us, and took on their own duties as soon as they were old enough. Paul mans the collecting-ring gate on dressage and

showjumping days to make sure that only people with the appropriate passes go in; then on cross-country day, he and his brother Barry are out on the course helping with crowd control.

'When the Queen was a regular visitor both Derek and Nigel found themselves being put to the test by special branch officers. Nigel had to remove a persistent gentleman from the grandstand area after he tried, on three occasions, to charge past without a ticket. As they bundled him outside he said he had a ticket in his inside pocket; when he opened up his jacket it revealed a shoulder holster complete with gun, and Nigel was mightily relieved when the offender quickly explained he was a special branch officer! Derek had a similar experience when a man tried to wander in without a ticket. He made a great fuss about how he couldn't tell which pocket his ticket was in because he was wearing so many coats; but when Derek said patiently that he would wait while the man removed his many outer garments in order to find the ticket, he too produced his special branch badge and congratulated the team on their thoroughness. Both families feel they could easily produce a book of excuses given them by people hoping to gain entry to forbidden areas!

'One of the nicest things about working at Badminton is the way you renew acquaintance with so many of its visitors each year. Regular spectators tend to buy the same seats each time, and so we catch up on all the news over the past year, and then look forward to seeing them the following year. In fact we see very little of the event's "action", and have to get friends to video it for us!

'My own father worked with Harry Norris's father-in-law, and he roped us into it in the same way as we rope our own children in. My brother Derek and his wife have done the same thing, and their children are now involved as well – and so it goes on; I don't think our children know what a year is without Badminton! And we certainly hope it is one thing that will never pack up – as far as we are concerned, when we pass on, our children will hopefully carry on in our place!'

# The Badminton Army

**Bill Pritchard** Bill Pritchard's burly figure is a popular and well-known sight around Badminton: up until his retirement he was landlord of The Eagle pub at Pinkney, just a few miles from Badminton. As was the case with so many others, he was 'recruited' by his

uncle W. H. Pritchard, and is now well suited to his involvement in security during the event:

'I used to be "on the door" for the Horse Trials dance at Westonbirt school, which meant that on those occasions I worked all day and nearly all night! I have a team of men whose loyalty and commitment I can count on, and we liaise with the police force and any other security people. Originally the royal box was a wagon inside the main arena and our job was quite easy then; but now the royal box is in the grandstand, and generally there are far more people, and a far greater area, to keep an eye on. My son helps me – so when Uncle Bill Pritchard was alive there were three generations of us involved for a while! Badminton is always a good opportunity to pick up a few new jokes each year as well!'

Bill's most abiding memories of Badminton are far removed from the fears and responsibilities of the security men's job: he can still clearly picture the Queen and the Queen Mother stopping to thank him so sincerely each year they attended. And he well remembers Mrs Allhusen asking if she could vacate her grandstand seat and watch her husband Derek from the side of the arena. You could see her virtually jumping every fence with her husband, so intense was her concentration and encouragement!

**Bill and Ben the ticket men** form Badminton's very own double act. For twenty-three years John Price and Derek Taylor's irreverent sense of humour has amused Badminton spectators. As John says,

'You only come this way once and you might as well make the best of it. We try to be as helpful as possible and this is usually easier if you humour and entertain people.'

John and Derek can be found taking tickets for the West Stand during dressage and showjumping days, and selling programmes on cross-country day. They, in turn, are well looked after by their 'customers' who keep them supplied with drinks, food and gifts throughout the event. With their quick wit and endless supply of terrible jokes, even the Duke of Beaufort manages to find a spare half hour to stop and be entertained by Badminton's own comedy act. The next time there is a long hold on the course the commentary team might be well advised to make use of the free entertainment!

**Dr Lewsey: chief medical officer** Tetbury general practitioner Dr Lewsey was another to 'inherit' his role at Badminton: 'I took over as chief medical officer from my senior partner about twenty years ago, and as the event has grown it has required a far greater team to service it. At one time, if a rider had a fall you could just drive down the middle of the course to get to them, but that would be impossible now, given the number of spectators and the fact that the track is roped off. So we have a doctor in each cross-country sector, where there is also a vet and course-builder stationed, and they look after any incidents in their area. We also have a number of mobile units which carry resuscitation and other specialist equipment which I direct from my station in the "field hospital". We used to be responsible for the "care" of the crowds as well, but now they are looked after by the Red Cross. A doctor is

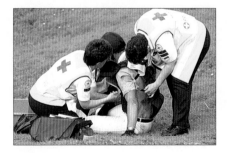

on duty during the dressage days, and we offer all competitors an "on-call" service. In recent years we have introduced the skills of physiotherapists which in our view riders should make more use of, particularly at the end of cross-country day'.

**Rowe Veterinary Group: veterinary consultants** The importance attached to the welfare of the horse throughout the Badminton Three-Day Event is evident in the veterinary care and expertise provided. There is a veterinary committee consisting of two vets whose job it is to advise the Ground Jury throughout the event, and in particular during the horse inspections. Any final decision is made by the Ground Jury, but it will be based on the advice they are given by the veterinary committee.

Badminton's veterinary consultants are brother and sister Richard and Helen Rowe, of the Rowe Veterinary Group: 'Our role is to look after the health of the horses throughout the competition, and to advise the Badminton committee on veterinary matters, such as the type of equipment that should be provided. A recent example of this is the supply of ice to be used to chill water for washing down in the ten-minute box. We used to hire ice-making machines, but since the veterinary trials for the 1996 Atlanta Olympics showed the benefits of using chilled water, we now organise the supply of several tonnes on a lorry. Horses are not well equipped to get rid of body heat quickly, so in hot weather it is essential that their body temperature is brought down as quickly as possible after the exertions of the speed and endurance phases.

'We work either independently or alongside the team vets and the competitors' own vets. The main thing is to ensure that the horse's welfare comes first, and competitors are welcome to use their own vets – we may be asked to help them or to provide drugs or equipment for them to use. One of the most common "health" problems for the event horse is azoturia, or "tying up"; this shows as stiffness or cramp of the muscles of the back and the hindquarters, and is most likely to occur in the ten-minute box before

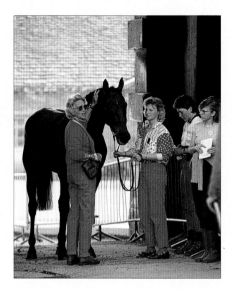

Far left: Bill Pritchard

Left: 'Bill and Ben': Derek Taylor and John Price

Below left: Owen Moore receives first aid after his fall on the cross-country course in 1995

Above: Before the vet check: a comforting pat for Get Smart from Elaine Straker and daughter Karen

Right: Cross-country control

the horse starts the cross-country. The actual cause is not known, but the result is an increase in enzyme concentration in the blood, and muscle damage.

'Another procedure which is becoming increasingly common is the use of "drips" to get essential fluids back into the horse's body after he has completed the speed and endurance phases. This is a preventative procedure which hopefully helps to produce a horse that is fresher and happier for the showjumping phase the following day.

'Treating horses within a competition environment adds a different kind of stress to a vet's life! Whilst the welfare of the horse comes first, the vet is also trying to treat the horse in such a way that he may still be able to complete the competition. Having owned an event horse ourselves we know the time, money and effort that has gone into producing a horse up to this level. But having said that, the eventing community is very good at not losing sight of the fact that the horse comes first, and the owner and rider are usu-

ally the first to agree with any decision the vet makes as to whether it should remain in the competition or not.

'During the dressage we are either at Badminton or "on call". On Saturday [cross-country day] we personally are based in the stables ready to treat any cuts, bruises or other injuries sustained during the day. Other vets are stationed in the different cross-country sectors, alongside a doctor and a course-builder ready to deal with any problems on their "patch". On the showjumping day we are inside the main arena so that should there be an accident we are instantly on hand.

'As vets at Badminton, most of the time we are dealing with the usual problems routinely associated with fit, competing horses, the only difference to a "normal day" being the higher profile of the situation you find yourself in.'

**George Weldon: cross-country control** Situated just outside the ten-minute box, cross-country control is the nerve centre of the event on speed and endurance day. Communications come into the control centre from all over the course, by telephone and radio, from the fence judges, doctors and vets, and stewards on the roads and tracks.

George Weldon, son of Badminton's most famous director, admits that his is the sort of job where, if all goes well, there is very little to do. But if there is a problem his team is caught right in the middle of it. 'An obvious priority is to ensure a fast response to any major incident, such as injury to horse and rider. Our task was made so much easier when television cameras were introduced to Badminton as we can now see much of what is happening, very often before the fence judge has had a chance to report back to us. This is particularly useful when you have to decide whether or not to stop a competitor on the cross-country course while another incident is being dealt with, such as an injury or a major fence repair. Experience usually tells you whether a fall is one where the rider will be up on their feet in a few minutes, or whether they are going to be immobile for a while. We try to keep delays to a minimum so that the competition is as fair as possible –

arguments still rage as to whether it is an advantage or disadvantage to be held on the course! If there is a major delay we would first have to stop any more horses starting out on Phase D [cross-country], and we may have to stop them setting off on Phase A [roads and tracks] to avoid a "pile up" in the ten-minute box. This is a last resort; once this happens, every competitor has to be given a new set of times for each phase and everyone's timetable is upset.'

Considering his father's role, helping out at Badminton was a natural step for George. He does recall with some embarrassment the day he tried to help his father, who was competing: 'I was watching the showjumping and one poor competitor had just been

eliminated for starting before the bell. Completely unaware of how professional my father was – and of his particular standing within the sport – I rushed out to tell him to be careful not to make the same mistake!

'Father used to be in charge of cross-country control, but as the event grew it became obvious that the director needed to be free to deal with other things, and I took over from him. Prior to that I had the role of interrogator, stationed in the ten-minute box and responsible for collaring each rider as they finished to find out if they had jumped clear, or how many faults they had. I would usually listen to the commentary as well, because riders have a habit of forgetting to mention the bits that go wrong! The information I gathered was used to help work out a provisional score so that provisional results could swiftly be given out over the public address. Nowadays each fence judge communicates directly with cross-country control as each horse tackles their particular fence, so the interrogator is redundant!'

# Score Sheets 1949–1999

Dr= dressage    Spd&End = speed and endurance    Pen= penalty (time+jumping)    B= bonus    SJ = showjumping

## 1949 (22 ran)

| | Horse and rider | Dr | Spd & End Pen | B | SJ | Total |
|---|---|---|---|---|---|---|
| 1 | Golden Willow (J. Shedden) | 90 | – | 63 | 10 | 37 |
| 2 | Sea Lark (I.H.Dudgeon) | 114.5 | – | 51 | – | 63.5 |
| 3 | Titus III (Brig L. Bolton) | 95.5 | 20 | 42 | 31.5 | 105 |
| 4 | Lucky Chance (Lt-Col P. Leech) | 89 | 20 | 24 | 34.5 | 119.5 |
| 5 | Neptune (Miss V.L. Machin-Goodall) | 172 | – | 54 | 10 | 128 |
| 6 | Remus (Capt T. Collings) | 56 | 70 | 9 | 34.5 | 151.5 |
| 7 | Minster Green (Maj J.J. Crotty) | 146 | – | 18 | 40 | 168 |
| 8 | Fritzy (Earl of Westmorland) | 125 | 100 | 27 | 10 | 208 |
| 9 | Nuthatch (Sgt-Maj L. Lungley) | 137 | 120 | 27 | 20 | 250 |
| 10 | Cool Star (Lt E.A. Boylan) | 114.5 | 160 | – | 10 | 284.5 |

## 1950 (30 ran)

| | Horse and rider | Dr | Spd & End Pen | B | SJ | Total |
|---|---|---|---|---|---|---|
| 1 | Remus (Capt T. Collings) | 44.5 | – | 30 | 12.75 | 27.25 |
| 2 | Kingpin (Capt J. Shedden) | 85 | 20 | 75 | 20 | 30 |
| 3 | Minster Green (Capt P.F. Arkwright) | 80.5 | 20 | 69 | 20 | 31.5 |
| 4 | P. McCann's Lily (Miss P. Hildebrand) | 59 | – | 33 | 10 | 36 |
| 5 | Golden Willow (Capt J. Shedden) | 95.5 | 20 | 57 | 1.75 | 40.25 |
| 6 | J. R. Hindley's Stealaway | 83.5 | – | 66 | 34.75 | 52.25 |
| 7 | Eildon (I. H. Dudgeon) | 119 | – | 48 | 20 | 91 |
| 8 | Salome (Miss E.Knox-Thompson) | 124.5 | 20 | 39 | 11 | 116.5 |
| 9 | Guinea Fowl (S.C.M. Thompson) | 91 | 80 | 51 | 22 | 142 |
| 10 | Quetta (Mrs J. Watherston) | 119 | 20 | 60 | 65.75 | 144.75 |

## 1951 (38 ran)

| | Horse and rider | Dr | Spd & End Pen | B | SJ | Total |
|---|---|---|---|---|---|---|
| 1 | Vae Victis (Capt H. Schwarzenbach) | 80.5 | – | 9 | 10 | 81.5 |
| 2 | Happy Knight (Miss J. Drummond-Hay) | 128.5 | 20 | 48 | – | 100.5 |
| 3 | Nerantsoula (H.M. Van Loon) | 106 | – | 39 | 42.25 | 109.25 |
| 4 | Werwolf (Lt A.S. Bühler) | 134.5 | 20 | 45 | 4.75 | 114.25 |
| 5 | Torloisk (A.C.M. Thompson) | 173.25 | – | 75 | 20 | 118.25 |
| 6 | Mahmud (Capt A. Blaser) | 48.75 | 60 | 24 | 40.25 | 125 |
| 7 | Stella (Maj J. Miller) | 157 | 20 | 51 | 10 | 136 |
| 8 | Euphrona (O. Schwarz) | 129.5 | 60 | 63 | 10.5 | 137 |
| 9 | Richard (Capt H. Bühler) | 108 | 60 | 36 | 20.25 | 162.25 |
| 10 | Tambour (S. Koechlin) | 78.25 | 80 | 48 | 59.5 | 169.75 |

## 1952 (26 ran)

| | Horse and rider | Dr | Spd & End Pen | B | SJ | Total |
|---|---|---|---|---|---|---|
| 1 | Emily Little (Capt M.A.Q. Darley) | 151.25 | 20 | 45 | – | 126.25 |
| 2 | Dandy (B. Young) | 135 | – | 27 | 20.25 | 128.25 |
| 3 | Greylag (Brig L. Bolton) | 120.25 | 20 | 42 | 30.5 | 128.75 |
| 4 | Hope (I.H.Dudgeon)* | 149.5 | 20 | 36 | 0.5 | 134 |
| 5 | Vigilant (Miss P. Moreton) | 100.25 | 40 | 33 | 31 | 138.25 |
| 6 | Cuchulain (H. Freeman-Jackson) | 160.25 | 40 | 51 | – | 149.25 |
| 7 | Abundance (J. Shedden) | 139 | 40 | 27 | – | 152 |
| 8 | Lionheart (Lt W.R. Thompson) | 152.5 | 30 | 36 | 10 | 156.5 |
| 9 | Garth Royal (Miss V. Pardoe) | 129.75 | 80 | 18 | 43.75 | 235.5 |
| 10 | Fitz (Maj R. Hern) | 121 | 130 | 9 | – | 242 |

* An error was later discovered which eliminated Ian Dudgeon and caused everyone else to move up a place.

## 1953 (40 ran)

| | Horse and rider | Dr | Spd & End Pen | B | SJ | Total |
|---|---|---|---|---|---|---|
| 1 | Starlight XV (Maj L. Rook) | 81 | – | 96.3 | 10 | +5.3 |
| 2 | Kilbarry (Maj F.W.C. Weldon) | 89 | – | 60 | 10 | 39 |
| 3 | Vae Victis (Capt H. Schwarzenbach) | 87 | – | 38.1 | – | 48.9 |
| 4 | Iller (J. Asker) | 84.5 | – | 71.4 | 40.75 | 53.85 |
| 5 | Neptune (Miss V.L. Machin-Goodall) | 142.5 | – | 78.6 | – | 63.9 |
| 6 | Speculation (J. R. Hindley) | 138 | – | 67.6 | 10.25 | 80.75 |
| 7 | Owenmore (Lt C.W.D. Morgan) | 122 | 40 | 66.9 | 10 | 105.1 |
| 8 | Flanagan (Brig L. Bolton) | 127.5 | 20 | 45.9 | 10 | 111.6 |
| 9 | Heavy Weather (Lt C.W.D. Morgan) | 142 | 20 | 46.2 | – | 115.8 |
| 10 | Sunbeam (Mrs A. Huot) | 175 | – | 40.2 | 10 | 144.8 |

## 1954 (36 ran)

| | Horse and rider | Dr | Spd & End Pen | B | SJ | Total |
|---|---|---|---|---|---|---|
| 1 | Bambi V (Miss M. Hough) | 104 | 20 | 59.7 | – | 64.3 |
| 2 | Kilbarry (Maj F.W.C. Weldon) | 135 | – | 89.1 | 20 | 65.9 |
| 3 | Tramella (Miss D. Mason) | 106 | 20 | 56.4 | – | 69.6 |
| 4 | Late Final (Capt A.J. Castle) | 152.67 | – | 79.2 | 20 | 93.47 |
| 5 | Brown Sugar (H. Freeman-Jackson) | 156 | – | 52.8 | 10 | 113.2 |
| 6 | Spahi (I.H. Dudgeon) | 130.67 | 40 | 50.1 | – | 120.57 |
| 7 | Strathcona (Capt G.L. Wathen) | 153.34 | 20 | 48.9 | – | 124.44 |
| 8 | Killultagh (Lt N. Arthur) | 190.67 | 20 | 76.2 | – | 134.47 |
| 9 | Crispin (E.E. Marsh) | 177.34 | 20 | 74.1 | 24 | 147.24 |
| 10 | Sandy Boy (Miss J. Bennett) | 180.67 | 60 | 79.5 | – | 161.17 |

## 1955 (51 ran)

| | Horse and rider | Dr | Spd & End Pen | B | SJ | Total |
|---|---|---|---|---|---|---|
| 1 | Kilbarry (Maj F.W.C. Weldon) | 79.334 | – | 84.01 | – | +4.676 |
| 2 | Radar (Lt-Com J.S.K. Oram) | 97.334 | – | 60.23 | – | 37.104 |
| 3 | Countryman III (A.E. Hill) | 114 | 20 | 90 | 10 | 54 |
| 4 | Gold Ross (L.R. Morgan) | 132.666 | – | 73.54 | – | 59.126 |
| 5 | Trux Von Kamax (O. Rothe) | 108 | – | 53.8 | 20 | 74.2 |
| 6 | Uranus (A.S. Bühler) | 100 | – | 33.31 | 10 | 76.69 |
| 7 | Jubal (Capt H.V. Blixen-Finecke) | 82 | 80 | 91.92 | 10 | 80.08 |
| 8 | Charleville (I.H. Dudgeon) | 145.334 | 40 | 84.01 | – | 101.324 |
| 9 | Richard (H. Bühler) | 144 | – | 2.4 19.89 | – | 126.51 |
| 10 | Brown Sugar (H. Freeman-Jackson) | 186.666 | – | 54.9 | – | 131.776 |

## 1956 (35 ran)

| | Horse and rider | Dr | Spd & End Pen | B | SJ | Total |
|---|---|---|---|---|---|---|
| 1 | Kilbarry (Lt-Col F.W.C. Weldon) | 56.22 | – | 108 | – | +51.78 |
| 2 | High and Mighty (Miss S.M. Willcox) | 57.78 | – | 108 | – | +50.22 |
| 3 | Gold Ross (L.R. Morgan) | 73.33 | 20 | 107.69 | 20 | 5.64 |
| 4 | Countryman III (A.E. Hill) | 125.44 | – | 91.87 | – | 27.44 |
| 5 | Copper Coin (Miss P. Moreton) | 120.78 | – | 108 | 10 | 28.91 |
| 6 | Trident (Miss A. Drummond-Hay) | 125.44 | – | 95.57 | – | 29.87 |
| 7 | Delagyle (Maj J.N.D. Birtwistle) | 123.9 | 60 | 99.01 | – | 84.89 |
| 8 | Just William (Miss G. Morrison) | 183.78 | – | 108 | 10 | 85.78 |
| 9 | Radar (B. Crago) | 104.44 | 20 | 44.9 | 10 | 89.54 |
| 10 | Wild Venture (E.E. Marsh) | 179.56 | – | 99.98 | 10 | 89.88 |

## 1957 (38 ran)

| | Horse and rider | Dr | Spd & End Pen | B | SJ | Total |
|---|---|---|---|---|---|---|
| 1 | High and Mighty (Miss S.M. Willcox) | 24.33 | – | 103.7 | – | +79.37 |
| 2 | Red Sea (Miss P. Moreton) | 50.33 | – | 103.91 | – | +53.58 |
| 3 | Wild Venture (E.E. Marsh) | 44.67 | – | 108 | 20 | +43.33 |
| 4 | Benjamin Bunny (Miss G. M. Morrison) | 63.33 | – | 108 | 10 | +34.67 |
| 5 | Charleville (I.H. Dudgeon) | 48.33 | – | 84.01 | 10 | +25.68 |
| 6 | Pampas Cat (Miss K. Tatham-Warter) | 32 | 20 | 97.01 | 22.25 | +22.76 |
| 7 | Scamperdale (Capt R.W. Scott) | 69 | – | 102.26 | 11.75 | +21.51 |
| 8 | Bandoola (Miss P. Molteno) | 55.67 | – | 84.75 | 10 | +19.08 |
| 9 | Cellarstown (H. Freeman-Jackson) | 57.33 | 20 | 103.5 | 10 | +16.17 |
| 10 | Souvenir II (W.G. Henson) | 72.67 | – | 101.33 | 20 | +8.66 |

# Score Sheets 1949–1999

Dr= dressage    Spd&End = speed and endurance    P= penalty (time+jumping)    B= bonus    SJ = showjumping

## 1958 (57 ran)

| Horse and rider | Dr | Pen | B | SJ | Total |
|---|---|---|---|---|---|
| 1 High and Mighty (Miss S.M. Willcox) | 37 | – | 115.2 | 10 | +68.2 |
| 2 Laurien (Maj D.S. Allhusen) | 70 | – | 101.2 | – | +21.2 |
| 3 Pluto (Miss A. Drummond-Hay) | 62.33 | – | 88.4 | 20 | +6.07 |
| 4 Copperplate (Com J.S.K. Oram) | 81.67 | – | 96 | 10 | +4.33 |
| 5 Jungle Queen (Miss V. Gilligan) | 65 | 20 | 106 | 20 | +1 |
| 6 Wild Venture (E.E. Marsh) | 59.67 | 20 | 90.4 | 10 | +0.73 |
| 7 Countryman III (D. Somerset) | 91 | – | 105.2 | 20 | 5.8 |
| 8 Benjamin Bunny (Miss G. Morrison) | 112.67 | – | 107.2 | 10 | 15.47 |
| 9 Absalom (S.H. Walford) | 113.33 | – | 86 | – | 27.33 |
| 10 Dear Brutus (Miss E. Colquhoun) | 100 | 20 | 87.6 | – | 32.4 |

## 1959 Great Badminton (24 ran)

| Horse and rider | Dr | Pen | B | SJ | Total |
|---|---|---|---|---|---|
| 1 Airs and Graces (Mrs J. Waddington) | 38.34 | – | 34 | 10 | 4.34 |
| 2 Countryman III (D. Somerset) | 95.34 | – | 88.4 | 10 | 10.94 |
| 3 Wild Venture (E.E. Marsh) | 80 | – | 68.8 | 10 | 21.2 |
| 4 Laurien (Maj D.S. Allhusen) | 69 | – | 38.8 | – | 30.2 |
| 5 Samuel Johnson (Col Weldon) | 101.34 | – | 68.4 | 10 | 42.94 |
| 6 Blue Jeans (E.E. Marsh) | 87.66 | 20 | 63.2 | – | 44.46 |
| 7 Fulmer Folly (J.J. Beale) | 62 | – | 26.4 | 10 | 45.6 |
| 8 St Finbarr (H. Freeman-Jackson) | 99 | – | 49.2 | 10 | 59.8 |
| 9 Fermoy (Lt-Col F.W.C. Weldon) | 97 | 20 | 46.8 | – | 70.2 |
| 10 Dear Brutus (Miss E. Colquhoun) | 92.56 | 40 | 43.2 | – | 79.46 |

## 1959 Little Badminton (27 ran)

| Horse and rider | Dr | Pen | B | SJ | Total |
|---|---|---|---|---|---|
| 1 Double Diamond (Miss S. Kesler) | 121.66 | – | 54.8 | 10 | 76.86 |
| 2 Robinwood II (Mrs J.O. McMillen) | 98 | – | 60.8 | 40 | 77.2 |
| 3 Free As Air (Mr Goddard Watts) | 111.6 | – | 37.6 | 10 | 84.06 |
| 4 Frigorifico (Capt J. Arthur) | 39.34 | 67.2 | 18.4 | 10 | 98.14 |
| 5 Happy Wanderer (Capt M.F. Whiteley) | 84.66 | 29.6 | 14 | – | 100.26 |
| 6 Merry Messenger (D. Nicholson) | 82.34 | 40 | 26.4 | 10 | 105.94 |
| 7 Sandyman (P. Nicholson) | 80.34 | 20 | 24 | 30 | 106.34 |
| 8 Marcus Adair (B. Young) | 65 | 23.6 | – | 30 | 118.6 |
| 9 Troubadour (Miss M.C. Newton) | 57.66 | 88.8 | – | 10 | 156.46 |
| 10 Tobruk (Mr Van de Vater) | 75.34 | 43.6 | 40.5 | – | 159.44 |

## 1960 Great Badminton (24 ran)

| Horse and rider | Dr | Pen | B | SJ | Total |
|---|---|---|---|---|---|
| 1 Our Solo (W. Roycroft) | 90.33 | – | 123.6 | – | +33.27 |
| 2 Salad Days (L.R. Morgan) | 88.33 | – | 108 | – | +29.67 |
| 3 Perhaps (Miss A. Drummond-Hay) | 69.67 | – | 107.6 | 20 | +17.93 |
| 4 Mirrabooka (N.J. Lavis) | 86.67 | – | 109.6 | 10 | +12.93 |
| 5 Blue Jeans (Capt N. Arthur) | 100 | – | 131.2 | 10 | +11.2 |
| 6 Fulmer Folly (J.J. Beale) | 86.67 | – | 94.4 | – | +7.73 |
| 7 Samuel Johnson (Lt-Col F.W.C. Weldon) | 96.33 | – | 123.6 | 20 | +7.27 |
| 8 Frigorifico (Capt J.N.S. Arthur) | 93 | 20 | 111.2 | 20 | 21.8 |
| 9 Sea Breeze (M. Bullen) | 97.67 | 20 | 104.8 | 10 | 22.87 |
| 10 Adlai (J. W. Kelly) | 86.67 | 60 | 100 | 20 | 66.67 |

## 1960 Little Badminton (21 ran)

| Horse and rider | Dr | Pen | B | SJ | Total |
|---|---|---|---|---|---|
| 1 Peggoty (Capt M.F. Whiteley) | 90.33 | 40 | 84.4 | 10 | 55.93 |
| 2 Robinwood II (Mrs J.O. McMillen) | 120.67 | – | 89.2 | 30 | 61.47 |
| 3 Top Twig III (Miss R. Greville Williams) | 98.67 | – | 82 | 50.5 | 67.17 |
| 4 Marcus Adair (B.A. Young) | 112 | – | 50.8 | 30.5 | 91.7 |
| 5 Carte Blanche (Lt-Col D.D.P Smyly) | 119.33 | 40 | 76.8 | 10 | 92.53 |
| 6 Athleague (Miss J. Stevens) | 136.33 | – | 54.8 | 30 | 111.53 |
| 7 Gipsy Love (Capt M.Q. Fraser) | 116.67 | 16 | 37.6 | 30 | 125.07 |
| 8 Counting House (Miss H. White) | 128.33 | 80 | 68 | 10 | 150.33 |
| 9 King Midas (Miss C. Ross Taylor) | 90.33 | 80 | 40.8 | 30 | 159.53 |
| 10 Sultana (W. G. Henson) | 147 | – | 45.6 | 86.5 | 187.9 |

## 1961 Great Badminton (27 ran)

| Horse and rider | Dr | Pen | B | SJ | Total |
|---|---|---|---|---|---|
| 1 Salad Days (L.R. Morgan) | 102.67 | – | 118.4 | 0.75 | +14.98 |
| 2 St Finbarr (Capt H. Freeman-Jackson) | 77.33 | – | 88.4 | – | +11.97 |
| 3 Cottage Romance (M. Bullen) | 61.33 | 60 | 114.4 | 10 | 16.93 |
| 4 Sea Breeze (M. Bullen) | 76.67 | 60 | 115.6 | – | 21.07 |
| 5 Benjamin Bunny (J.G.A. Tulloch) | 120.67 | – | 94.4 | 10.25 | 36.52 |
| 6 Sherpa (Sgt R.S. Jones) | 103.33 | – | 65.6 | – | 37.73 |
| 7 Merry Messenger (D. Nicholson) | 117.33 | – | 90.4 | 11.5 | 38.43 |
| 8 The Gladiator (Miss S.G. Fleet) | 76.67 | 60 | 77.2 | 1 | 60.47 |
| 9 Violette G (M. Cochenet) | 106.67 | – | 44 | – | 62.67 |
| 10 Mr Wister (Miss L. du Pont) | 91.33 | – | 37.2 | 11.25 | 65.38 |

## 1961 Little Badminton (32 ran)

| Horse and rider | Dr | Pen | B | SJ | Total |
|---|---|---|---|---|---|
| 1 Mr Wilson (Capt J.P.E. Welch) | 95.33 | – | 102 | 10 | +51.73 |
| 2 Ryebrooks (Miss J. Wykeham-Musgrave) | 78.67 | – | 84 | 2.5 | +2.83 |
| 3 Dispatch (Miss S. Clifford) | 108 | 20 | 80.8 | – | 47.2 |
| 4 Gipsy Love (Lt T.W. Ritson) | 118.67 | – | 107.6 | 51.25 | 62.22 |
| 5 King Midas (Miss C. Ross-Taylor) | 75.33 | 60 | 70 | 2 | 67.33 |
| 6 High Jinks (P.V. Hervey) | 133.33 | 20 | 63.2 | 13.75 | 103.88 |
| 7 Botany Degree (J.G.A. Tulloch) | 110 | 60 | 62.4 | 11.25 | 118.85 |
| 8 Granite (Miss V. Freeman-Jackson) | 157.33 | – | 47.6 | 12 | 121.73 |
| 9 Anonymous (Mrs J.J. Beale) | 88 | 60 | 26.4 | 1 | 122.6 |
| 10 Hansel II (Miss J. Graham-Clark) | 86 | 71.6 | 7.2 | – | 150.4 |

## 1962 Great Badminton (19 ran)

| Horse and rider | Dr | Pen | B | SJ | Total |
|---|---|---|---|---|---|
| 1 Merely-A-Monarch (Miss A. Drummond-Hay) | 56.67 | – | 118.4 | 10 | +51.73 |
| 2 Young Pretender (Lt-Col F.W.C. Weldon) | 95.67 | – | 118.4 | 10 | +9.73 |
| 3 Sea Breeze (M. Bullen) | 110.67 | – | 118.4 | – | +7.73 |
| 4 Dignity (A. Cameron) | 99.33 | – | 99.6 | – | +0.27 |
| 5 Red Dawn (Miss P Green) | 108.67 | – | 91.2 | – | 17.47 |
| 6 Peggoty (Capt M.F. Whiteley) | 126 | – | 87.6 | – | 38.4 |
| 7 Ballyhoo (Lt the Hon P.T. Connolly-Carew) | 123.33 | – | 72.8 | – | 50.53 |
| 8 Souvenir (D. Nicholson) | 134.67 | – | 82.8 | – | 51.87 |
| 9 High Jinks (P.V. Hervey) | 140.67 | – | 103.2 | – | 57.97 |
| 10 Mr Wilson (Capt J.P.E. Welch) | 114.67 | 40 | 93.2 | – | 61.47 |

## 1962 Little Badminton (16 ran)

| Horse and rider | Dr | Pen | B | SJ | Total |
|---|---|---|---|---|---|
| 1 Priam (Mrs P. Crofts) | 132.67 | – | 107.2 | – | 25.47 |
| 2 M'Lord Connelly (Capt J.R. Templer) | 130.67 | 20 | 118.4 | – | 32.27 |
| 3 Granite (Miss V. Freeman-Jackson) | 144.67 | – | 76.4 | 10 | 78.27 |
| 4 Hansel II (Miss J. Graham-Clark) | 128.67 | – | 52.8 | 10 | 85.87 |
| 5 Grey Gander (Miss J. Crawford) | 182 | – | 70.8 | – | 111.2 |
| 6 Goldwave (Maj J.N.D. Birtwistle) | 118 | 14.4 | 13.6 | 1 | 119.8 |
| 7 Anzac (P. N. Simpson) | 134 | 40 | 54.8 | 1.25 | 120.45 |
| 8 The Zephyr (Van de Vater) | 139.33 | 24.8 | 24.8 | 10 | 149.33 |
| 9 Highwayman (T. Allhusen) | 122.67 | 100 | 54.4 | – | 168.27 |
| 10 Lanark (Sgt R.S. Jones) | 96 | 64 | 8.1 | 20 | 171.6 |

# Score Sheets 1949–1999

Dr= dressage   Spd&End = speed and endurance   S'ch=steeplechase   P= penalty (time+jumping)   J=jump   T=time   B= bonus   SJ = showjumping

## 1963 ONE DAY EVENT ONLY

## 1964 Great Badminton (27 ran)

| Horse and rider | Dr | Spd & End Pen | B | SJ | Total |
|---|---|---|---|---|---|
| 1 M'Lord Connelly (Capt J.R. Templer) | 75 | | 108 | | +33 |
| 2 By Golly (J.D. Smith-Bingham) | 53.5 | | 70 | 10 | +6.5 |
| 3 Black Salmon (A. Cameron) | 90 | | 106.4 | 30 | 13.6 |
| 4 St Finbarr (Capt H. Freeman-Jackson) | 96 | | 69.2 | | 26.8 |
| 5 Sea Breeze (M. Bullen) | 95 | 20 | 88 | | 27 |
| 6 Young Pretender (M. Bullen) | 95.5 | | 94.8 | 30 | 30.7 |
| 7 Victoria Bridge (Capt Beale) | 82.5 | | 49.6 | 10 | 42.9 |
| 8 Merry Messenger (D. Nicholson) | 121.5 | | 86 | 10 | 45.5 |
| 9 Easter Bouquet (Miss B. Pearson) | 112 | | 76. | 10 | 46 |
| 10 Priam (Miss J. Graham-Clark) | 101.5 | | 43.6 | 13 | 70.9 |

## 1964 Little Badminton (25 ran)

| Horse and rider | Dr | Spd & End Pen | B | SJ | Total |
|---|---|---|---|---|---|
| 1 Glenamoy (Mrs J. Waddington) | 65.5 | | 86.8 | 20 | +1.3 |
| 2 Lough Druid (Miss P. Moreton) | 76 | | 64 | 10 | 22 |
| 3 Fenjirao (Miss C. Sheppard) | 83 | | 30.8 | 10.5 | 62.7 |
| 4 Kilmacthomas (Miss M. Macdonell) | 64.5 | | 18.8 | 20 | 65.7 |
| 5 Anna's Banner (Miss B. Pearson) | 111.5 | | 46.4 | 1.75 | 66.85 |
| 6 Happy Talk (Capt M.F. Whiteley) | 62 | 60 | 51.2 | | 70.8 |
| 7 The Viking (M. Tucker) | 98 | 20 | 62 | 30 | 86 |
| 8 Sunny Jim (Capt Beale) | 97 | | 37.2 | 34.75 | 94.55 |
| 9 Rise and Shine (Miss M. Speed) | 90.5 | 60 | 55.6 | | 94.9 |
| 10 Marshall Tudor (Hon W.R. Leigh) | 101.5 | 20 | 46 | 20 | 95.5 |

## 1965 Great Badminton (21 ran)

| Horse and rider | Dr | Spd & End Pen | B | SJ | Total |
|---|---|---|---|---|---|
| 1 Durlas Eile (Maj E.A. Boylan) | 45.5 | | 98.4 | 20 | +32.9 |
| 2 Eldorado (W. Roycroft) | 87.5 | | 113.2 | | +25.7 |
| 3 Glenamoy (Mrs S. Waddington) | 48.5 | | 84.8 | 11.25 | +25.05 |
| 4 Rise and Shine (Miss M. Speed) | 75.5 | | 104.44 | 10 | +18.9 |
| 5 Fenjirao (Miss C. Sheppard) | 66.5 | | 84.4 | 10 | +7.9 |
| 6 Stoney Crossing (W. Roycroft) | 81 | | 112.4 | 30 | +1.4 |
| 7 Nadine D (Mlle R. Cailleux) | 74 | | 78.8 | 10 | 5.2 |
| 8 Lochinvar (Maj D.S. Allhusen) | 76.5 | | 105.2 | 40 | 11.3 |
| 9 Sam Weller (Miss V. Freeman-Jackson) | 85.5 | | 96 | 30 | 19.5 |
| 10 French Frolic (Miss J. Graham-Clark) | 89 | | 75.2 | 10 | 23.8 |

## 1965 Little Badminton (17 ran)

| Horse and rider | Dr | Spd & End Pen | B | SJ | Total |
|---|---|---|---|---|---|
| 1 The Poacher (Capt M.F. Whiteley) | 94.5 | – | 76.4 | 20.25 | 38.35 |
| 2 Avatar (W. Roycroft) | 89.5 | 60 | 100.8 | 10 | 58.7 |
| 3 The Little Mermaid (Mrs T.W. Kopanski) | 88 | – | 18.8 | – | 69.2 |
| 4 Cornishman (Mrs C.M. Parker) | 87.5 | 20 | 52 | 20 | 75.5 |
| 5 Dreamy Dasher (T. Durston Smith) | 116.5 | 20 | 60.8 | 10.25 | 85.95 |
| 6 Freeman II (Mrs A. Oliver) | 56 | 62.4 | 30.4 | 1 | 89 |
| 7 The Viking (M. Tucker) | 101.5 | 60 | 73.6 | 10 | 97.9 |
| 8 Corrinwell (E. Thompson) | 127.5 | 20 | 20 | 10 | 137.5 |
| 9 Alouette (Miss V. Longmore) | 94.5 | 170.8 | 15.2 | 20 | 270.1 |

## 1966 EVENT CANCELLED

## 1967 (43 ran)

| Horse and rider | Dr | Spd & End Pen | B | SJ | Total |
|---|---|---|---|---|---|
| 1 Jonathan (Miss C. Ross-Taylor) | 39.33 | – | 105.2 | – | +65.87 |
| 2 Durlas Eile (Maj E.A. Boylan) | 31 | – | 106.4 | 20 | +55.4 |
| 3 Count Jasper (Miss P. Hely-Hutchinson) | 50.67 | 20 | 116.8 | – | +46.13 |
| 4 Mazaretta (Miss S. Clifford) | 52.33 | – | 104.4 | 11.75 | +40.32 |
| 5 Our Nobby (Miss J. Bullen) | 61.67 | 20 | 118 | – | +36.33 |
| 6 Turnstone (R. Meade) | 55.67 | – | 106 | 20 | +30.33 |
| 7 Foxdor (Sgt R.S. Jones) | 59.67 | – | 100 | 10 | +30.33 |
| 8 Nicholas Nickleby (Miss L. Sutherland) | 59.67 | – | 87.2 | – | +27.53 |
| 9 Cornishman (Mrs C.M. Parker) | 69.33 | – | 111.2 | 20 | +21.87 |
| 10 Evening Echo (Capt T.W. Ritson) | 62.33 | – | 105.6 | 21.5 | +21.77 |

## 1968 (55 ran)

| Horse and rider | Dr | X-country S'ch | J | T | SJ | Total |
|---|---|---|---|---|---|---|
| 1 Our Nobby (Miss J. Bullen) | 92.5 | +37.6 | | +86 | | +31.1 |
| 2 Turnstone (R.J.H. Meade) | 88.5 | +32.8 | | +83.6 | | +27.9 |
| 3 Foxdor (S/Sgt R.S. Jones) | 62 | +37.6 | | +56.8 | 10 | +22.4 |
| 4 Rock On (M. Phillips) | 90 | +37.6 | | +80.8 | 10 | +18.4 |
| 5 Lochinvar (Maj D. Allhusen) | 73.5 | +37.6 | | +60 | 10 | +14.1 |
| 6 Ballinkeele (Miss F.E. Pearson) | 66 | +37.6 | | +49.2 | 10 | +10.8 |
| 7 Char's Choice (P. Welch) | 96 | +32.8 | | +53.6 | | 9.6 |
| 8 Popadom (Miss L. Sutherland) | 86 | +33.6 | 20 | +44.8 | | 27.6 |
| 9 Plain Sailing (M. Plumb) | 64.5 | +3.2 | | +32.8 | | 28.5 |
| 10 Nicholas Nickleby (Miss L. Sutherland) | 95.5 | +13.6 | | +51.6 | | 30.3 |

## 1969 (48 ran)

| Horse and rider | Dr | X-country S'ch | J | T | SJ | Total |
|---|---|---|---|---|---|---|
| 1 Pasha (R. Walker) | 62.67 | +32 | | +70.8 | | +40.13 |
| 2 Grey Cloud (Miss A.Martin-Bird) | 67 | +37.6 | | +66 | | +36.6 |
| 3 Warrathoola (W. Roycroft) | 47.33 | +35.2 | 20 | +70.8 | 10 | +28.67 |
| 4 Furtive (W. Roycroft) | 70.33 | +37.6 | | +70.8 | 10 | +28.07 |
| 5 Count Jasper (Miss P. Hely-Hutchinson) | 79.67 | +37.6 | | +70 | | +27.93 |
| 6 Jonathan (Miss C. Ross-Taylor) | 69.33 | +37.6 | | +55.2 | | +23.47 |
| 7 Brown Duke (Miss S. Warwick) | 87 | +37.6 | | +70.8 | | +21.4 |
| 8 P.J.L-L. Esq (J. Smart) | 80.33 | +37.6 | | +70.8 | 10 | +18.07 |
| 9 Cornishman V (Miss M. Gordon-Watson) | 70 | +37.6 | | +70.8 | 26.25 | +12.15 |
| 10 Lane Trial (R. Walker) | 59 | +37.6 | 40 | +70.8 | 10 | 0.6 |

## 1970 (46 ran)

| Horse and rider | Dr | X-country S'ch | J | T | SJ | Total |
|---|---|---|---|---|---|---|
| 1 The Poacher (R. Meade) | 36 | +27.2 | | +28.4 | | +19.6 |
| 2 San Carlos (Capt R. McMahon) | 60 | +33.6 | | +41.6 | 10 | +15.2 |
| 3 Cornishman V (Miss M. Gordon-Watson) | 54 | +20.8 | | +30 | | 3.2 |
| 4 Gypsy Flame (Miss L.Sutherland) | 53.5 | +23.2 | | +16.4 | 10 | 23.9 |
| 5 Baccarat (Miss D. West) | 74.5 | +25.6 | | +23.6 | | 25.3 |
| 6 Henry the Navigator (T. Durston-Smith) | 88 | +24 | | +26 | | 38 |
| 7 Lynette (Miss M. Meakin) | 65 | +15.2 | | +12.8 | 10 | 47 |
| 8 Rembrandt (D. Goldie) | 90 | +32 | | +14 | 10 | 54 |
| 9 Richlieu (Mrs S. Johnson) | 104 | +32.8 | | +17.2 | 10 | 64 |
| 10 Mooncoin (Miss A. Sowden) | 104.5 | +30.4 | | +9.2 | | 64.9 |

## 1971 (48 ran)

| Horse and rider | Dr | X-country S'ch | J | T | SJ | Total |
|---|---|---|---|---|---|---|
| 1 Great Ovation (Lt M. Phillips) | 75.5 | 13.6 | | 36.8 | | 125.9 |
| 2 Cornishman V (Miss M.Gordon-Watson) | 88.5 | 8 | 20 | 29.2 | 10 | 155.7 |
| 3 Baccarat (Miss D. West) | 102.5 | 6.4 | 20 | 30 | | 158.9 |
| 4 Upper Strata (R. Walker) | 94.1 | 12 | 20 | 23.6 | 10 | 159.61 |
| 5 Doublet (HRH Princess Anne) | 82.5 | 32 | | 42.4 | 10 | 166.9 |
| 6 Farmer Giles (M. Tucker) | 111.5 | 20.8 | | 35.6 | | 170.9 |
| 7 Mooncoin (Miss A. Sowden) | 99 | 18.4 | | 50.8 | | 168.2 |
| 8 Henry the Navigator (T. Durston-Smith) | 114.5 | 20.8 | | 35.6 | | 170.9 |
| 9 Mary Poppins II (Miss H. Booth) | 98 | 16 | 20 | 38.4 | | 172.4 |
| 10 Deemster (Miss H. Booth) | 93.5 | 24 | 20 | 48.4 | | 185.9 |

# Score Sheets 1949–1999

Dr=dressage  S'ch =steeplechase  J=jump  T=time  SJ=showjumping

## 1972 (60 ran)

| Horse and rider | Dr | X-country | | | SJ | Total |
| | | S'ch | J | T | | |
|---|---|---|---|---|---|---|
| 1 Great Ovation (Lt M. Phillips) | 59 | 8.8 | – | 38.8 | – | 106.6 |
| 2 Laurieston (R. Meade) | 66 | 2.4 | – | 37.6 | 1.25 | 107.25 |
| 3 Cornish Gold (Mrs C.M. Parker) | 79.5 | – | 20 | 42 | – | 141.5 |
| 4 Baccarat (Miss D. West) | 73.5 | 12 | – | 59.6 | – | 145.1 |
| 5 Be Fair (Miss L. Prior-Palmer) | 83 | 4.8 | 20 | 37.6 | – | 145.4 |
| 6 Classic Chips (S.T.R. Stevens) | 93 | – | 20 | 33.2 | – | 146.2 |
| 7 Wayfarer II (R. Meade) | 79 | 4.8 | – | 45.6 | 20 | 149.4 |
| 8 Mary Poppins II (Miss H. Booth) | 101 | – | – | 21.6 | 30 | 152.6 |
| 9 Deemster (Miss H. Booth) | 100.5 | 10.4 | – | 54 | – | 164.9 |
| 10 Larkspur (Miss J. Hodgson) | 104.5 | 14.5 | – | 46.4 | – | 165.3 |

## 1973 (69 ran)

| Horse and rider | Dr | X-country | | | SJ | Total |
| | | S'ch | J | T | | |
|---|---|---|---|---|---|---|
| 1 Be Fair (Miss L. Prior-Palmer) | 42 | – | – | 14 | – | 56 |
| 2 Eagle Rock (R. Meade) | 60 | – | – | 18.4 | – | 78.4 |
| 3 Cornish Duke (Miss V. Thompson) | 58 | – | – | 33.2 | 10 | 101.2 |
| 4 Lynette (Miss M. Meakin) | 55.75 | – | – | 45.6 | – | 101.35 |
| 5 Farewell (Mrs R. Jones) | 69.75 | – | – | 34.4 | – | 104.15 |
| 6 Cornishman V (Miss M. Gordon-Watson) | 47.25 | – | 60 | – | – | 107.25 |
| 7 The Ghillie (Mrs M. Comerford) | 61 | – | – | 17.2 | 30 | 108.2 |
| 8 Goodwill (HRH Princess Anne) | 53.5 | 7.2 | 20 | 34 | – | 114.7 |
| 9 Harley (Miss S. Hatherley) | 63.75 | 1.6 | 20 | 33.6 | – | 118.95 |
| 10 Little Extra (Miss P.A. Biden) | 57.5 | – | 20 | 50.8 | – | 128.3 |

## 1974 (60 ran)

| Horse and rider | Dr | X-country | | | SJ | Total |
| | | S'ch | J | T | | |
|---|---|---|---|---|---|---|
| 1 Columbus (Capt M. Phillips) | 40.33 | – | – | – | – | 40.33 |
| 2 Larkspur (Miss J. Hodgson) | 53 | – | – | – | – | 53 |
| 3 Irish Cap (B. Davidson) | 41.67 | – | – | 13.6 | – | 55.27 |
| 4 Goodwill (HRH Princess Anne) | 58.67 | – | – | – | – | 58.67 |
| 5 The Ghillie (Mrs M. Comerford) | 46.33 | 5.6 | – | 12.4 | – | 58.73 |
| 6 Wayfarer II (R. Meade) | 44.33 | – | – | 10 | – | 59.93 |
| 7 Baccarat (Miss D. West) | 60 | – | – | – | – | 60 |
| 8 Playamar (H. Thomas) | 63.67 | – | – | – | – | 63.67 |
| 9 Smokey VI (C. D. Collins) | 56.67 | – | – | – | 10 | 66.67 |
| 10 Centurian (C. D. Collins) | 59 | – | – | 13.2 | – | 72.2 |

## 1975 EVENT ABANDONED AFTER THE DRESSAGE

## 1976 (70 ran)

| Horse and rider | Dr | X-country | | | SJ | Total |
| | | S'ch | J | T | | |
|---|---|---|---|---|---|---|
| 1 Wideawake (Miss L. Prior-Palmer) | 50 | – | – | 18.8 | – | 68.8 |
| 2 Playamar (H. Thomas) | 58 | – | – | 23.6 | – | 81.6 |
| 3 Favour (Capt M. Phillips) | 57 | – | – | 25.2 | – | 82.2 |
| 4 Jacob Jones (R. Meade) | 60.33 | – | – | 22.8 | – | 83.13 |
| 5 Merry Sovereign (Miss C. Strachan) | 56.67 | – | – | 32 | 10 | 98.67 |
| 6 Larkspur (Miss J. Hodgson) | 48 | 7.2 | – | 43.6 | 10 | 108.8 |
| 7 Gamble (Mrs Charlotte Steel) | 68.67 | 3.2 | – | 43.6 | – | 115.47 |
| 8 Topper Too (Miss J Starkey) | 57.33 | – | – | 58.4 | – | 115.73 |
| 9 Demerara (M. Moffett) | 83.33 | – | – | 32.8 | – | 116.13 |
| 10 Smokey VI (C. Collins) | 83.33 | – | 20 | 12.4 | 20 | 135.73 |

## 1977 (45 ran)

| Horse and rider | Dr | X-country | | | SJ | Total |
| | | S'ch | J | T | | |
|---|---|---|---|---|---|---|
| 1 George (Miss L. Prior-Palmer) | 37.4 | – | – | – | 0.25 | 37.65 |
| 2 The Kingmaker (Miss D. Thorne) | 59 | – | – | – | – | 59 |
| 3 Killaire (Miss L. Prior-Palmer) | 47.4 | – | – | 13.2 | 5 | 65.6 |
| 4 Warrior (Mrs J. Holderness-Roddam) | 48.6 | 3.2 | – | 14 | – | 65.8 |
| 5 Carawich (Miss A. Pattinson) | 43.8 | – | – | 12.8 | 10 | 66.6 |
| 6 Smokey VI (C. Collins) | 51.6 | – | 20 | – | 5 | 76.6 |
| 7 Collingwood (Miss M. Frank) | 48.6 | – | – | 27.6 | 5 | 81.2 |
| 8 Drakenburg (Miss F. Moore) | 48.6 | – | 20 | 11.6 | 5 | 85.2 |
| 9 Madrigal (K. Schultz) | 28.8 | 0.8 | 20 | 45.2 | 5 | 99.8 |
| 10 Cheal Cloud (Mrs M. Comerford) | 60.4 | – | – | 30.8 | 10 | 101.2 |

## 1978 (42 ran)

| Horse and rider | Dr | X-country | | | SJ | Total |
| | | S'ch | J | T | | |
|---|---|---|---|---|---|---|
| 1 Warrior (Mrs T. Holderness-Roddam) | 52.8 | – | – | 4.4 | – | 57.2 |
| 2 Village Gossip (Miss L. Prior-Palmer) | 66.8 | – | – | – | – | 66.8 |
| 3 Topper Too (Miss J. Starkey) | 44.2 | – | – | 28 | – | 72.2 |
| 4 Felday Farmer (Miss E. Boone) | 71.4 | – | – | 7.6 | – | 79 |
| 5 Cambridge Blue (J. Watson) | 67.4 | – | – | 9.2 | 5 | 81.6 |
| 6 Bleak Hills (R. Meade) | 53.2 | 3.2 | – | 12.8 | 15 | 84.2 |
| 7 Jack Be Nimble (C. Bealby) | 70.4 | – | – | 23.6 | – | 94 |
| 8 Martha (Miss D. Clapham) | 56.8 | 20 | – | 24 | 5 | 105.8 |
| 9 Master Question (J. Seaman) | 69.2 | 8 | 20 | 19.6 | – | 116.8 |
| 10 Rescator (Mrs G. Fleming-Williams) | 62.8 | – | 20 | 38 | – | 120.8 |

## 1979 (41 ran)

| Horse and rider | Dr | X-country | | | SJ | Total |
| | | S'ch | J | T | | |
|---|---|---|---|---|---|---|
| 1 Killaire (Miss L.Prior-Palmer) | 49.4 | – | – | 6.8 | – | 56.2 |
| 2 Monacle II (Miss S. Hatherley) | 59.4 | – | – | – | – | 59.4 |
| 3 Columbus (Capt M. Phillips) | 66 | – | – | – | – | 66 |
| 4 Carawich (J. Wofford) | 53 | 2.4 | – | 5.6 | 10 | 71 |
| 5 Merry Sovereign (Miss C. Strachan) | 56.4 | 2.4 | – | 13.2 | 5 | 77 |
| 6 Goodwill (HRH Princess Anne) | 84.2 | – | – | – | 5 | 89.2 |
| 7 Village Gossip (Miss L. Prior-Palmer) | 72 | – | 20 | – | 5 | 97 |
| 8 Topper Too (Miss J. Starkey) | 49.6 | – | – | 53.2 | 10 | 112.8 |
| 9 Monaco (N. Haagensen) | 50.6 | – | 40 | 17.2 | 5 | 112.8 |
| 10 March Brown (Miss K. Lende) | 70 | – | 20 | 12.4 | 20 | 122.4 |

## 1980 (68 ran)

| Horse and rider | Dr | X-country | | | SJ | Total |
| | | S'ch | J | T | | |
|---|---|---|---|---|---|---|
| 1 Southern Comfort (M. Todd) | 64.6 | – | – | – | – | 64.6 |
| 2 Killaire (Miss L. Prior-Palmer) | 53.8 | – | – | 7.6 | 5 | 66.4 |
| 3 Ultimus (G. Breisner) | 74.6 | – | – | – | – | 74.6 |
| 4 Merganser II (Mrs H Butler) | 57 | – | – | – | 20 | 77 |
| 5 Flying Solo (Miss J Wilson) | 63.8 | – | 20 | 4 | – | 87.8 |
| 6 Lincoln (Capt M. Phillips) | 57.4 | – | 40 | – | – | 97.4 |
| 7 Monaco (N.Haagensen) | 53.2 | 7.2 | 20 | 13.6 | 5 | 99 |
| 8 Kilcashel (R. Meade) | 56 | – | – | 44.4 | – | 100.4 |
| 9 The Mountaineer (Miss T. Martin-Bird) | 73.2 | – | 20 | 12 | 5 | 110.2 |
| 10 Bilbo Baggins II (C. Wares) | 71.4 | – | 20 | 11.2 | 10 | 112.6 |

## 1981 (80 ran)

| Horse and rider | Dr | X-country | | | SJ | Total |
| | | S'ch | J | T | | |
|---|---|---|---|---|---|---|
| 1 Lincoln (Capt M. Phillips) | 57.8 | – | – | 1.2 | 5 | 64 |
| 2 Free Scot (Miss S. Pflueger) | 61.2 | – | – | 2 | 10 | 73.2 |
| 3 Kilcashel (R. Meade) | 48.8 | – | – | 17.6 | 10 | 76.4 |
| 4 Ultimus (G. Breisner) | 77.2 | – | – | 8.8 | – | 86 |
| 5 Amoy (Mrs J. Harrington) | 75 | – | – | 12.8 | – | 87.8 |
| 6 Windjammer II (Miss D. Clapham) | 65 | 5.6 | – | 15.6 | 5 | 91.2 |
| 7 Darius III (J-P. Lagrassiere) | 66.4 | – | – | 15.6 | 10 | 92 |
| 8 Priceless (Miss V. Holgate) | 53.2 | – | – | 34.4 | 5.25 | 92.85 |
| 9 Peter The Great (Mrs L. Purbrick) | 71.6 | – | – | 16.4 | 5 | 93 |
| 10 Killaire (Miss L. Prior-Palmer) | 65 | 4.8 | – | 23.2 | – | 93 |

# Score Sheets 1949–1999

Dr=dressage   S'ch =steeplechase   J=jump   T=time   SJ=showjumping

## 1982 (79 ran)

| | Horse and rider | Dr | X-country S'ch | J | T | SJ | Total |
|---|---|---|---|---|---|---|---|
| 1 | Speculator III (R. Meade) | 37.6 | – | – | – | – | 37.6 |
| 2 | J.J. Babu (B. Davidson) | 39.4 | – | – | – | – | 39.4 |
| 3 | Mystic Minstrel (Miss R. Bayliss) | 33.6 | – | – | 7.2 | 5 | 45.8 |
| 4 | Priceless (Miss V. Holgate) | 45.4 | – | – | – | 5 | 50.4 |
| 5 | Gemma Jay (Mrs S. Benson) | 45.6 | – | – | 5.6 | – | 51.2 |
| 6 | Mairangi Bay (D. Green) | 59 | – | – | – | – | 59 |
| 7 | Regal Realm (Mrs L. Green) | 60.8 | – | – | – | – | 60.8 |
| 8 | Beagle Bay (Mrs L.Green) | 58.2 | – | – | – | 5 | 63.2 |
| 9 | Primmore Hill (Miss N. Stephens) | 68.4 | – | – | – | 5 | 73.4 |
| 10 | Ultimus (G. Breisner) | 74.6 | – | – | – | – | 74.6 |

## 1983 (67 ran)

| | Horse and rider | Dr | X-country S'ch | J | T | SJ | Total |
|---|---|---|---|---|---|---|---|
| 1 | Regal Realm (Mrs L. Green) | 51.2 | – | – | – | 5 | 56.20 |
| 2 | General Bugle (M. Tucker) | 50.8 | – | – | 2.4 | 6 | 59.20 |
| 3 | Amoy (Mrs J. Harrington) | 59.8 | – | – | – | 5 | 64.80 |
| 4 | Danville (Mrs L. Clarke) | 44.4 | 3.2 | – | 17.2 | – | 64.80 |
| 5 | Beagle Bay (Mrs L. Green) | 47.4 | – | – | 11.2 | 10 | 68.60 |
| 6 | Ultimus (G. Breisner) | 64.4 | 2.4 | – | – | 5 | 71.80 |
| 7 | Dalwhinnie (M. Tucker) | 57.0 | – | – | 6 | 20.5 | 83.50 |
| 8 | Dylan II (Miss P. Schwerdt) | 72.2 | – | – | 6.4 | 5 | 83.60 |
| 9 | Felix Too (M. Todd) | 65.0 | – | – | 17.2 | 1.5 | 83.70 |
| 10 | Squires Holt (Miss F. Moore) | 51.8 | – | 20 | 13.6 | 5 | 90.4 |

## 1984 (75 ran)

| | Horse and rider | Dr | X-country S'ch | J | T | SJ | Total |
|---|---|---|---|---|---|---|---|
| 1 | Beagle Bay (Mrs L. Green) | 51.4 | – | – | – | – | 51.4 |
| 2 | Charisma (M. Todd) | 57.4 | – | – | – | – | 57.4 |
| 3 | Oxford Blue (I. Stark) | 58.2 | – | – | – | – | 58.2 |
| 4 | Danville (Mrs L. Clark) | 60.6 | – | – | – | – | 60.6 |
| 5 | Village Gossip (Mrs L. Green) | 61.8 | – | – | – | – | 61.8 |
| 6 | Sir Wattie (I. Stark) | 58.6 | – | – | – | 5 | 63.8 |
| 7 | The Gamesmaster (R. Lemieux]) | 58.8 | – | – | 0.8 | 5 | 64.6 |
| 8 | Pomeroy (R. Powell) | 62.8 | – | – | – | 5 | 67.8 |
| 9 | The Dark Imp (Mrs M. Lucey) | 66.8 | 4.8 | – | 3.2 | – | 74.8 |
| 10 | Bugsy Malone (Miss M. Hunter) | 68.4 | – | – | 7.6 | – | 76.0 |

## 1985 (76 ran)

| | Horse and rider | Dr | X-country S'ch | J | T | SJ | Total |
|---|---|---|---|---|---|---|---|
| 1 | Priceless (Miss V. Holgate) | 59.75 | – | – | – | – | 59.75 |
| 2 | Charisma (M. Todd) | 55.75 | – | – | – | 5 | 60.75 |
| 3 | Night Cap II (Miss V. Holgate) | 58.5 | – | 4.0 | – | 0.75 | 63.25 |
| 4 | Finvarra (Mrs T. Watkins-Fleischmann) | 55.5 | 2.4 | – | – | 10 | 67.90 |
| 5 | Pomeroy (R. Powell) | 73.25 | – | 4.0 | – | – | 77.25 |
| 6 | Fair Lady (C. Erhorn) | 73.75 | – | 0.8 | – | 5 | 79.55 |
| 7 | Divers Rock (Miss M. Thomson) | 81 | – | – | – | 5 | 86.00 |
| 8 | Ben Arthur (Miss K. Stives) | 64.5 | – | 17.2 | – | 5 | 86.70 |
| 9 | Myross (Mrs L. Clarke) | 81.5 | – | 2.8 | – | 5 | 89.30 |
| 10 | Windjammer II (Miss D. Clapham) | 70.75 | – | – | 20 | 5 | 95.75 |

## 1986 (62 ran)

| | Horse and rider | Dr | X-country S'ch | J | T | SJ | Total |
|---|---|---|---|---|---|---|---|
| 1 | Sir Wattie (Ian Stark) | 46.80 | 0.8 | – | 20.4 | 5 | 73.00 |
| 2 | Piglet II (Rachel Hunt) | 74.80 | – | – | 2.8 | 5 | 82.60 |
| 3 | Pomeroy (Rodney Powell) | 65.80 | 0.8 | – | 13.2 | 10 | 89.80 |
| 4 | Night Cap II (Virginia Leng) | 42.20 | – | 20 | 32.0 | – | 94.20 |
| 5 | Any Chance (Mark Todd) | 59.20 | – | 20 | 19.2 | – | 98.40 |
| 6 | JJ Babu (Bruce Davidson) | 40.60 | – | 20 | 35.2 | 5 | 100.80 |
| 7 | The Dark Imp (Miranda Lucey) | 65.00 | 3.2 | – | 44.4 | – | 112.60 |
| 8 | Marsh Heron (Jane Thelwall) | 60.00 | 5.6 | – | 49.6 | – | 115.20 |
| 9 | Buckley (Jane Starkey) | 57.80 | – | – | 49.2 | 10 | 117.00 |
| 10 | Streetlighter (Helen Ogden) | 52.60 | – | 20 | 42.8 | 5 | 120.00 |

## 1987 EVENT WAS CANCELLED

## 1988 (57 ran)

| | Horse and rider | Dr | X-country S'ch | J | T | SJ | Total |
|---|---|---|---|---|---|---|---|
| 1 | Sir Wattie (Ian Stark) | 48.0 | – | – | – | – | 48.00 |
| 2 | Glenburnie (Ian Stark) | 52.4 | – | – | – | 5 | 57.40 |
| 3 | Master Craftsman (Virginia Leng) | 54.4 | – | – | 6.8 | 1.25 | 62.45 |
| 4 | Volunteer (Tinks Pottinger) | 65.8 | – | – | – | – | 65.80 |
| 5 | Get Smart (Karen Straker) | 57.0 | – | – | 6.4 | 5 | 68.40 |
| 6 | Barnabus Brown (Paddy Muir) | 66.8 | – | – | 2.8 | – | 69.60 |
| 7 | Friday Fox (Rachel Hunt) | 67.2 | – | – | 3.2 | 5 | 75.40 |
| 8 | Special Appointment (Rodney Powell) | 71.4 | – | – | – | 5 | 76.40 |
| 9 | Horton Point (Ros Bevan) | 60.0 | – | – | 17.2 | – | 77.20 |
| 10 | Fearliath Mor (Lorna Clarke) | 83.4 | – | – | – | – | 83.40 |

## 1989 (58 ran)

| | Horse and rider | Dr | X-country S'ch | J | T | SJ | Total |
|---|---|---|---|---|---|---|---|
| 1 | Master Craftsman (Virginia Leng) | 49.0 | 1.6 | – | 7.2 | – | 57.80 |
| 2 | King Boris (Mary Thomson) | 56.2 | – | – | 5.2 | – | 61.40 |
| 3 | The Irishman II (Mark Todd) | 57.4 | – | – | – | 5 | 62.40 |
| 4 | Glenburnie (Ian Stark) | 61.6 | – | – | – | 5 | 66.60 |
| 5 | Murphy Himself (Ian Stark) | 57.8 | – | – | 5.6 | 5 | 68.40 |
| 6 | Get Smart (Karen Straker) | 59.0 | – | – | 10.0 | – | 69.00 |
| 7 | McDuff III (Nicola May) | 60.0 | – | – | 2.0 | 10 | 72.00 |
| 8 | Welton Apollo (Leslie Law) | 58.4 | – | – | 4.0 | 10.75 | 73.15 |
| 9 | Highland Road (Polly Lyon) | 67.6 | – | – | 6.4 | 5 | 79.00 |
| 10 | Phoenix (Michael Huber) | 69.2 | – | – | 4.4 | 6 | 79.60 |

## 1990 (74 ran)

| | Horse and rider | Dr | X-country S'ch | J | T | SJ | Total |
|---|---|---|---|---|---|---|---|
| 1 | Middle Road (Nicola McIrvine) | 48.2 | – | – | 1.6 | 0.5 | 50.30 |
| 2 | Messiah (Blyth Tait) | 54.4 | – | – | 0.8 | – | 55.20 |
| 3 | King Boris (Mary Thomson) | 50.6 | – | – | – | 5 | 55.60 |
| 4 | Barnabus Brown (Paddy Muir) | 52.0 | – | – | 4.4 | 5 | 61.40 |
| 5 | Sir Barnaby (Pippa Nolan) | 50.8 | – | – | 5.6 | 5 | 61.40 |
| 6 | The Irishman II (Rodney Powell) | 56.6 | – | – | – | 5 | 61.60 |
| 7 | Master Marius (Susanna Macaire) | 57.4 | – | – | – | 5 | 62.40 |
| 8 | King Cuthbert (Mary Thomson) | 55.2 | – | – | – | 10 | 65.20 |
| 9 | Get Smart (Karen Straker) | 60.2 | 1.6 | – | – | 5 | 66.80 |
| 10 | Griffin (Virginia Leng) | 52.0 | – | – | 20.0 | – | 72.00 |

## 1991 (83 ran)

| | Horse and rider | Dr | X-country S'ch | J | T | SJ | Total |
|---|---|---|---|---|---|---|---|
| 1 | The Irishman II (Rodney Powell) | 54.8 | 1.6 | – | – | – | 56.40 |
| 2 | Murphy Himself (Ian Stark) | 52.2 | – | – | 1.6 | 5 | 58.80 |
| 3 | Troubleshooter (Helen Bell) | 49.8 | – | – | 8.8 | 5.25 | 63.85 |
| 4 | King's Jester (Lorna Clarke) | 63.4 | – | – | 3.6 | – | 67.00 |
| 5 | Just An Ace (Mark Todd) | 58.2 | – | – | 8.8 | – | 67.00 |
| 6 | Glenburnie (Ian Stark) | 62.0 | – | – | 4.4 | 5 | 71.40 |
| 7 | Master Marius (Susanna Macaire) | 58.2 | – | – | 10.8 | 5 | 74.00 |
| 8 | Tekainga Fred (Greg Watson) | 70.0 | – | – | 1.6 | 5 | 76.60 |
| 9 | Chief (Victoria Latta) | 63.4 | 4.0 | – | 9.2 | – | 76.60 |
| 10 | Get Smart (Karen Straker) | 70.0 | – | – | 3.2 | 5 | 78.20 |

# Score Sheets 1949–1999

Dr=dressage   S'ch =steeplechase   J=jump   T=time   SJ=showjumping

## 1992 (82 ran)

| Horse and rider | Dr | S'ch | J | T | SJ | Total |
|---|---|---|---|---|---|---|
| 1 King William (Mary Thomson) | 42.2 | — | — | 13.6 | 5 | 60.80 |
| 2 Master Craftsman (Virginia Leng) | 50.2 | — | — | 14.8 | 0.25 | 65.25 |
| 3 Chief (Victoria Latta) | 51.4 | 0.8 | — | 32.8 | — | 85.00 |
| 4 Duncan II (David Green) | 53.2 | — | — | 25.6 | 10 | 88.80 |
| 5 Alfred the Great (Mark Todd) | 64.4 | — | — | 25.6 | — | 90.00 |
| 6 Arctic Goose (Lucinda Murray) | 51.6 | — | — | 40.4 | — | 92.00 |
| 7 Wilton Fair (David O'Connor) | 44.0 | 0.8 | — | 34.8 | 15.50 | 95.10 |
| 8 Kibah Tic Toc (Matt Ryan) | 49.8 | 1.6 | — | 17.6 | 28 | 97.00 |
| 9 Fair Share (Claire Bowley) | 73.4 | — | — | 24.0 | 0.75 | 98.15 |
| 10 Song and Dance Man (Kristina Gifford) | 79.8 | — | — | 23.2 | — | 103.00 |

## 1993 (79 ran)

| Horse and rider | Dr | S'ch | J | T | SJ | Total |
|---|---|---|---|---|---|---|
| 1 Welton Houdini (Virginia Leng) | 43.0 | — | — | — | — | 43.00 |
| 2 Ricochet (Blyth Tait) | 44.8 | — | — | — | — | 44.80 |
| 3 Watkins (Tanya Cleverly) | 43.2 | — | — | — | 5 | 48.20 |
| 4 Chief (Victoria Latta) | 46.8 | — | — | 3.2 | — | 50.00 |
| 5 Mr Punch (Anna Hermann) | 54.4 | — | — | — | — | 54.40 |
| 6 Quart du Placineau (Marie-Christine Duroy) | 44.2 | 1.6 | — | 8.8 | 1.25 | 55.85 |
| 7 Chaka (William Fox-Pitt) | 51.0 | — | — | — | 5.25 | 56.25 |
| 8 The Cool Customer (Charlotte Hollingsworth) | 56.6 | — | — | — | — | 56.60 |
| 9 Bertie Blunt (Nick Burton) | 49.6 | — | — | 2.4 | 5 | 57.00 |
| 10 Troubleshooter (Helen Bell) | 52.2 | — | — | 4.0 | 1.5 | 57.70 |

## 1994 (79 ran)

| Horse and rider | Dr | S'ch | J | T | SJ | Total |
|---|---|---|---|---|---|---|
| 1 Horton Point (Mark Todd) | 40.6 | 0.8 | — | — | — | 41.40 |
| 2 Delta III (Blyth Tait) | 53.8 | — | — | — | — | 53.80 |
| 3 Bounce (Vaughn Jefferis) | 57.0 | — | — | — | — | 57.00 |
| 4 Eagle Lion (Bruce Davidson) | 55.0 | — | — | 2.0 | — | 57.00 |
| 5 Just An Ace (Mark Todd) | 57.2 | — | — | — | 5 | 62.20 |
| 6 Get Smart (Karen Dixon) | 48.4 | — | — | — | 15 | 63.40 |
| 7 General Jock (Kristina Gifford) | 58.4 | — | — | — | 10.25 | 68.65 |
| 8 King's Jester (Mandy Stibbe) | 55.4 | — | — | 2.0 | 11.75 | 69.15 |
| 9 Troubleshooter (Helen Bell) | 56.0 | — | — | 13.6 | 3.5 | 73.10 |
| 10 Carmody St. (Felicity Cribb) | 47.2 | — | 20 | 6.0 | — | 73.20 |

## 1995 (78 ran)

| Horse and rider | Dr | S'ch | J | T | SJ | Total |
|---|---|---|---|---|---|---|
| 1 Eagle Lion (Bruce Davidson) | 46.6 | — | — | — | — | 46.60 |
| 2 Kibah Tic Toc (Matt Ryan) | 42.8 | — | — | — | 5.5 | 48.30 |
| 3 Biko (Karen O'Connor) | 51.0 | — | — | — | — | 51.00 |
| 4 Just An Ace (Mark Todd) | 49.0 | — | — | 4.8 | — | 53.80 |
| 5 General Jock (Kristina Gifford) | 50.2 | — | — | — | 5 | 55.20 |
| 6 True Blue Girdwood (Phillip Dutton) | 56.2 | — | — | — | 0.25 | 56.45 |
| 7 Midnight Blue II (Kristina Gifford) | 51.0 | — | — | 2.0 | 5 | 58.00 |
| 8 Summersong BF (Marie-Christine Duroy) | 52.6 | — | — | 6.8 | 0.5 | 59.90 |
| 9 Elektra Spiritus (Anna Hermann) | 63.6 | — | — | — | — | 63.60 |
| 10 Caliber (Ian Stark) | 50.2 | — | — | — | 15 | 65.20 |

## 1996 (77 ran)

| Horse and rider | Dr | S'ch | J | T | SJ | Total |
|---|---|---|---|---|---|---|
| 1 Bertie Blunt (Mark Todd) | 41.2 | — | — | 0.8 | — | 42.00 |
| 2 Bounce (Vaughn Jefferis) | 43.0 | — | — | — | — | 43.00 |
| 3 Custom Made (David O'Connor) | 40.4 | — | — | 0.4 | 5 | 45.80 |
| 4 New Flavour (Leslie Law) | 46.2 | — | — | — | 0.25 | 46.45 |
| 5 Chesterfield (Blyth Tait) | 49.2 | — | — | — | — | 49.20 |
| 6 Stanwick Ghost (Ian Stark) | 40.6 | — | — | — | 10 | 50.60 |
| 7 Broadcast News (Victoria Latta) | 44.4 | — | — | 2.0 | 10 | 56.40 |
| 8 Buckley Province (Andrew Nicholson) | 51.6 | — | — | — | 5 | 56.60 |
| 9 Archie Brown (Paddy Muir) | 52.6 | — | — | 4.8 | 5 | 62.40 |
| 10 Darien Powers (Andrew Hoy) | 58.2 | — | — | — | 5 | 63.20 |

## 1997 (80 ran)

| Horse and rider | Dr | S'ch | J | T | SJ | Total |
|---|---|---|---|---|---|---|
| 1 Custom Made (David O'Connor) | 48.6 | — | — | 0.4 | 0.25 | 49.25 |
| 2 Star Appeal (Mary King) | 50.0 | — | — | — | 5 | 55.00 |
| 3 Cosmopolitan II (William Fox-Pitt) | 55.6 | — | — | — | — | 55.60 |
| 4 Chesterfield (Blyth Tait) | 56.2 | — | — | — | — | 56.20 |
| 5 Lafayett (Linda Algotsson) | 48.6 | — | — | 3.6 | 5 | 57.20 |
| 6 Squirrel Hill (Sally Clark) | 61.4 | — | — | — | — | 61.40 |
| 7 Headley Bravo (Daisy Dick) | 49.6 | — | — | 12.4 | — | 62.00 |
| 8 Eagle Lion (Bruce Davidson) | 64.2 | — | — | — | — | 64.20 |
| 9 Bits and Pieces (Pippa Funnell) | 60.0 | — | — | — | 5 | 65.00 |
| 10 Bounce (Vaughn Jefferis) | 62.0 | — | — | 3.2 | — | 65.20 |

## 1998 (79 ran)

| Horse and rider | Dr | S'ch | J | T | SJ | Total |
|---|---|---|---|---|---|---|
| 1 Word Perfect II (Chris Bartle) | 36.6 | — | — | — | 0.50 | 37.10 |
| 2 Broadcast News (Mark Todd) | 35.2 | — | — | — | 5 | 40.20 |
| 3 Eagle Lion (Bruce Davidson) | 45.0 | — | — | — | — | 45.00 |
| 4 Bounce (Vaughn Jefferis) | 45.6 | — | — | — | — | 45.60 |
| 5 Prince Panache (Karen O'Connor) | 37.0 | 0.8 | — | 8.4 | — | 46.20 |
| 6 General Jock (Kristina Gifford) | 44.2 | — | — | — | 5 | 49.20 |
| 7 Market Venture (Stuart Black) | 33.8 | 4.0 | — | 12.4 | 5 | 55.20 |
| 8 Welton Molecule (Lucy Thompson) | 42.4 | — | — | 8.0 | 5 | 55.40 |
| 9 Aspyring (Blyth Tait) | 51.8 | — | — | — | 5 | 56.80 |
| 10 Sas Monaghan (Paula Törnquist) | 52.8 | — | — | — | 5 | 57.80 |

## 1999 ( ran)

| Horse and rider | Dr | S'ch | J | T | SJ | Total |
|---|---|---|---|---|---|---|
| 1 | | | | | | |
| 2 | | | | | | |
| 3 | | | | | | |
| 4 | | | | | | |
| 5 | | | | | | |
| 6 | | | | | | |
| 7 | | | | | | |
| 8 | | | | | | |
| 9 | | | | | | |
| 10 | | | | | | |

# Index

Page numbers in *italic* indicate illustrations

# Index/Acknowledgements

## Acknowledgements

It has been a great pleasure to write this book which I hope reflects the spirit of Badminton and the character of the many people who are its history and its future. I am truly grateful to everyone who has so willingly shared with me their own Badminton story and I hope they enjoy the result as much as I have enjoyed the research. I would also like to thank His Grace the Duke of Beaufort and Hugh Thomas for allowing me to take on this project. And my husband Martin, for somehow keeping the rest of our lives on track throughout the researching and writing of this book.

The author would particularly like to thank Kit Houghton and Jim Gilmore for their help in supplying photographs, and the publishers would like to thank Debbie Cook at Kit Houghton Photography for turning her stock of photographs upside down on numerous occasions, with never a grumble heard!

The author would also like to thank the following for the loan of photographs: Edwina Norris pp14, 32(top), 228(btm rt); Jim Gilmore at The Badminton Press Office pp15, 48, 70, 110, 146, 204, 217, 218–19; Bee Joynson pp16, 22–3(mid & btm lft & rt), 40(btm), 44, 53, 55, 59, 61, 83; Isobel Reid p25; Major Derrick Dyson pp50, 114; Virginia Lady Petersham pp64–5, 80(lft), 85; Jo Challens p81; Polly Lochore p93; Angela Craddock p103; Col Ronnie McMahon p106; Bridget Parker p117; Carol Alexander p160; Adrian and Elaine Cantwell p224(btm); Liz Sampson p226(top)

Peter Harding: pp2, 14, 15, 18, 21, 22–3, 24, 27, 29, 30, 34, 40(top), 40(btm), 41, 42, 47, 48, 51, 52, 55, 56, 57, 58, 60, 62, 66, 67, 69, 72, 73, 74(lft), 76, 77, 78, 80(rt), 82, 84, 86, 87, 88, 89, 90, 91, 100, 101, 107, 108–9, 111, 119, 121, 125, 146, 165

Kit Houghton: pp1, 3, 4–5, 6, 7, 8–9, 10(btm), 11(btm), 13(btm), 50(btm), 71, 74(rt), 75, 83(lft), 96, 98–9, 112, 115, 118, 130–1, 134–5, 139, 140–1, 142, 143, 146(btm), 147, 148–9, 152, 153, 154, 156, 157, 158, 159, 161, 162, 163, 164, 166, 167(rt), 168, 169(except rt), 170–1, 172–3, 174, 175, 176–7, 178, 179, 180–1, 182, 183, 184, 185, 186, 187, 188–9, 190, 191, 192–3, 195, 196, 197, 198, 200–1, 202–3, 205, 206, 207, 208, 209, 211, 212–13, 214, 216, 220, 222, 223, 224(top), 225, 226, 227, 228(top mid & top rt), 230(btm), 231

P.M. Antrobus p103; Jean Bridel p83; Bristol Evening Post pp44, 228; Central Press Photos pp61, 114; Derek Croucher pp10(top), 17, 92, 97; Srdja Dukanovic pp11(top), 194; Eventing/IPC pp126, 127(Leslie Lane), 128, 129(E.D. Lacey); Mark Fiennes p117(top); David Fraser pp12, 13(top & mid); Michael Gilmore p120; Keystone Press Agency pp16, 22–3(mid & btm lft & rt), 53, 59; Leslie Lane p110; Bob Langrish pp132–3, 150–1; Mitschke p106; Monty pp 50, 64–5, 80(lft); Helen Revington pp94, 228(lft); Riding Magazine pp35, 36, 38–9, 102, 104–5, 113, 116, 122–3, 124; Shaw-Shot pp144–5, 169(rt), 210; Stephen Sparkes pp167, 228(mid btm), 230(top rt); The Willow Studios p85

Line illustrations on pp137 and 138 by Caroline Bromley-Gardner. By kind permission of Badminton Horse Trials Office.